# A LIFE OF

# Significance

# A LIFE OF

# *Significance*

ORDINARY PEOPLE FULFILLING THE
*Extraordinary Call of God*

---

# RENEE MARINI

REDEMPTION
PRESS

Published by Redemption Press, PO Box 427, Enumclaw, WA 98022.
Toll-Free (844) 2REDEEM (273-3336)

Redemption Press is honored to present this title in partnership with the author. The views expressed or implied in this work are those of the author. Redemption Press provides our imprint seal representing design excellence, creative content, and high-quality production.

The author has tried to recreate events, locales, and conversations from memories of them. In order to maintain their anonymity, in some instances the names of individuals, some identifying characteristics, and some details may have been changed, such as physical properties, occupations, and places of residence.

ISBN 13: 978-1-64645-590-4 (Paperback)
978-1-64645-589-8 (ePub)
978-1-64645-588-1 (Mobi)

Library of Congress Catalog Card Number: 2022911408

For All Those Who Hear and Obey

*The two most important days in your life are the day you are born and the day you find out why.*

—Mark Twain

# Preface

IN SEPTEMBER 2019, PASTOR DALE O'SHIELDS, SENIOR PASTOR AT Church of the Redeemer in Gaithersburg, Maryland, taught a series entitled *Ten Lessons for a Life of Significance*. The first lesson, "Be Prepared," had me captivated from the first few sentences. He stated that there are three levels of living: Survival, Success, and Significance. None of them are bad; they're just different levels of experiencing our time on this earth.

A life of Survival is where we just make it day to day. It reminds me of living paycheck to paycheck, like when my husband, Sal, and I first got married and started raising our family. It's not bad, compared to the alternative of *not* surviving, but it is not what we humans seek.

A life of Success is where we have achieved something. It usually means that, according to the world's standards, we have financial stability. For Sal and me, that happened in our forties. We finally had stability—a family house, a rental townhouse, careers, community, and church, with a little left in the budget for fun. Ah . . . life was good! I can't say we were ever without problems, but we were finally able to navigate through them.

You often hear of people at this level not feeling satisfied. That's why you regularly see celebrities, politicians, sports icons, and business tycoons striving for something bigger. They are still looking for that third level of living: the life of Significance.

It's not enough to merely survive or achieve success, because God calls us to a life of Significance. Unfortunately, many people never find the third level.

A life of Significance is where we make a difference for other people. It has an impact that will outlive us. Pastor Dale said, "Success is something that happens *to* you, but Significance is something that happens *through* you."

Hearing that lesson, I started to ponder about the life Sal and I have lived. It was then that I got serious about sharing the story.

# Chapter 1

I WAS A MISTAKE.

The year was 1955. My father had returned from the Korean War, and my mom found herself pregnant at the age of thirty-six. With three sons—ages fifteen, fourteen, and eleven—she opted to make the most of the situation. She prayed for a girl and even made a deal with Jesus, promising to name her after His mother, Mary.

So Mary Ethlarine was born. *Mary* to fulfill the promise, and *Ethlarine* after my maternal grandmother. Her name had been inspired by two friends of my great-grandmother: Ethel and Lorraine. Despite the name on my birth certificate, everyone called me Renee.

The first event I recall happened when I was three. I fell down a flight of stairs and hit my head on the closet door at the bottom. The culprit was a hole in the worn-out carpet at the very top step. I remember crying and being comforted on the lap of a man with a head of dark hair. I assume that was my dad.

For the next ten years, the results of that fall consumed my life. My eyes had crossed, so I spent those years in glasses with what seemed like never-ending trips to the eye doctor for exams, patches, and more glasses. Not cool glasses either. Back then, the choices for someone so small were limited to one style and three colors: blue, pink, or white.

My first surgery was at the age of five, on both eyes. I remember being in the hospital with bandages over my eyes and my mother teaching me nursery rhymes. I would sit in my hospital bed, eyes covered, and recite nursery rhymes, not knowing at the time that I often had an audience of passersby stopping to listen and smile at the "cute little patient."

I remember the age of seven well. Not only was it the year of my second eye surgery, this time on the right eye only, but also of my first attention from a member of the opposite sex. I was in second grade and received my first Valentine's Day gift, from a boy named Billy—a small box with a ring from the bubble-gum machine and a candy heart that said "Be My Valentine." It was very special to me and caused a bit of a spark between us.

One day in the schoolyard at recess, he decided to demonstrate that spark by pushing me as he ran by. I fell flat on my face, breaking my newly acquired permanent two front teeth. Bleeding and crying, I picked up the pieces and was escorted into the main office.

Many factors—such as discipline from the principal, meetings and phone calls between our parents, financial responsibility, and the daily evidence every time I smiled—played a part in separating us. To this day, Billy and I have never spoken again. So much for first love.

Two other milestones occurred at age seven. I made my first Holy Communion, and my dad brought home a bicycle for me. My aunt Lo—who, along with my uncle Joe and two cousins, Sue and Jay, had moved in with my grandmother in the other half of the duplex we lived in—was the one who taught me how to ride.

A third surgery on the left eye happened at age nine during summer vacation. Summers were spent mostly in the backyard pool that my dad had bought for me. In spite of surgery, patches, and glasses, this was something I could enjoy. I spent hours in that pool with Sue and Jay, then we'd run when we heard the ice cream truck. We loved it when the driver rang the bell, announcing his arrival, then waited while we made our selection for the day.

At age eleven, I received my new front teeth: two porcelain crowns to make my smile complete, just in time to be a junior bridesmaid for my brother Jim's wedding. As for my eyes, there were now brown glasses and a couple of different shapes to choose from.

During my early school years, I often questioned God about why these things had happened to me—why I had to wear glasses, and for how long, and why I had to be made fun of about the glasses and the missing teeth. But He never answered me.

At thirteen, I was devastated to receive the news that I needed another surgery on both eyes. This one, however, was optional, as it was merely for cosmetic reasons, to make sure my eyeballs were stabilized and moved together.

It was more than I could take. I decided to let God know exactly how I felt. I cried and I yelled, but once again there was no answer.

That night I had a dream. I seldom remember my dreams, but that one I remember vividly. In my dream, I walked into eighth grade *without glasses!* When I got to my desk, everyone came around to congratulate me and look at me without glasses and with a tooth-filled smile. It was that dream that helped me decide to go through one more surgery.

But right before they wheeled me into the operating room, I almost backed out. My dad was ready to stop them from taking his baby girl.

It was my mother who forcefully stepped in and said, "No, she's going to have the surgery."

I owe my mom a debt of gratitude for her decision that day. It was the right choice. My eyes and mouth are the parts of me that were "fixed." I have used my eyes over the years to see and recognize the stepping stones in God's plan, and my mouth to encourage, teach, preach, and share the Word—both one-on-one and in speaking engagements.

And guess what? When I walked into eighth grade without glasses, many of my fellow students gathered round to congratulate me.

High school was a good time. A newfound confidence came with my new face. I began to try more activities and clubs. I made the cheerleading squad for our basketball team and was captain my senior year. I joined the Red Cross Club and served a year as president and was also a member of the Spirit Club. I even participated in our school play, went to our junior-senior prom, and was voted the Sweetest Senior.

At age sixteen, I applied for a work permit in order to get my first job. When I asked my mother for my birth certificate, I discovered that my name was not Renee! How could I possibly live the rest of my life as Mary Ethlarine when I had spent the last sixteen years as Renee?

My mother's solution, bless her heart, was to trot off to Vital Statistics and have "Renee" put in front of the whole mess for a whopping two bucks. Problem solved. Renee Mary Ethlarine it was.

I got my first part-time job as an EKG technician at St. Francis Hospital.

On to college at Slippery Rock State, which lasted only one semester. They canceled my major, early childhood education. A little confused now that my plan to be a preschool teacher had been taken away, I decided to transfer back home to Duquesne University in the nursing degree program.

Since I had previously worked at St. Francis Hospital, they agreed to hire me back part time while I attended college. I always liked the hospital and working with patients, so nursing seemed like a good choice.

Little did I know it was God's Providence—not only changing careers but bringing me back to the place where I would meet my husband.

Sal was an orderly on a rehab floor, and since we were both in college, our shifts coincided. I would cut through the third floor where he worked whenever I had to get from the south wing of the hospital to the north wing in order to complete the list of Sunday admissions that needed EKGs prior to Monday-morning surgeries.

Toward the end of July 1974, Sal finally asked me on a date. It was a church dance that not only required a long gown, but his *entire* family would be attending. I said yes, and forty-six years later, I still admit it was the best decision of my life. Well, maybe the *second* best, but I'll get to that.

We had a wonderful time at the dance and won a lunch at a very exclusive restaurant on top of Mount Washington, overlooking downtown Pittsburgh. Committed to that as a second date, we went to lunch, and the lookout at Mount Washington became one of our favorite places. It was there that we shared all our hopes and dreams for the future.

We began seeing each other daily—during work, after work, and on days off. We went to church on Sundays and had breakfast at my house afterward.

After about three weeks, he left for a week's vacation to Canada with his mom, dad, and brother, Rick. It was like part of me was missing!

Before he returned, I went for Labor Day weekend to a nearby hotel with my parents.

When Sal returned from Canada, he immediately called the hotel where we were staying.

My father said, "Tell him to come and meet us for dinner."

My parents went to the hotel restaurant while I waited in the room for Sal. When he knocked on the door, my heart skipped. I raced to answer and jumped into his arms. I am only four eleven, so I literally jumped up to give him a big hug.

Thankfully, he reciprocated and caught me. He still says that was his defining moment. He asked me to marry him on our next date at our place on top of Mount Washington. Three weeks of being together, and we both knew we were meant for each other.

We still needed to finish school and plan a big wedding. Sal had spent the first two years after high school at the College of Steubenville, where he joined a fraternity and didn't concentrate much on his studies. He then transferred to the University of Pittsburgh to get serious and spent two more years preparing for a career as a physical therapist. Devastated when he wasn't accepted into the PT program, he decided to quit school and get a job.

While he contemplated his future career, the city of Pittsburgh was starting a new emergency care system with personnel specifically trained for ambulance and first response. They started a new 9-1-1 call system and wanted medical personnel to handle emergency ambulance and rescue calls instead of the previously deployed police officers and firefighters. They even started a two-year education program at the local community college in emergency medical services.

After I encouraged him to apply, he was accepted to start in September 1975. That put both of us on track to graduate together in May of 1977, me with a BS in nursing and him with an AS in emergency medical services. All seemed right with the world, and plans were working out nicely.

There was just one problem—we didn't want to wait two more years to get married.

# Chapter 2

THE BICENTENNIAL RED-WHITE-AND-BLUE WEDDING TOOK PLACE on June 4, 1976, the summer prior to our last year of school. We moved into a one-bedroom apartment close to where we worked part time and began our life together as husband and wife and as college students.

Another unexpected surprise occurred in July when I found myself pregnant. Not the best timing, but the news was welcome nonetheless. Shaun Michael was born on March 5, 1977, nine months and one day after we said "I do." That's significant, because that meant the hospital bill for the delivery would be covered by medical insurance. For two struggling students, that was important!

Thankfully, my mother agreed to take care of Shaun while I finished school.

Graduation occurred in May 1977 for both Sal and me, but I was the only one who had a job waiting for me—at the same hospital where I had worked since I was sixteen. I was hired at St. Francis Medical Center as an evening charge nurse on a twenty-eight-bed surgical floor. Sal, however, had to be unemployed in order to get on with the City of Pittsburgh EMS (Emergency Medical Services), so he agreed to take care of Shaun and the house while I worked. This was back in the day when roles were pretty well set and men did not stay home.

By September, Sal was hired by the City of Pittsburgh EMS as a paramedic.

Over the next ten years, much happened. First of all, we moved into a two-bedroom apartment, once again near the hospital where I worked, and also close to my mother, who was now our babysitter. A year later, when I was pregnant with our second son, we moved into a rental house with two bedrooms, a basement, and a yard.

Scott Matthew was born on May 4, 1979. We found a babysitter right around the corner, who watched the boys while we worked. We lived in that house for five years while planning the dream house we wanted to build.

Our careers flourished. I transferred to a neurological unit for a year, then became a nursing instructor for the Alvernia School of Practical Nursing. I was hired to be the foundations instructor and loved every minute of it! I was responsible for teaching all the nursing procedures, both in the classroom and during practical labs. I was also one of the med-surg instructors responsible for gastrointestinal and cardiovascular. I loved teaching and still do.

That position lasted five years, until my love for GI nursing opened the doors for me to become an enterostomal therapist (ET), or ostomy nurse. I was selected to go to Cleveland Clinic for a five-week course, then passed my certification exams and returned to St. Francis to replace the ET, who was supposed to retire. She changed her mind, and since there was only an allotment for one ET position, I decided to leave St. Francis. I took a position as an ET at Mercy Hospital, on the outskirts of downtown Pittsburgh.

During that time, Sal worked on both the ambulance and rescue units. He enjoyed caring for patients as well as the adventure and risk of successfully completing daring rescues.

As I look back and remember his sense of defeat when he failed to get into the physical therapy program at the University of Pittsburgh, I chuckle at how boring that job would have been for him. Sal was promoted to crew chief, overseeing a team of three.

By 1983, our careers were advancing nicely, and the time felt right to build our dream house. Sal's uncle Sam owned Marini Construction Company, and all the brothers worked for him, including Sal's dad. It made sense to utilize the family talents to build our house. The only restriction was that it had to be inside the Pittsburgh city limits, because Sal worked for the city's EMS department. Finding an affordable plot of land inside the city was challenging, but we found a very inexpensive piece on what we affectionately called Marini Hill.

Sal's grandparents had immigrated from Italy and bought a very large piece of property. Over the years, they subdivided the land into plots for each son and daughter. I think there are about nine properties all on the hill. Imagine all the cousins going to school and playing games and sports together. And everyone was able to enjoy Grandma's homemade bread every Saturday, not to mention the homemade wine from the grape arbor and, of course, the hot sausage they packed themselves.

Our property was around the bend and out of sight of all the other properties, snuggled in a grove of trees. The only drawback seemed to be a small neighborhood cemetery from years past that was fairly close. But the property was affordable and allowed us to live in the city, and Sal's father and uncles would be our builders.

I designed the layout of the ranch-style house with three bedrooms, one bathroom with separate master access, a sunken living room with a stone fireplace, a dining room with sliding-door access to a top deck, a sizable eat-in kitchen with floor-to-ceiling cabinets, a full basement with family room and laundry, and a two-car garage. The top deck at the back was the length of the house with a full covered porch underneath.

Everything was our selection, from the color of the brick and mortar to the windows, doors, flooring, and kitchen cabinets. Sal's father built the stone fireplace with a built-in log box on each side. An added bonus was that my father, an established steamfitter, was able to install our energy-efficient, hot-water baseboard heating system, which was connected to an Aqua Grate in the fireplace.

We planned for this to be the home we would stay in until death. Where we would raise our children and entertain family and friends with cookouts, Super Bowl parties, and holiday dinners. We were finally settling into a place where we could put down roots and continue to grow.

But it was not to be. Our time there lasted only five years. What I didn't realize was that God's hand was in everything from the beginning. He had a master plan that I was yet to discover.

During those five years, we continued to work, and our boys started school at the local Catholic elementary school. Sal coached little league, and I ran the concession stand.

I did help teach the boys how to bat, however. I was determined to be part of my boys' lives, and since I had no girls, I dove in wherever I could.

I loved holidays and tried to make them both memorable and fun. Fourth of July had to be celebrated with fireworks. Halloween had dress-up and trick-or-treating. And Thanksgiving was filled with food, family, and football. The buildup throughout the year culminated at Christmas, with decorating, shopping, tree trimming, and gift wrapping. Then came the Marini Christmas Eve Italian dinner, midnight Mass, Christmas morning with Santa, and Christmas dinner with my family.

During those years, Sal took night courses at the University of Pittsburgh and completed his bachelor of science in health-related professions. He took a part-time job teaching evening classes at the university in the paramedic program, and it was there that his love for teaching became apparent.

Life was good . . . very busy but good!

Then suddenly, things came to a halt for Sal.

One snowy winter night on a call with Medic 2, he was carrying a patient on a stretcher down some icy steps. He lost his footing and landed on his back with the stretcher on top of him. Bracing himself and the patient with his arms, he tore the rotator cuff in his right shoulder. That injury required orthopedic surgery and subsequent physical therapy, all with time off work, which, thankfully, was covered under workers' compensation.

The light in the tunnel at this time was the birth of our third son, Mark Jeffrey, on April 6, 1985. It was an enjoyable family time for all of us, with Sal and me both off work at the same time and home with all the boys.

After six long months, Sal made a full recovery. Being a man who *has* to work, Sal was very eager to return to his unit and crew. He was a happy man again.

But before long, he lifted a stretcher and felt a severe shooting pain in his right shoulder. Not wanting to cause injury to any patients, he reluctantly agreed to see the orthopedic surgeon again. The surgeon told Sal that he had torn the rotator cuff again, and unfortunately, this time there was nothing he could do.

Sal was devastated! What about his career?

He told me, "Hun, I'm thirty-five years old, and I can't spend the rest of my life on disability."

No, sitting around collecting money and not being useful was not an option for my husband. But he could not continue working on the medic unit. What was the solution? There were no full-time teaching positions available at the university where he'd taught a couple evenings a week, supplementing his EMS salary.

I realized there was nothing confining us to Pittsburgh . . . except our families and our house. We would have to give up proximity to our parents, brothers, and extended family and be willing to leave the perfect house we had put so much of ourselves into.

The decision, however, was much easier than I thought. How important was Sal to me? Did my career, my family, or my possessions mean more to me than him? The answer was a resounding *no*. So we started the hunt for a teaching position in EMS that he was qualified for, anywhere in the US.

That search led us to three choices: Hahnemann University in Philadelphia, the University of Dallas, and George Washington University in DC. We traveled to each of the cities in order to make a joint decision. Sal went to interview, and I tagged along to see the area. We went with real estate agents to view possible homes, discovered the cost of living in each area, walked the streets, and assessed the travel options and distance from family. We found out that western Pennsylvania is quite different from the eastern side of the state, especially when it came to food, language accents, and slang.

Philadelphia and Pittsburgh, two of the major cities, are not just miles apart in distance but also in thinking and ways of living. And of course, there was the rivalry of the Philadelphia Eagles versus the Pittsburgh Steelers! No, Philadelphia was not for us.

Dallas was warm, had no snow, and boasted a lower cost of living. We would even be able to afford a house with a pool for the kids. The position and salary were not comparable to DC, and of course, the rivalry between the Dallas Cowboys and the Pittsburgh Steelers also came up. But the determining factor for not taking the job in Dallas was the distance from family.

George Washington University was a good opportunity with a nice salary. Sal would be able to get his master's degree, and there seemed to be room for advancement.

We found a suburb in Maryland that reminded us a bit of Pittsburgh. The icing on top was that travel time to family was only three hours by car.

Selling the house that we had custom built was a bit difficult, but sacrifices are made for those we love.

"A house is only a house," I told myself. "But you can make a home anywhere."

I also had to leave my ET job in Pittsburgh. Surprisingly, that was not as hard as I anticipated.

## Chapter 3

WE ARRIVED IN OUR NEW LOCATION IN AUGUST 1988, JUST IN TIME to get the boys settled into their new school. Shaun was going into sixth grade and Scott into grade four. I had to find a day care for three-year-old Mark and a new job for myself.

We moved into a community in Gaithersburg, Maryland, called Montgomery Village. We rented a three-level, three-bedroom townhouse on a cul-de-sac, very convenient to the grocery store, the kids' new school, and a Catholic church. Also, there was a Montessori day care–preschool within walking distance. A large shopping mall was only five minutes away. Travel distance for Sal to DC was forty-five minutes. Seemed like a perfect location.

Sal began his new position at George Washington University in the Emergency Medicine Degree Program and prepared to teach his first class.

Once everyone was settled, everything was unpacked, and the house became a home, I began my job search. I found a nighttime position at Sibley Memorial Hospital in Northwest DC as a charge nurse on one of their medical units. I thought nights would give me adequate time with the kids, plus it included a salary bonus.

Unfortunately, this wound up being the only job in my entire career that I walked out on—after completing my shift, of course. It only took three weeks.

We had a patient in an isolation room who was near death's door. I could handle the technical aspects of his care and his terminal condition. What I couldn't handle was his diagnosis. He was dying of AIDS.

In 1988, not a lot was known about HIV and AIDS. This was my first encounter—my first patient. All I knew was that I had a three-year-old at home, and with one fateful slip of a needle, I could die. I decided that this was not the job for me.

Back to the classifieds once again.

While looking in the nursing section of the newspaper, I saw an advertisement:

Nurses . . . Try Real Estate!

Intrigued, I read on. They were offering a training course taught by one of the managers of a well-established real estate firm. At the end of the three-week course, you would sit for the real estate licensure exam. You would then be able to affiliate with any agency and operate as an agent. Three weeks of training, making my own calendar, and booking according to Sal's work schedule and family needs sounded great.

I signed up and drove to Bethesda, Maryland, for the class. It was there that I met my soon-to-be forever friend, Roberta. Our meeting that day has taken us on an incredible journey of ups and downs over the last three-plus decades. Another God-directed appointment!

I finished the course, took the exam, and became a licensed real estate agent. Roberta and I became real estate partners and started working in a local firm in Damascus, Maryland, about twenty minutes from Gaithersburg.

While showing houses to prospective buyers, I found a four-bedroom, two-story home with a finished basement and fenced backyard. Sal and I purchased it. Interest rates in 1989 were through the roof, and the only way we could manage was with an 18 percent adjustable-rate mortgage.

In hindsight . . . what a mistake. We should have waited, but after selling our dream house back in Pittsburgh, we were eager to be home-owners again.

Within two years, we were about to go into foreclosure. So we relinquished the house and moved into a rental townhouse on the other side of Damascus. It was a three-level, three-bedroom townhouse with a deck and small backyard, situated on a cul-de-sac.

It was during that year, 1991, that trouble began.

One day we received a call from the school telling us that Scott, who was in seventh grade, had gotten into a car with some other students and left in the middle of the day. They had found out that the driver was seventeen, but they would not give us his name. We immediately called the police. An officer came to our house to take information and discuss the situation.

A few hours later, he called to tell us they had talked with the driver and found out that he had dropped the kids off in Tacoma Park, which is near Washington, DC.

What did my twelve-year-old son know about that area? Nothing!

Sal somehow managed to find the names of the other kids and contact numbers for their parents. He called each one, but they were either unable or unwilling to join in the search.

Sal and Shaun got in the car and drove to the intersection in Tacoma Park where the police officer had told us the driver had dropped the kids.

By the time they got there, it was getting dark. There was nothing around the intersection except a movie theatre. Sal's thought as he waited in the vehicle was that maybe they had gone into the theatre. Sure enough, when the movie let out, there were Scott and five of his runaway buddies.

Very relieved to find them alive and well, Sal wordlessly loaded them into the car and dropped each kid at their home.

There would be a strong discussion with Scott when morning came, but for that night, it was enough to have him home safe. The police officer who'd been working with us was notified, and everyone breathed a sigh of relief.

For the next three years, life with Scott was not easy. He played sports, continuing baseball and soccer and trying football. But he found his passion and gifting when he became involved with theatre.

During eighth grade, he started with a local community drama group called Imagination Station and began traveling to neighborhood grade schools, putting on performances.

Having discovered a passion for theatre, especially Shakespeare, Scott became the youngest member ever to work in the Maryland Renaissance

Festival, at age fourteen. The festival is a massive annual event from August to October. There are jousting tournaments, food vendors, craftsmen, and performances on twenty-seven acres, portraying life in a sixteenth-century English village. Scott participated in the festival for two years in a row.

When he entered ninth grade at Damascus High School, his love for theatre spilled over into drama classes. In tenth grade, he played King Pellinore in *Camelot*. The reason he did not get the lead role of King Arthur was because it was a musical, and Scott did not sing. He did an awesome job with his character role and was quite memorable.

All his teachers thought he had a future in acting. He even started taking voice lessons.

However . . .

A few problems had arisen after his seventh-grade runaway escapade. First, he started smoking cigarettes, which made it easy to start smoking marijuana. Marijuana had an adverse effect on his personality. I used to say it was like there were two boys, Scott and the "other Scott."

Next was skipping school, then lying to cover up whatever behavior he was trying to hide.

During this time, we tried all kinds of interventions: individual counseling, family counseling, and even drug rehab in a day facility. The problem with all these was that, being a great actor, Scott always knew what to say and how to act. He fooled everyone. Later, he even bragged about smoking marijuana in the bathroom of his drug rehab facility.

The only class he managed to attend was theatre. It got so bad that the teachers walked him from class to class so he wouldn't be disqualified from participating in *Camelot*. That intervention only worked until the play was over. After that, he just quit school completely.

I tried everything and was devastated to find that Maryland's dropout age was sixteen. I couldn't even get help to keep my son in school. Sal and I decided to try a school of the performing arts for him.

In October of what would have been his junior year, we took him to Duke Ellington High School of Performing Arts in Washington, DC, to discuss the possibility of enrollment. They were reluctant to admit him after the year had already begun, but were willing to offer him an audition.

As Sal and I sat in the office and waited, they took him for an impromptu audition. Upon their return, they told us he had undeniable talent, and they enrolled him that very day. He started classes immediately and quickly procured one of the leads in the school play. He traveled back and forth each day by metro and told us how much he loved the school.

We went to the school play, and he did a great job.

Before the December break, the school had an open house for parents to meet teachers. Sal and I went with Scott. The first class was theatre, and his teacher spoke highly of him, as well as his performance in the school play.

From there, it all went downhill.

In the next class, there seemed to be a mistake. Scott's name was not on the roster. The same with the next class. We turned to question Scott, and he immediately took off running down the steps and out the door.

Our hearts sank once again. We later found out that theatre was the only class he ever attended. He spent the rest of the day in a nearby park, playing chess with the old men. Needless to say, he did not go back to school, and the school never missed him.

During this time, Shaun exceled in school, taking advanced placement classes. He continued with soccer, playing for both Damascus High School and a travel team. He got a job at sixteen at the local Roy Rogers restaurant and within months was given manager duties. He was a "good" kid . . . until he reached eighteen and something snapped. It was like someone opened the door of the cage and let the monster out.

He started along the same path as Scott, although he decided to sell marijuana instead of smoking it. Shaun became one of the dealers in Damascus, all without our knowledge. He had a pager, so no one ever called our house or came to the door. He handled business through codes on the pager.

It wasn't until I went to leave for work one morning and found all the windows in his car smashed and all his tires slashed that I became aware that something was really wrong. Soon after that, I found a large bag of weed hidden in their room and flushed it down the toilet. When I told Scott what I had done, he freaked out.

The fear in his eyes told the story. "Mom, what have you done? They'll kill us!"

Dramatic effect or not, I panicked and, naturally, called the police. I told them what I had done and how I had put both of my sons in jeopardy. The police soon arrived at our house to handle the situation.

Their answer was to put a wire on Scott and send him out to help catch a bigger fish by buying drugs from him. My son wore the wire and met up with the dealer. He secretly showed him the wire, and I'm not sure what else transpired, but the police thanked him, and that was the end of it. Neither of my sons were ever charged or arrested. Really . . . everywhere I turned, I was unable to find help.

Sal and I each worked two jobs to make ends meet and continued to take care of our youngest son, Mark, as well as managing our household. There was a lot of stress during that time.

Sal completed his master of arts degree in education and human development through George Washington University. He worked overseeing an offshoot of the main university, still teaching paramedic classes but now in Fairfax, Virginia, at a location called CPEC, short for Commonwealth Paramedic Education Center.

I supplemented real estate for a while as a home health nurse until I found a position at a newly opened urgent care center in Damascus. I started as a nurse and ended up the clinical coordinator for what eventually turned out to be a total of five centers in different locations.

Between the drugs and skipping school, our two older sons both started leaving the house before we came home from work and coming home after we were in bed.

Scott was about to turn eighteen, and I felt I was going to lose him forever if I didn't do something, especially after what had transpired with Shaun's coming of age. To say I was at my wit's end is an understatement. I had no clue what to do.

## Chapter 4

MY FRIEND ROBERTA TOLD ME THAT SHE WAS SENDING HER SON, Justin, to a week-long church camp at Damascus Camp Meeting. She suggested I send Scott too.

I was intrigued. "What's a camp meeting?"

"Oh, they read the Bible a lot and pray."

I thought a moment. "You know what? I have tried everything else . . . why not God!"

I packed his clothes and forcefully told my seventeen-year-old son to get in the car . . . and he did! I was stunned but managed to drive him to Damascus Camp Meeting.

The grounds were dotted with little white cabins and an outside tabernacle. After registering him, I quickly left. All the way home, I cried.

It didn't take long for me to begin to feel guilty, thanks to my good Catholic upbringing. Thoughts kept popping into my head.

*Where did I put him?*

*What are they going to teach him?*

*What if it's a cult?*

I called Roberta the next morning, and she suggested we attend the evening service, which was open to anyone. I quickly agreed. We showed up and found seats in the middle of the outdoor tabernacle. All I really remember is that when the preacher asked a question—I don't even remember what it was—a loud voice from behind me rang out.

"I have been called to preach!"

I froze, then looked at Roberta. "Was that my son?"

"Yep." She beamed. "It sure was!"

I burst into tears!

At that moment, the preacher made an altar call.

Roberta looked at me and the tears streaming down my face. "You should go."

Wasting no time, I made my way to the altar rail. I knelt down and was led in the sinner's prayer, accepting Jesus as my Lord and Savior. The best part about it was that Scott knelt down next to me and accepted Jesus at the very same time.

It was August 1996. I left that night satisfied that my son was finally in the right place to get help. I didn't know what that meant or how things were going to pan out, but leaving him there for the rest of the week felt like the right thing to do.

Over the course of the week, I bombarded Roberta with questions. She brought me a Bible and said to start reading the book of John. And to find a good church.

I said, "I can't go back to the Catholic church. Where do I go?"

"Well, there is a church right at the camp meeting. Why don't you go there?"

That sounded good, but then the bigger question came out. "How do I tell Sal?"

Sal listened to my story. Although he never stopped me from doing what I wanted to do, he wasn't going to go with me. So the following Sunday morning, I went to the church at the campgrounds, Damascus Wesleyan Church, alone.

I was warmly greeted and ushered to a seat. A few people asked if this was my first time and welcomed me. I felt like they really meant it. No one had ever talked to us when we'd attended the local Catholic church . . . ever.

The service was very different from the Catholic Mass that I was used to. They had a full band on the altar, including a piano, drums, guitar, and bass. Our folk Mass had a guitar; otherwise, an organ and choir was what I was used to.

When they prayed, it was not a rote prayer in unison, but uplifted individual voices in personal prayers . . . all together, out loud. And they clapped their hands and loudly praised the Lord. Everyone smiled and seemed happy to be there.

The sermon was good, and Pastor Jerry was warm and friendly. At the end, he stood at the door to say goodbye to everyone. He asked my name, thanked me for coming, and told me he hoped to see me the next week. The way I was treated made me want to come back. I actually looked forward to the next Sunday. Maybe it was me who needed the help!

When I arrived the next week, Pastor Jerry smiled. "Hello, Renee." He shook my hand. "I'm glad you came back."

He knew my name. He remembered me! That did it . . . this was where I was supposed to be. Now if I could only get Sal to go with me.

A Catholic Mass is an hour long and quite comfortable for Sal. There was no way he would sit for a two-hour service. But on Sunday nights, there was a one-hour prayer service with praise and worship. Sal had been in a band back in his teens and still played the keyboard, so I figured he would love the music. I decided this would be a perfect introduction to this new church. When I told him about it, he was intrigued and agreed to go.

After going to the Sunday-night prayer service a few times, I watched Sal walk right up to Pastor Jerry at the front of the church.

"Yes, Sal." Pastor Jerry gave him a warm smile. "What can I do for you?"

Sal sighed. "Let's get this over with."

"Get what over with, Sal?"

"This 'saved' thing . . ." he explained. "Let's get this over with."

Pastor Jerry walked him through the prayer. On October 6, 1996, my husband received Jesus Christ as his Lord and Savior.

Mark, who was eleven at the time, received Jesus as his Savior during the children's church service. Nell, Pastor Jerry's daughter-in-law, did a wonderful job as children's pastor, and Mark loved it!

Scott occasionally came out to youth group with Pastor Clark, who was Pastor Jerry's son-in-law and also Nell's brother. Pastor Clark was very committed to young people and their challenges, and Scott found himself wanting to come if even only now and then.

The only holdout was Shaun, who thought we were all nuts. The boys were still not doing right things, but somehow it was a little easier to live through since we had found a personal relationship with Jesus and support from our new church family.

Two weeks after Sal received Jesus as his personal Savior, there was a video presentation during the prayer service about a ministry in Zambia, Africa. The missionary was working as a maintenance man at a small mission hospital while he waited to find land to base the mission on. As photos of the hospital were shown on the screen, something came over me. I had no idea what I was feeling. All I knew was that I would be going there. Tears filled my eyes.

At that moment, Sal leaned over and spoke in my ear. "When are we going?"

I froze. Why had he asked me right at that moment? We had *never* talked of going out of the country, let alone to *Africa*. The farthest we ever talked about traveling was to Hawaii.

The second we got into the car after the service, I brought it up. "Why did you ask me right at that moment?"

"I don't know." He shrugged. "I just felt like we were going there."

A warm feeling overtook me. "Do you think that was God?"

He looked at me with raised brows, then pondered in silence.

We didn't bring it up again. We continued to go to the Sunday-night services and started attending the two-hour morning service as well.

November 10, 1996, was about to become Miracle Sunday. During the morning service, Pastor Jerry told the congregation that the missionary in Zambia had found the land for the ministry. He said that we needed to raise a quarter of a million dollars to buy the ten thousand acres. There were two parcels—one with a main house and other buildings, and the other with four thousand acres of open bush. The missionary named the two parcels of land James and John, so according to Mark 3:17, the name Sons of Thunder was penned.

> James the son of Zebedee and John the brother of James, to whom He gave the name Boanerges, that is, "Sons of Thunder." (Mark 3:17 NKJV)

Pastor Jerry told the story of how his brother-in-law had seen the land in a dream. He had told Jerry that he saw not only outbuildings but also a railroad track and a river.

The first piece of land that the missionary had found was only five thousand acres and did not have a railroad track or a river.

Pastor Jerry had told him, "It's the wrong land. Keep looking."

This ten-thousand-acre farm not only had outbuildings but also a railroad track and the Maramba River.

So Pastor Jerry had declared, "That's the one!"

After hearing the story, Sal and I witnessed the raising of $250,000 in pledges from the congregation in that one morning service. I could feel something different in the atmosphere, which I later came to know as the presence of the Lord.

By February of the following year, Sal had become an usher. He was seated in the back with the other ushers on the left-hand side of the church. I was in the front on the right-hand side. Pastor Jerry started talking about how the missionary in Zambia had moved onto the property, which was now paid in full, and into the main house with his family. Then Pastor Jerry said those fateful words I will never forget.

"The poor missionary wife keeps getting knocks at the door for Tylenol and Band-Aids."

That feeling came over me again. I knew with my entire being that we were supposed to start a clinic on the farm.

I don't know how else to explain it. I could not contain myself in that seat.

I got up and made my way to the ladies' room. Once inside, I burst into tears. "How can You ask me to do that? I can't go to Africa."

After a few minutes, I realized I wasn't accomplishing anything, so I dried my eyes and exited the bathroom. I was unable to return to my seat, however, because my good Catholic upbringing wouldn't let me go down front while the pastor was speaking. Spotting an empty seat next to Sal, I made my way over to him.

Before I could even settle in, Sal leaned over and said, "I know, we are supposed to start a clinic on the farm."

I almost screamed! How did he know? He used the exact same words that I'd heard in my spirit just a few moments earlier. It was all I could do to sit still for the rest of the service.

## Chapter 5

*START A CLINIC ON THE FARM.*

In Zambia, Africa! Oh my!

If I wasn't sure it was God speaking to my spirit that Sunday night during the video, there was no doubt now that the Almighty God of the Universe had just given us both an assignment to complete.

How could we possibly say no?

*So now what do we do?*

I decided to make an appointment with Pastor Jerry.

Sitting in his office, I blurted it out. "I think Sal and I are supposed to go to Zambia."

"Renee . . ." Knowing that we had been saved less than six months before, he cautioned me. "Africa is not a place you want to—"

"I never said I *wanted* to go." I held up a hand. "I said, 'I think we are *supposed* to go.'"

"Okay." He smiled kindly. "We have a work team going in August. You and Sal can go along. You just need five thousand dollars. That will include both airfares, travel shots, housing, food, and tourist activities."

Sounded easy. The only problem was, we didn't have any money. No savings. None. Yes, we each worked full time and even had part-time jobs to supplement, but we were in serious credit card debt. We'd applied for credit cards to pay off other credit cards. We were literally living paycheck to paycheck.

But listening to the sermons every Sunday and reading the Bible, I kept hearing that God is Jehovah Jireh, the God who provides. Since this was His idea in the first place, I told Sal, "If God wants us to go, He will provide the money."

Sure enough, it happened. Soon after, we went to our accountant to have our taxes done. We had owed money the previous year, and no changes had taken place during the current year. We held the same jobs, made the same salaries, lived in the same house, had the same expenses, and even used the same accountant.

This time however, after reviewing our documents, she said, "How does six thousand eight hundred dollars sound?"

I gulped. "We owe that much?"

"No." The accountant grinned. "That's your refund!"

Sal and I looked at each other in amazement.

Back then, you had to mail hard copies to the IRS, so we'd have to wait for a call to pick up the paperwork.

Once in the car, we just stared at each other. God had provided! It was another confirmation that we were indeed supposed to go to Zambia to start a clinic.

We scheduled our flights and appointments for travel shots. Altogether, the cost for the entire mission trip to Zambia was going to be fifty-eight hundred dollars. Our tax refund was going to be a thousand more than we needed!

Then the accountant called, only not to tell us the paperwork was done but that she had made a mistake in her calculations. Our hearts sank as we listened on speaker phone, waiting for the dreaded news. We knew it had been too good to be true.

Now what would we do?

After taking a deep breath, she said that she was sorry, but the amount was not going to be sixty-eight hundred as she thought.

"The correct refund is fifty-eight hundred."

We looked at each other and smiled. God was providing exactly what we needed, and He was making sure we knew it was Him.

In August of 1997, we started off on our three-week mission trip to Zambia, with Pastor Jerry and a team of volunteers from our church in Damascus. We left Mark, who was twelve years old, with family in

Pittsburgh, but our eighteen- and twenty-year-old sons were another story. We locked the doors to our house and told them to find another place to stay for those three weeks. That may seem harsh, but they had already been staying out and not coming home, and we didn't want partying and drugs and problems in our house.

We asked Roberta and her husband, Skip, to monitor our house and to be available if our kids needed anything. Since both of them had a work history of dealing with troubled young people, we felt secure enough to leave. Besides, it was God's job to watch over our kids back home, since this was His idea.

Two days and three planes later, when we entered the guesthouse at Sons of Thunder, a message was waiting for us from Roberta. She had called to tell us that our sons had broken into the house as soon as we left, but everything was under control. She and Skip would be monitoring both the house and the boys.

Since there was nothing we could do from eight thousand miles away, we let it slip to the back of our minds to be dealt with upon our return to the States. We needed to concentrate on the job at hand.

We had packed two suitcases each, one for our clothes and one with whatever medical supplies we thought would be needed to start a clinic. The first night and the next day were spent settling in, getting acclimated to the time difference, and overcoming jet lag.

After taking a tour of the farm and existing outbuildings, it became apparent that there was no place readily available to establish a clinic. We had been scheduled, however, to go to the hospital we had seen on the video from church and work for four days alongside the two old missionary doctors and their wives.

Besides talking about what life was like on the mission field, making rounds at the hospital, and going out for emergency calls in the middle of bush fires, Sal was asked to assist with a cesarean delivery. He was handed the baby after the surgery to give to the midwife, who would assess the newborn's status.

However, the midwife backed away, waiting to see if the child would start breathing on its own. Sal ended up resuscitating the newborn.

As for me, I didn't do much except take it all in.

The hospital itself was like a Motel 6 with open wards. Even the TB ward had multiple patients and open windows and doors instead of isolation rooms with gowns and masks like I was accustomed to in the United States. The operating room, which they called the "theatre," was also a bit shocking. There were bugs crawling all over the utility room, or scrub room, as well as catheters and tubes for all orifices in the body soaking together in the same disinfectant container. Lab technicians collected patients' blood with syringes, then placed the specimens in old medicine bottles instead of vacutainers and blood tubes.

One day we had to drive an hour and fifteen minutes to the hospital in Livingstone just to borrow a couple of IVs. No . . . this was not America. Medical care in a developing nation was quite different. But then again, so was life itself.

Out in the rural communities, as well as back on the farm, people lived in small huts made of grass. They didn't have electricity, but some used candles, solar panels, or car batteries to add light to their houses. They didn't have toilets. Some dug holes near their house for a pit latrine, but others just relieved themselves outside in the African bush. They used either firewood or handmade charcoal to cook.

People were very thin, some even emaciated. Most didn't have shoes. Children played with balls made of trash or handmade toy vehicles made of wire. A lot of kids had swollen bellies due to malnutrition.

Shopping in town consisted of local open markets and a couple of small neighborhood grocery stores. When the missionary wife needed to do bulk shopping for visitors, she would cross the border into Zimbabwe to go to a small supermarket.

One day, a young boy came to the guesthouse at the farm to see me, escorted by a translator. I found out that the boy's name was Tom, and he was ten years old. He couldn't speak any English, but he rolled up his pant leg and showed me a gaping, draining wound on his lower leg. Since I wasn't allowed to bring anyone into the guesthouse, I had him wait on the front porch while I collected the medical supplies I would need.

Upon my return, I cleaned his wound with hydrogen peroxide, applied Neosporin, then bandaged it. I smiled and told him in sign language to return the next day at the same time. The translator also repeated my instructions in Chetonga. Tom smiled and nodded.

He came the next day, and every day, eventually without the translator, to have his dressing changed. The wound was no longer draining and was getting smaller and smaller. When the time came for us to return to America, I asked the missionary wife to continue the dressings until the wound was completely healed. That was my only medical contribution to our trip.

Sal and I went home, a bit discouraged that we had not fulfilled God's call to "start a clinic on the farm." But looking back, it makes me laugh. What were we thinking? How unrealistic to think we could start a clinic in a developing country and be done and ready to go home in three weeks!

All these years later, I also realize God's call to *start* a clinic was all we could handle at the time. "Starting" a clinic had nothing to do with staying and working in it.

Once on US soil again, we explained to God that we had been willing to obey His command, but the circumstances in Zambia—with the lack of a building, personnel, and medical supplies—had made it impossible. Three weeks was not enough time to carry out His vision.

So we decided to wait until we heard from Him again. He needed to tell us the way forward. In the meantime, we decided to carry on with our lives, our family, our jobs, and our relationship with Him.

For the next eight years, that was exactly what we did. In hindsight, it was a time of preparation. God had a lot of work to do to get us ready for the call and life He had in store for us.

## Chapter 6

AS I REFLECT ON OUR EIGHT YEARS OF PREPARATION, FROM 1997 TO 2005, I see that they were definitely years of waiting. We had to wait for God to say, *The time is now*, not knowing if that time would ever come but always anticipating its arrival. All we knew for sure was that we had not completed what God had commanded us to do. We needed to wait on *God's timing*.

People would frequently ask *when* we were going to Zambia. After a while, they asked *if* we were going. Eventually, they stopped asking altogether.

We stayed busy during those years, while waiting on God. Our prayer was that we would hear Him and obey. These things did not happen all at once, but God prepared us, without our knowledge or understanding. We made mistakes and didn't always hear or follow His instructions readily, but we both had a willing spirit and a desire to please Him. We had trials and difficulties, but He was always faithful and always there. He spoke in different ways to each of us, and He pushed or got louder when we didn't move fast enough.

In order to carry out what God had purposed for us, we were going to need to take on the role of a servant, being submissive to divine authority and obedient to His direction, never sharing His glory. We were also going to need to submit to the governing authorities.

He started with cleansing.

First, our hearts were cleansed with confession, repentance, and removal of idols.

Sal was teaching paramedics at the satellite campus of George Washington University in Fairfax, Virginia, and had plaques all over his office and the halls of the training center. The plaques had been given to him by students over the years, praising and thanking him for a job well done. He removed them all from the walls one day and packed them in a box. He added all his Boy Scout paraphernalia and sports trophies that had been stored in the attic, and he went to the garbage dump.

My idol was a little harder. It was Christmas.

I loved decorating, baking cookies, spending too much money on gifts, wrapping presents, buying poinsettias, watching Christmas movies, and going to look at lights. I even decorated two Christmas trees, a larger one for the family and a smaller one for me. No one was allowed to touch Mom's tree!

We always put up the artificial trees the day after Thanksgiving and took them down after Super Bowl Sunday in mid-January. That way, we could enjoy Christmas longer. I thoroughly enjoyed the commercialism and all the hustle and bustle of the season. I didn't realize it was an idol for me until one fateful year.

Our basement flooded one day while we were all out. When we surveyed the damage, we found that the water had entered the storage area where we had the Christmas decorations, ruining the family Christmas tree.

When it came time to decorate that year, I decided to put up my tree in place of the family tree, since the kids were older and really didn't care. After I had decorated my tree to perfection in the living room of our townhouse, Scott was horsing around. He fell backward into the tree, breaking the artificial branches, lights, and ornaments beyond repair. The nativity set, however, was untouched.

The first Christmas tree had been destroyed in a flood a couple months before Christmas. The remaining one had been demolished. And the nativity set survived.

As I sat there on the floor in tears because of the tree, angry at my son for messing up my Christmas, I realized I had never celebrated its true meaning. I bought a Ray Boltz Christmas CD and played the song "A Perfect Tree" over and over again. I finally realized what God was trying to tell me. I repented, and that year we did not have a Christmas tree. Instead, I bought poinsettias and made a display around the nativity scene. I set it up in the kitchen, where I would see it often and be reminded of the true meaning of Christmas—the birth of Jesus Christ.

The song played all that year, reminding me of His sacrifice for me. As I look back, it's now clear that God was preparing me for a life without Christmas as I knew it.

After cleansing our hearts, it was time for our home.

The first step we made was to clean out all the alcohol in our house. We realized that neither one of us had a desire or a taste for even a beer or a glass of wine anymore. It was like the Holy Spirit had taken it away. So down the drain it all went!

Next, we cleaned out our reading material. Being avid readers, we enjoyed crime thrillers, dark mysteries, science fiction, and fantasy. Despite not really knowing why, we felt led to remove them from our house, so we did, giving some to the community library and some to a thrift shop in town.

After cleansing, the next thing God worked on was submission.

We decided to join a Bible study at church. The lesson being presented was from a book by John Bevere called *Under Cover*. Sal was so impacted by the study on submission and spiritual authority and the divine protection it brings that he purchased all the materials and went through the series a couple of times on his own.

I, however, was about to learn about submission the hard way. First, with my husband.

I thought our marriage was a partnership, and we always discussed problems, plans, and situations before making final decisions. I didn't realize that submission only comes into play when both parties disagree. Otherwise, it is just agreement. So I had to come to the realization that I could voice my opinion, even strongly, but the final decision over a situation rested with Sal.

We had been married for more than twenty years at this point, so we already agreed on most things. The one area we did not always agree on was money. Every Sunday, we would sit over the bills together, but

I would write checks and make decisions. That had been the way it was for our entire marriage.

Sal had started to take a leadership role with our finances after some sermons on the topic at church. One Sunday, he sat down to write checks, but I looked over his shoulder, mouthing my displeasure over something he'd decided to do. All at once, something happened.

Believe it or not, I could not see. I was blinded. Literally, everything was black!

I screamed in panic. "I can't see!" He didn't believe me at first, so I repeated myself. "Sal, I can't see!"

I immediately lifted my eyes from the paper and stood up. Remarkably, my eyesight returned.

I was so scared that I backed away. "I don't think God wants me to be involved with our finances. That's for you. You need to do it by yourself, taking your place as head of our household."

To this day, I have never again looked at or interfered with our personal finances. What I didn't realize at the time was that God was beginning to divide our areas of responsibility: Sal with our personal finances in the USA, and me with the accounting of Sons of Thunder in Zambia.

The second test I endured was with my pastor.

During this time, I felt God telling me I was to be financial secretary of the church. I was already adept in QuickBooks and inputting financial data, so I went to Pastor Jerry and told him how I felt God directing me.

He, however, told me I was wrong and that he thought I should be church secretary, which involved handling visitors and the pastor's calendar, as well as writing and printing the bulletin.

I had no desire to be someone's secretary, nor did I know anything about writing and printing bulletins, but I submitted. It was a job with flexible hours, and it gave us some extra money at a time when we were in need. I definitely was more qualified for the financial position, but it turned out that my being the church secretary was a test of humility. It also held the position for someone who really needed it and for whom it was well suited.

A year or so after completing my interim time in the church secretary position, I was asked by the volunteer treasurer of Sons of Thunder, USA, if I would consider doing the books for a year while he took a sabbatical. I agreed and ended up handling the accounts where donations were collected, recorded, and sent to Sons of Thunder, Zambia, for their operations.

What I didn't realize at the time was that God was giving me a bird's-eye view of how things operated behind the scenes in the United States. It was going to help me later on to understand operations better and answer donors' questions from both perspectives.

In another act of submission, we learned about tithing. We were in church at a Wednesday-night service when the assistant pastor started preaching. He quoted Malachi 3:9–10.

> "You are under a curse—your whole nation—because you are robbing me. Bring the whole tithe into the storehouse, that there may be food in my house. Test me in this," says the LORD Almighty, "and see if I will not throw open the floodgates of heaven and pour out so much blessing that there will not be room enough to store it."

The pastor added, "You can't outgive God. It's the only time God tells you to test Him. So why not try Him?"

Sal and I looked at each other. We both felt convicted. We were learning about tithing—giving 10 percent of our income to our church—for the first time. We always paid the bills first, then gave whatever small amount was left to God. Now we were hearing to give to God first, then pay the bills. So when our next paychecks came, we closed our eyes and bit our lips, and Sal wrote the check for 10 percent of the total.

Wow, it was scary. But somehow, we still managed to pay all the bills that month and every month since. I don't know how it works. I just know it does. You really can't outgive God!

Sal and I were and still are take-charge people, not only in our careers but also in our home and with each other. We were always striving to be independent decision makers and had been trained in our positions to tell others what to do. And we both did it well. The problem was, to live in Christ means to be dependent, submit to authority, and follow His direction. These were all things we had to learn in this new Jesus-centered life. But as you walk in humility, it brings great reward, and I was about to see that fulfilled in my life.

As it says in Luke 14:11 ESV, "For everyone who exalts himself will be humbled, and he who humbles himself will be exalted."

Both of us were working hard, but we were still struggling with credit card debt and bill collectors. Not knowing what else to do, I walked into our neighborhood bank and asked to see someone about financial advice. To my surprise, they ushered me into the office of the president of the bank. What did I have to lose?

I told him how, despite our being working professionals with good salaries, we had no savings and were finding it difficult to pay the bills and manage our money. I asked for some kind of financial help or budget-making guidance. I laid before him a pile of papers that I thought he might need to see. As he attentively listened, I felt very comfortable in his office. I did not feel judged. I felt like he understood and was taking me seriously.

After I completed my tale of woe, he looked me in the eye without viewing any of the papers and sincerely said, "What you need to do is buy a house."

"I don't think you understand," I sputtered. "We don't have any savings. There's absolutely nothing for a down payment. We can't afford to buy a house."

Calmly, he replied, "I have a house I want you to look at that we have received in foreclosure. It is an end-unit townhouse in the Plantations development. We don't need a down payment. Just someone to take over monthly payments."

I sat there, amazed.

He continued. "You already told me your employment history and salaries, and just from your visit here, I see you are financially responsible. I think the house is the solution to your problem."

I was dumbfounded. Plantations was the community where Roberta lived! It had a community association and a swimming pool. It would be awesome.

I had walked into his office with the weight of the world on my shoulders and no solution in sight, and I walked out with an answer I never expected.

I immediately called Sal, and we went to look at the three-level, three-bedroom townhouse with a finished walkout basement and small fenced yard. It was perfect! So we became homeowners once again.

That townhome was a blessing when we needed it the most, and years later when we purchased a single-family home, we were able to keep it as a rental property.

Over the years, it ended up being a blessing to three other families who were in need of help, including our son Scott.

# Chapter 7

LITTLE DID WE KNOW THAT GOD WAS PREPARING US FOR THE long haul.

Both Sal and I had a lot to learn, and we were hungry for more. Just like every new Christian, we learned about quiet time, plans for daily Bible reading, devotions, prayer, praise and worship, being thankful, practicing presence, Bible studies, baptism, spiritual warfare, and numerous other lessons.

It all seemed overwhelming at times, especially since we were still dealing with our two older sons. They continued to live opposite our schedules. They would be in bed when we left early in the morning for work and were gone when we got home. They did not return home until we were in bed. So the cycle continued.

In an attempt to break the cycle, Sal decided to try something bold. We woke the boys up at six a.m. and made them come to breakfast and morning devotions. At least I knew they ate one good meal. After we dismissed them, they would go back to bed, and we would go to work. Circumstances did not change overnight, but we had hope.

Things came to a head on Memorial Day weekend, 1998. Sal and I were awakened by the urgent shouts of our two older sons. We found Shaun and Scott bloody and beaten at the foot of the stairs. We called 9-1-1, and they were taken to the emergency room. There were broken ribs, a broken nose, head trauma, and marks from a baseball bat on their heads and bodies. CT scans, x-rays, stitches, and bandages were the order of the day.

It was definitely a parent's nightmare, but I think it was a turning point in the lives of our sons. Scott started going more regularly to youth group, with Shaun occasionally by his side. By camp meeting in August 1998, Shaun got saved! God was faithful, and prayers were being answered.

Around this time, God started teaching me about fasting. Everywhere I turned, there was a sermon, a book, or someone talking about it. The problem was, I didn't know how to fast. Sure, I could skip a meal like anyone, but a true fast was something I had never done.

I started researching the different kinds of fasts, and I guess I was taking too long. I walked into work one morning at the endoscopy center, where I was the clinical manager, and I greeted Harvey, one of the techs. Harvey was a born-again Christian, very open with his faith and very spirit-filled. He would often read the Word during lunch.

That day as I greeted him, he said, "Renee, fast."

I had not discussed fasting with him or told anyone, for that matter, about what I felt God saying in my own quiet time.

I stopped dead in my tracks. "Why are you telling me that?"

Harvey shrugged. "I dreamt about you last night. In the dream, God told me to tell you to fast. So I am telling you, Renee: fast!"

I was so shaken that I left work and went directly to our church in Damascus. I prayed on the way. "Please, let Pastor Jerry be there."

When I pulled into the parking lot, Pastor Jerry's car wasn't there. I just sat outside in my car and prayed. "Please, let Pastor Jerry come."

After about ten minutes, Pastor Jerry drove in and found me in my car. I got out and told him the story and asked him to teach me how to fast.

That day, I went home and started fasting by only drinking liquids.

During those years of waiting and preparation, I learned how to fast, attempting different lengths of time and different types. Prayer and fasting became a way of life for me as I sought to get closer and closer to God.

For a season, Sal and I would go to church in the mornings together to pray. A young man in the church at that time was having difficulties with his car. He needed a vehicle for work, but the one he had was old and always breaking down. Sal felt led to give him one of ours to use but was still seeking confirmation and waiting for an answer.

When we were praying at church one morning, Sal suddenly looked up and said, "I just got a billboard!"

Confused, I asked, "What are you talking about?"

Sal eagerly explained. "I saw a billboard, and it said *give car now*!"

He immediately called the young man and asked him to come to the church. When he came, Sal handed him the keys to the vehicle. "This car is yours. We will handle the paperwork later. Could you drive Renee and me home?"

Once Sal was clear about what God had told him, he immediately obeyed.

During those years of preparation, I came upon the book *The Mary Miracle*, by Jack Hayford. I was totally absorbed in the book and its message. I feel a strong bond to Mary somehow. Maybe it's my Catholic roots or because Mary is my birth name.

According to the book, God comes *to* you, to grow *in* you, to be delivered *through* you to change the world *around* you. Jack Hayford says that God gives each of us an opportunity for a Mary Miracle. The Mary Miracle comes to the ordinary and doesn't require anything you can accomplish by yourself. The only qualifier is faith, believing God can do anything, and trusting Him. When He comes to you with an invitation or call, you listen, receive, and believe. You just need to respond, then the Holy Spirit will come upon you, and the power of the Most High will overshadow you. Once you hear, don't doubt but actively wait.

That was exactly what I felt Sal and I were going through. God came to us that day at church to call us to Zambia to start a clinic. We were just ordinary people, a man and a woman, a husband and a wife, a mom and a dad, a paramedic and a nurse. We were nothing special. But that day, we said yes, we listened, we heard, we received, we believed, and we did not doubt.

Now we were actively waiting for the time to come—for the Holy Spirit to come upon us and the power of the Most High to overshadow us. We surrendered our will for His and were hungry for more. Just as Mary waited nine months, we were waiting for our time to come.

Pastor Jerry stepped down as senior pastor of the church in order to be involved full time with Sons of Thunder. His son-in-law—Clark, the youth pastor—took over the lead position. Under the new leadership, there became more of a message that the church was not inside the building, so we were led to move in outreach activities.

Trying to submit to authority but being very uncomfortable with the idea of evangelizing, Sal verbalized what we were both thinking. "I can't do this."

We were supposed to go one Saturday as a group to a lower-income housing area near the church that was known for drugs and crime. We were to take a grill and cook hamburgers, as well as put new nets on the basketball hoops, play with kids, and pray for people.

As Sal was having second thoughts, I said, "Sal, if we can't go to our local neighborhood and minister, how are we going to go eight thousand miles away to Africa?"

He looked at me and thought for a moment. "You're right," he said. "Let's go."

So even though we were uncomfortable at first, we participated in whatever outreach opportunity was presented.

## Chapter 8

GOD HAD TO ALSO TEACH US HOW TO RECOGNIZE HIM WHEN HE spoke. It says in John 10:27, "My sheep listen to my voice: I know them, and they follow me."

Over and over again, God gave us opportunities to listen and obey, both individually and as a couple. Sometimes we did that better than other times. Sometimes it was a very small thing, and other times it was something a whole lot bigger.

In 1998, things became difficult for Sal at his job. Top leadership in the education program at GWU had changed, and he was being challenged and felt added pressure. Unfounded allegations were being made regarding discrimination with grades. It was during this time that God led Sal to start his own education company.

Sal, however, was not receptive to the idea, since he had always worked within an already established organization. He'd always had a boss. Starting his own company was scary, especially financially. But when it looked like he was going to lose his position at GWU, we went to a lawyer to start up a company. Associates in Emergency Care (AEC) was begun.

Once Sal was obedient to God and began the groundwork to start the company, everything fell into place. The issues at GWU were resolved, and Sal was cleared of all suspicions of discrimination. Policies had been followed equally for all. But after feeling God's push, Sal decided to leave GWU in order to put all his attention and effort into the new venture.

Once he handed in his resignation, the dean and other management at the university asked him to stay on for a year as a consultant. God provided him with not only the time to devote to starting and establishing AEC but also a full year's salary to do it.

We set up the company with Sal and me as employees. Sal began as the only instructor for the company and did marketing and scheduling, while I handled all the data entry, payroll, and accounting. Day by day, course by course, the business grew. God showed us how John the Baptist had gone to the School of the Holy Spirit and lived in the desert on locusts and honey so he would not owe anybody anything. No one had provided his financial support. That was exactly what God had in mind for us in Zambia. AEC was going to establish us as self-supporting missionaries, allowing us to raise funds for the entire ministry instead of ourselves.

One of the next directions given to me was to homeschool Mark through high school. Scott had dropped out of school after sophomore year. He later went on to get his GED, but it had been a struggle to get him to sit in a classroom. He could pass tests without ever studying, but going to school was a challenge.

We were afraid that Mark would have the same outcome as Scott, not because he couldn't manage academically but because he also struggled with staying inside a building all day. That was just not conducive to his type of learning.

So after much prayer and what I perceived as God's direction to homeschool, I went to part-time status at my job.

I admit, I found it difficult to trust God with the financial ramifications of my staying home, so instead of quitting outright, I backed down to half salary. Sal and I were both receiving small salaries from AEC. God had provided a year's salary from GWU, but that was coming to an end, and I feared not having enough to make the bills. But God was faithful, as business kept increasing for Sal and the company.

Once I saw that we could manage on half my salary, I quit completely and trusted God for the outcome. That decision gave me four years of individual attention and time with my youngest son. God knew we were going to leave Mark behind in Maryland at the age of twenty while we went on to answer the call to Zambia. Looking back, I see His love and care to make sure I was not left with a mother's guilt.

During the 1999–2000 school year, while teaching American history, I decided to concentrate on the Civil War, since we lived in an area full of battlegrounds, monuments, and historical sites.

One day as Mark and Sal and I were preparing to leave for a tour of one of these sites, Sal and I got into an argument. I don't remember what it was about, but it was enough to cancel the tour for the day. For some reason, Mark mentioned a housing development that was being constructed in New Market. We had gone the previous year and even filled out a financial application which, unfortunately, had been denied.

Having a weakness for viewing houses from my old real estate days, and as a way of making up, we decided to all go for a ride to see the progress, then stop for ice cream. We fell in love with one of the houses in the new section that had just been completed. It was a four-bedroom house with a loft outside the master bedroom, two and a half bathrooms, living room, dining room, kitchen, family room, breakfast nook, laundry room off the kitchen, unfinished basement, and two-car garage. This was the very house in the community called the Meadows at New Market that would become our new home!

This time we were approved for the loan without even selling our townhouse. To this day, I have no idea why, because all the numbers were the same as the year before. The only difference was that God had a plan for *this* particular house.

When we moved in, we didn't have enough furniture to fill all the rooms. But we felt strongly that we were supposed to stay liquid. We were not to buy any furniture in case we got called to Zambia. We already had furniture for three bedrooms. The fourth bedroom we made into an office for the business and had custom cabinets and counters installed. The loft, we left empty. As for the main floor, we put our furniture in the family room and dining room, leaving the living room empty.

We closed in part of the deck off the dining room, making a sunroom, and bought furniture for it. That became my favorite room to sit and read and seek God.

When we were looking at furniture for the sunroom, we came across a small living room set that would fit perfectly in the loft outside the master bedroom. Unable to resist, we purchased it. It was beautiful and did indeed fit perfectly. The only problem was, every time I walked past it, I felt guilty.

After a couple of days, I couldn't stand it any longer, so I called the store and asked to speak to the manager. I told him I had to return the furniture.

He asked, "Why, ma'am? Is there a problem?"

"No, sir. It's perfect. I love it."

"Then . . ." There was a moment of puzzled silence. "Why do you want to return it?"

I thought before responding. "Sir, are you a Christian?"

"Yes, I am."

"Then maybe you will understand. You see, I felt God say not to buy furniture, but I went ahead and did it, because I wanted it. Now every time I walk past the room, I'm reminded of my disobedience. Even if I don't get my money back, I just can't keep it. I made a mistake."

The manager sighed. "I understand, ma'am. I'll send the truck to pick it up, and you will get your full refund."

The next day, the guys from the store came and removed the furniture from the loft, and I felt like a load had been lifted.

As they carried the furniture past the empty living room and out the door, one of them said to me, "Don't worry, ma'am. You'll be able to get more furniture someday."

They were so sweet, but I had to chuckle. They thought the furniture was being repossessed!

One of the hardest things we had to do happened in 2002. According to the missionaries that were at Sons of Thunder, there was a severe drought and famine in Zambia. Pastor Jerry came into a Sunday service and told the congregation that we needed to raise money to prevent starvation at Sons of Thunder and the communities surrounding the farm.

Immediately, people started raising their hands and stating pledges or pulling dollar bills out of their pockets to put in the collection basket that was being passed around. Sal also wanted to raise his hand in pledge, but something told me "No," so I stopped him.

We had just received money from refinancing our house in order to put a built-in swimming pool in the side yard. As I sat there that morning, listening to the report of hunger and starvation, I felt strongly that our plans for a swimming pool were about to be topped by God's plan.

As we were leaving the service, Pastor Jerry took me aside. "When you can talk, I want to know what God said to you."

I was stunned . . . was I that obvious?

After talking with Sal in the car on the way home, we agreed to give the entire refinancing amount to Sons of Thunder for food and to forget the pool. We decided to follow God's plan instead of our own.

Before we could have second thoughts, we called Pastor Jerry and told him the whole story. That year, Sons of Thunder, Zambia, imported a large truckload of mealie meal from Zimbabwe to make it to the next harvest and prevent people from dying of hunger. The missionaries on-site also started a feeding program serving a meal three days a week to vulnerable people in the surrounding communities. People's lives were saved.

We had seen all our sons come to salvation, accepting the Lord Jesus as their personal Savior. Shaun and Scott were redeemed and delivered from their old life of drugs, then became youth leaders in the church with powerful testimonies of God's redeeming love. They each married a Christian girl from our church and started their families.

Because I was homeschooling Mark, I was available to provide childcare to three of our grandkids, giving me special "grandma time" with the children I would have to watch grow up from a distance.

Mark graduated from high school. My eighty-three-year-old mother passed away after a grueling year trying to recover from a car accident in which the airbag deployed and damaged her lungs. A history of cigarette smoking complicated her pulmonary condition, so she spent the last months of her life in a nursing home on a ventilator, alert, with a fully functioning mind, adamantly refusing to come home with me.

My father had passed away at home at the age of seventy-six from asbestosis of the lung in 1996. So after Mom's funeral and Mark's graduation, both in 2003, God said, *Now is the time.* He said it and confirmed it in many different ways.

A woman from church who was very sensitive to the leading of the Holy Spirit handed me a CD. She said, "I felt like God wanted me to give this to you."

It was a music CD by Lindell Cooley called *Open Up the Sky*. The most significant part was one of the songs titled, "It's Time." The words confirmed: "I hear the calling. It's time."[1]

The other surefire way we knew it was time was when I was sitting quietly by myself in the sunroom at dusk looking at the sky. In the cloud formation, I saw something. I called for Sal to come quickly.

"Look up." I pointed. "What do you see?"

"Oh wow." He gasped. "That looks like a nine-month fetus!"

My heart warmed at the confirmations. "Hun, I think our time has come."

## Chapter 9

WALKING OUT THE CALL ON YOUR LIFE—THE PURPOSE FOR WHICH you were born—will definitely lead you through times of difficulties, challenges, and obstacles. During those times, God wants you to be faith filled and sure that He will be your all in all, to lead you and walk with you through those times. It's during those times that faith grows.

Two weeks after we announced our plans to go to Zambia full time, Sal noticed a bulge in his abdomen. I told him it was probably a ventral hernia but that he should make an appointment to schedule any surgical repair if needed before we went to Zambia.

At the appointment, the physician said, "This is no hernia," and scheduled further diagnostic studies.

After all the tests, she informed us that Sal had non-Hodgkin's lymphoma. He was going to need his very enlarged spleen removed as soon as possible.

This came as quite a shock. Would Sal live? What would his life expectancy be? What if this lymphoma had spread? Would he need chemotherapy? Would we still be able to go to Zambia? How did this fit into God's plan for a medical clinic?

Looking back, I can see it was a time of testing. Would we trust God for the outcome? Did we believe He was healer? He already had proven Himself as provider. Would we trust Him? Would we have unwavering faith? Would we stand firm and see the deliverance of the Lord?

October 16, 2003, was the date scheduled for Sal to have his spleen removed. The week prior to his surgery, I was supposed to participate in a dance conference in Arkansas with our dance team from church. Flights had already been booked and plans made. Sal encouraged me to go.

Sitting on the plane with my friend Dawn from the team, I held my iPod and had my headphones on. A flight attendant asked what I was listening to, and I quickly replied, "Music." I did not elaborate any further.

She immediately handed me a portable CD player and said, "Listen to this." She then proceeded up the aisle.

Feeling I had no choice, I started to listen. It was a woman's voice speaking faith-filled Scripture. It surprised me, as I was not wearing a sign that said "Christian." I listened intently, writing down the name of the CD and the artist: *Who I Am in You* by Robyn Murphy. I quickly scribbled these notes in my journal:

Believe in the Word. God does not lie. All His promises are yes and amen.

At the very moment it ended, the flight attendant reappeared. She smiled and took the player.

When we landed, I wanted to say thank you, so Dawn and I looked for the flight attendant. She wasn't on the plane, and the other flight attendants told us there was no one else.

Dumbfounded, I said to Dawn, "Do you think that was an angel?"

Looking back, I know in my heart that God sent that angel to me. It was not a coincidence that she handed me a CD with everything He wanted to remind me of. He knew my heart and saw my obedience to keep on, even when my world had been shaken. He wanted me to know He was right there. He wanted me to remember His promises. He wanted me to trust Him through it all.

I returned from the conference, and Sal had surgery. His spleen was removed, and no further treatment was needed at that time. No chemotherapy. Nothing. Sal just needed to recuperate from abdominal surgery.

God had been faithful!

We made plans once again to go to Zambia full time in early 2004. Everything and everyone on the US side of Sons of Thunder was agreeable to the timetable. The Zambia side, however, was another story. The missionary there asked us to wait another year.

What? Why all these obstacles? Had God changed His mind?

It was decided that once Sal recovered from surgery, we would go there again on a mission trip and stay longer than the other volunteers. The thought was that we would see how life would be without a team of people.

One day while Sal was still recuperating, we went to the mall for a bit of walking. They had a new vehicle on display in a roped-off area. It was a Humvee.

As we were inspecting it and joking about how it would work in the African bush, a gray-haired man dressed in farm overalls came up to us and asked, "Why are you looking at a vehicle like this?"

I smiled and told him my husband and I were going to Africa as missionaries.

"Well." He grunted. "If you're going to Africa, you want a Land Rover out of England."

Neither Sal nor I had any idea what a Land Rover was, so when we got home, we looked it up on the computer.

"Sal," I said, "this is it. This is what we are supposed to get."

We would wait on God to show us the way.

In March of 2004, Shaun decided to come to work for Associates in Emergency Care. We already had existing contracts and part-time instructors, so we needed an administrator to take over while we were in Africa. Someone to be in charge of hiring and firing, scheduling, financials, accreditation requirements, and marketing. This would give us a year to work alongside him, making sure he was ready to take over when we departed for Zambia. He was also our choice for someone to handle all our personal affairs.

We spent a good portion of that year making sure that when we left for Zambia, things were going to carry on smoothly. Working with Shaun for a year also gave adequate time for clients to get to know and trust him. Things were working out well.

We returned to Africa in 2004 on a four-week mission trip to see if God had changed His mind. One of our first days there, God gave me the confirmation I was seeking.

Sal and I asked the missionary at Sons of Thunder if there were any Land Rover dealers in town. Being a Toyota advocate, he reluctantly told us about Foley's Garage in Livingstone, which sold and repaired only used Land Rover vehicles.

When we went to the shop to take a look, they directed us to a man inside. We found him under a vehicle working on it. When he slid out, stood up, and started talking, I smiled. There was a very heavy British accent! I remembered the old man's words: "A Land Rover out of England." Yep, we were in the right place.

We told him that we were looking for a Land Rover Defender 110 and that we would be coming the following year in August. We told him our price range and asked him to look for one for us. We exchanged emails and left, feeling like God was indeed directing our steps.

The next confirmation happened when I went by myself to the little church on the farm before service one Sunday morning to pray. When I stepped through the doorway, I was a bit surprised to see someone already walking around inside. He was a young man, dressed in a crisp long-sleeved white shirt with a tie, dress pants, and dress shoes, holding an open Bible. I smiled at him.

He returned the smile. "Madam, have you been here before?"

"Yes," I said. "As a matter of fact, I have."

"I thought so." He pulled up the leg of his pants, revealing a scar. "You healed me."

"No." I broke into a smile. "Jesus healed you, but I remember."

This was Tom, the little boy with the draining wound that I met on that first mission trip in 1997. The little boy who could not speak English but who faithfully came every day for his dressing change. Tom was ten back then. Now he was seventeen, spoke perfect English, and was one of the Sunday-school teachers at church. He was there that morning preparing his lesson. Oh my! God is good, and He had not changed His mind.

That was my sign that we were still called to come and start that medical clinic. I still didn't understand the obstacles, but I trusted that God's timing is perfect. I couldn't wait to tell Sal.

On the heels of that confirmation, we were informed that one of the American missionaries in town had died of a heart attack as his wife was driving him to the teaching hospital in Lusaka, five hours away, seeking medical care. He was only in his fifties.

We attended his funeral, and within a couple of days, we went to the widow's house. She was selling everything in order to quickly go back to the United States. We bought a bedroom set, a dining room set, end tables and a coffee table, dinnerware and cooking utensils, lamps, and a few other odd and ends. We arranged to store all the items on the farm until our anticipated return in 2005.

While we were still in Zambia, Shaun's townhouse flooded, creating an obnoxious musty smell. Since he had a two-month-old, he had concerns about staying in the house while a cleaning company came in. Since Sal and I were in Africa and Shaun knew the other bedrooms were empty, he moved his family into our house. So not only did we arrive home from Zambia with a renewed outlook, knowing for sure that God still had a purpose for us, we also had the surprise of Shaun and his family living with us.

I began to ponder how Shaun's situation fit into God's plan. After much thought and a bit of prayer, we suggested to Shaun that he move his family into our house and rent out their townhouse. Sal and I were going to Zambia, and Mark had plans to relocate for school. The office for the business was in the house, making it convenient for Shaun to work from home.

We saw that our living room, which had no furniture in it because God had said to stay liquid, would accommodate his living room furniture perfectly. The kitchen was big enough to hold our supplies and theirs. The bedrooms were empty, so their furniture would fit there also.

After discussion with his wife, they agreed it looked like God's plan. So they moved in permanently. It was definitely a God-directed step.

As the time grew closer, we started feeling fearful and inadequate in our knowledge and skill in medicine, and we listened to well-meaning people tell us we needed to take a course in tropical medicine.

I found a course in North Carolina at a place called Equip Inc. It was specifically meant to equip missionaries to be ready for whatever they might face on the mission field. The section we were interested in was a two-week medical-mission-intensive program. We signed up and went for two weeks, living in a propane-gas-heated hut and using an outside compost toilet.

We had case studies to diagnose and treat according to certain algorithms for different tropical diseases. We practiced suturing and casting techniques, reviewed maternity and baby deliveries, and had a wonderful experience.

About a month after our training, in May 2005, Sal went alone to Zambia once again with an American pediatric doctor. They spent two weeks at Sons of Thunder and saw twenty-one patients, as well as doing physicals on all the children at the orphanage. Sal met with both the district and provincial government health officers and collected his Zambian clinical officer license.

But the most significant thing that happened when he was there was that one of the orphanage workers was diagnosed with TB and was found to be HIV positive. That was Sal's first encounter with HIV and all the necessary procedures needed at that time to try to get medication. So even though we were unaware, God had given a foreshadowing to Sal of what the primary ministry of the clinic was going to be. He had spent his time on the first trip in 1997 with the delivery of a newborn infant and the last trip before our arrival together with an HIV patient. He was sowing those seeds for the harvest ahead!

While we waited to depart for whatever future awaited us in Zambia, we got to be at home for the birth of our two most recent grandchildren. Looking back, I think maybe that was why we had to wait another year.

As I sat with our newest grandbaby, thinking about each of them, God showed me how they were gifts to Sal and me. Our first grandchild, Daniel Scott, had been born on October 9, 2002. In the Bible, Daniel was a man of "Vision."

When God called Sal and me, the first thing He gave us was a "Vision." When God is going to use you, He must first tell you the vision. Oftentimes it is very big—so big, in fact, that you have a tendency to dismiss it. Sal and I were told at the time of our calling and during the years of preparation to *Start a clinic on the farm, raise the standard, and feed a nation.* That's quite a vision.

Next came Brooke Abigail, on June 29, 2004. Brooke Abigail means a "River of God's Joy."

Once you have said yes to whatever God is calling you to do, you must have strength for the journey. It says in God's Word that "the joy of the Lord is your strength" (Nehemiah 8:10). God gave Sal and me a whole "river of joy" when He gave us Brooke.

Daniel's brother, Phinehas Luke, was born on February 10, 2005. The Phinehas of the Bible was a man "Zealous for the Lord."

In order to continue with radical obedience to whatever the Lord leads you to do, you need a passion, a love, a holy "zeal"—something God gave Sal and me when He gave us Finn.

Faith Elisabeth joined the family on July 29, 2005, less than one month away from our departure.

Now God had given Sal and me Faith—faith to believe all that He was going to do with and through us to bring glory to Himself.

God says in His Word that He equips those He calls. With the arrival of Faith, I believed we were armed and ready to get on that plane on August 22, 2005 . . . armed with the Vision of the Lord . . . armed with Strength for the Journey . . . armed with a Holy Zeal for the will of the Lord . . . and now armed with the Faith to Believe.

## Chapter 10

WHEN THE PLANE LANDED AT LIVINGSTONE AIRPORT ON AUGUST 24, 2005, a feeling of relief was coupled with a bit of uncertainty. We were on our own with God alone as our guide. There was no one at the airport to greet us except the Land Rover dealer, who had our Defender 110 fueled up and ready to go.

After handling our visa requirements and collecting our luggage, Sal and I packed the vehicle and proceeded to Sons of Thunder. Crossing the threshold of the iron gate with the word *Boanerges* (Sons of Thunder) over it, we felt prepared for whatever God had in store for us.

As Sal drove the Land Rover down the dirt road toward the compound, I looked out at the dry, cracked land on the right with a small grove of guava trees. On the left, I saw the citrus orchard with trees filled with lemons and oranges.

The scattering of buildings in the distance ahead consisted of an infant orphanage, an old tobacco barn, a small building used for a church, and a building with a couple of classrooms used by the primary school. Construction of a second orphanage building from a renovated chicken coop had been started during our absence; otherwise, not much had changed.

We pulled into the driveway, passing a six-foot grass fence surrounding the main house. The only part of the house itself that was visible over the fence was a large glass dome topping the structure, suggesting a history of Indian architecture. The house was constructed in 1964 and had three previous owners before being purchased by Sons of Thunder. All three were of Indian descent: a doctor, a pharmacist, and a dairy farmer.

A small porch with a vine-covered trellis, complete with a swing and a double glass door, graced the front of the house. As we were about to knock on the door, we were met by the missionary's wife, who welcomed us but directed us to continue on to a different location she had prepared.

It was a two-bedroom apartment on the end of the newly constructed building slotted for the orphanage. She had retrieved all the furniture we had purchased and stored during our last visit and furnished the space in a very comfortable and homey fashion. Curtains hung, appliances connected, dining room table and chairs in place, and bed made.

We had also purchased living room furniture, as well as medical supplies and other accessories in the US, and had them sent in a container that our church just happened to be sending months before we were scheduled to leave for Zambia. Those were still in the container, now on the farm, waiting to be unpacked.

I can honestly say it felt quite relieving as she spoke.

"Please take your time to settle in. You can come up to the house and join us for dinner at six. We can all talk more then."

A shower with hot water and a change of clothes felt so good. Whatever fatigue I felt from our long days of travel was replaced with a sense of excitement. We had finally arrived!

We started unpacking and saw a door that we hadn't noticed at first. We discovered a small hallway leading into the rest of the proposed building.

Excited for a little adventure, I grinned slyly. "Sal, let's take a look."

We toured the rest of the building. It had a very spacious open area in the center, surrounded by six rooms planned for bedrooms for the children, I guessed, and one small storage room. There were also two community bathrooms, complete with multiple toilets, shower stalls, and sinks, and one bathtub in each. I supposed one was for the girls and one for the boys. In the middle of the building, there were double wooden entry doors on both sides, a front and back entrance.

Standing in the middle of the main room, I said, "This would be perfect for the clinic." Looking all around, I continued. "This area would be registration and a waiting room. The four small rooms on the one side would be exam rooms and a lab. The two larger rooms would be for inpatients, and the bathrooms are already male and female. The double door entries could accommodate wheelchairs or stretchers. And the apartment where we would stay is right here when we get called out at night for rounds or emergencies."

Sal smiled and nodded in agreement. We both knew we had been given only one room at the end of the classroom block to set up the clinic, but I had the feeling God was showing us something a whole lot bigger!

Back in the apartment, we unpacked until it was time to go to the main house for dinner. The orphanage director and her husband were already there with the old missionary and his wife. They were the other two American couples on the farm.

The men were in the sitting room and the ladies in the kitchen, putting the final touches on dinner. They set the meal out buffet-style in the kitchen, and everyone proceeded with a full plate to one of the two dining room tables to eat.

"Thank you so much for setting up the apartment." I smiled and began the conversation. "It's perfect."

The missionary husband spoke up. "Don't get too comfortable. It's only temporary. That's going to be another orphanage building. When the new parents arrive, they will stay in that apartment."

I was stunned. We had just arrived and were being told our place was temporary. I picked up my fork, put my head down, and started to eat.

"We're excited to get set up." Sal beamed as he changed the subject. His gaze drifted in the direction of the one room at the end of the classroom building that he knew had been designated for the clinic. "We plan to be up and running as soon as possible."

The old missionary's demeanor subtly shifted. "There's one more thing for you to know." He cleared his throat before continuing. "Running the clinic will not be your only job."

Sal and I exchanged a look, and my stomach dropped. Opening and running the clinic already felt like we'd bitten off more than we could chew. How could we possibly handle anything extra?

I swallowed hard before asking, "What do you mean?"

"It's about the church." He directed his focus toward the window and the small building in the distance. "The pastor has been going through a time of personal difficulty and will be leaving at the end of the month. The church has no order or structure anywhere."

I stared at the missionary. What on earth was he getting at?

"The worship leader has been put on discipline." The old missionary shook his head as he continued. "There is no rhyme or reason to Sunday school. No teaching and no plan for preaching. The budget is almost nonexistent. Every aspect is struggling."

"I'm sorry to hear that." Sal's voice was filled with compassion. We both knew how critical the church was to the success of the entire ministry. "But what does that have to do with us?"

The old missionary mustered up a forced smile. "Sal, besides being in charge of the medical ministry, you are also being placed over the church."

My mouth fell open and our eyes met. Before either Sal or I could argue, we remembered *submission*. God had shown us all those lessons regarding submission, and I was beginning to understand why. Surprisingly, Sal said nothing.

Discerning a sense of mixed emotions and feeling a bit tired from the journey, we finished our meal and said good night, then headed over to the apartment to continue settling in.

As we unpacked, we remembered the two teachings we had placed in our suitcases that we knew we were supposed to bring but were frankly unsure why. One was the *Under Cover* teaching on spiritual authority, and the other a series of lessons called *Firm Foundations*. Maybe they were our direction for the church. During our time of restructuring, Sal could teach the *Under Cover* series to the adult Sunday-school class, followed by a full year of *Firm Foundations*.

Tomorrow would be another day. The beginning of nine months in Zambia until our first furlough back home. As we laid our heads on the pillow that night, one thing was clear—God had more in store for us than we anticipated.

## Chapter 11

IN THE MORNING, OUR SHORT PRAYER WAS "HERE WE ARE, GOD . . . now what?"

The truth was, we had not come with a plan of our own. The only plan was God's, and He had not revealed all the details yet. All we knew was that He wanted a medical clinic on the farm and transport to the bush. So like Abraham, we had come, trusting God to show us each step of the journey.

Besides the original call to *Start a clinic on the farm*, we had been told over time to also *Raise the standard* and *Feed a nation*. Not really understanding what God meant and seeking direction, we had also been told, *Don't look up! The need is too great, and you will be overwhelmed. Just do what I put in front of you.* So that was exactly what we planned to do—whatever He put in front of us!

We spent most of that first week in town attempting to set up our phones, satellite TV, and emails. Things took more than one trip to accomplish because they were either not done right the first time or computers were down or people were out for a two-hour lunch break. We quickly learned the phrase "Come back tomorrow."

We were welcomed by the pastor at church on Sunday and sat in the service that would be his last. After service, he came to the house and told Sal about his troubles and decision to leave. He confirmed that the worship leader had indeed been placed on discipline and proceeded to ask Sal to lead worship.

The first opportunity had presented itself. Sal accepted, walking in faith that God had given him that assignment.

In hindsight, I believe the assignments to oversee the church and to lead worship were made in hopes of Sal failing. But God equips those He calls, and even though we had no forewarning of this new challenge, He had already prepared us.

At our church back home in Maryland, Sal had been part of the worship team, and I'd served on the dance ministry. God had taught us the awesome responsibility of leading people into His presence through praise and worship, as well as the power it has as a means of prayer and spiritual warfare.

Overall, the job ahead felt quite gigantic—like a mountain too steep to climb. As we walked under authority with God's direction for the clinic and the church, we had no idea the things that were to transpire over the course of time.

At three a.m. Monday, we set out for Lusaka, which is approximately five hours away, to check on the status of our employment permit, find the General Nursing Council so I could register for the Zambian nursing exam, and, of course, shop some more.

The paperwork for our employment permit was found still sitting on a desk at the church office in Lusaka and had not been submitted to Immigration. But it was now in process, and there was still a lot of paperwork that needed to be obtained from the States and filed before I could take the nursing exam in December. We were discovering the difference between living in the US and in a developing country. There were going to be challenges ahead, to put it mildly.

Ten days after we touched ground in Zambia, our vehicle was registered, and Sal got a lot of practice driving on the left side of the road with the steering wheel on the right and the stick shift in the left hand. All our purchases sent on the container before our arrival had been located, the apartment was almost set up, and I had cooked three meals so far.

The TV was still not working, so we were watching DVDs that we'd brought from home. Our cell phones, thankfully, were operational, but email was only available at an internet café in town.

As soon as we began working on the clinic, people came. It didn't seem to matter to them that we had not really opened or that we didn't have the required licenses yet. They still came.

It was obvious to both of us that medical care in the rural area was definitely lacking. People came to us like starving people who had heard there was food. These people were very sick, and a lot were malnourished on top of it. It was hard to tell which came first. Were they malnourished because they were sick, or were they sick because they were malnourished?

There were children who had walked for miles with swollen bellies and bare feet, on stick legs with open sores, just to come to school on the farm. There were women who were eight months pregnant and had never had any prenatal care—no pelvic exam, no vitamins, no iron, no proper diet. These women planned on delivering their babies in their grass huts with the help of the older village women. Some of them already had a history of losing babies after delivery for unknown reasons.

There were men in their fifties walking around trying to work and provide for their families with wasting diseases like AIDS and TB. They had traveled from clinic to clinic seeking help and a cure . . . sometimes going to the "traditional healer" (witch doctor) for tattooing or charms (little cloth pouches with herbs in them that are tied around the waist, neck, wrist, or ankle). We saw many with scarring on different parts of their bodies from that procedure, which involves cutting the skin with a razor blade and placing different herbs and concoctions underneath the skin. These patients were continuing to seek answers because the tattooing procedure, of course, did not work.

I had to continually remind myself that it's not *what* we know but *Who* we know that's the key. Jesus is the One with all the answers. He is the only source of Hope. He is the Hope of the nations. The problems here were much bigger than Sal and I could ever hope to solve. There was nothing in our strength that we could do—it was all up to God. No wonder He'd told us, *Don't look up, for the need is too great. Just do what I put in front of you.*

Right outside the clinic, there was a covered shelter with small logs as makeshift seats. It functioned perfectly as a waiting room. The room next to the one we were given was empty, so we requested it once we saw the numbers and conditions of the people who came. Both rooms had to be scrubbed down, cracks grouted, walls painted, windows screened, cement floors sealed and polished, window coverings hung, and cabinets purchased. After that was done, we were able to unpack and stock shelves.

In a very short time, it became obvious that we would have registration and the taking of vital signs in the first room and exam and treatment in the second. Before we could establish regular clinic hours, we needed to hire an assistant, who would also be our interpreter. Anna was the daughter of Linah, the head orphanage supervisor, and was very excited to begin her new position.

With two rooms, we would also need two translators, so Bertha was hired to work in the registration room. She was taught vital signs with digital equipment brought from the States. Anna worked as an assistant in the exam-treatment room, learning medications, dressings, and whatever else was needed. We had a bed made in town and placed it in the registration room behind a portable stand with a curtain, in case we had to watch anyone for a few hours or even overnight.

One of the best things I did, both for myself and for our loved ones, was to set up a blog to keep people back home informed. Blogs were brand new back in 2005, and mine wound up being a terrific outlet for me as well as a convenient tool of communication, not only to tell stories but to send pictures.

This is an excerpt from an update I posted two weeks after our arrival in Zambia:

> Today is Friday, Sept 9, and we're getting used to our new life. It is very hot and dry right now. There's always dirt and dust coming into the house because we have to have the windows open and fans going.
>
> There are a lot of bugs here—spiders; flies that dive bomb you, trying to get at the water in your eyes and mouth; hornets; crawlers; things with hard shells; and who knows what else. The floors everywhere are cement, so you just squish them. We've even had to chase small lizards out of the clinic!
>
> Everything in Africa takes longer than we are used to. It's been ten days and five trips to town to try and get our satellite

TV and emails up and operational (which, by the way, has been unsuccessful) and two trips to town for our phones to be set up.

Cooking is a challenge because everything is from scratch. There is no box of Bisquick, no cake mix, no sour cream.

Currency here is kwacha, and it is interesting to pay at a store and figure out the bills. One dollar is equal to approximately 4,500 kwacha, and the rates change daily. We purchased an electric stove here for 2.1 million kwacha! Thank goodness they do not have coins!

We have been to the bank twice trying to figure out if we should open an account. Most of the missionaries don't have them. There is no federal safety net like at home, and frankly, people don't trust the banks.

Our vehicle is a used four-wheel drive Land Rover with an extended gas tank, a much-needed vehicle because there aren't always tarmacs (paved roads). Driving is a challenge to stay on the left side of the road.

Everything here is metric, like kilometers instead of miles, liters instead of gallons, kilograms instead of pounds, Celsius instead of Fahrenheit (and that's not only body temperature but also the dial on my oven).

We are comfortably settled in our apartment, so our focus has switched over to the clinic. We're starting to organize it and have seen patients already.

We are treating one little boy with sores on his legs from malnutrition. He is thirteen, looks nine, has sticks for legs, and is in the second grade here at the farm.

Sal was stirred to supplement his diet with a high-protein gruel, so he sent for his mother to get permission. When she came, we found out she also has four-month-old twins. She is breastfeeding and doesn't have enough milk for both babies, so one baby is doing okay, but the other is sickly and smaller. I can't imagine not being able to feed my babies. The missionaries told us we are going to see a lot of that, especially these next few months. There has been a drought, so crops did not do well and people will soon be hungry.

One of the missionary ladies heads up a feeding program here at the farm, and I'm sure we will be a part of it. Even if we were to give all we have, it would not be enough. This is too big a problem for us . . . but not for our very big God. With God, all things are possible, and as long as we have Jesus, there is always hope. Things are definitely challenging here.

After just three weeks, we had seen over two hundred patients with various complaints, including scabies, STDs, TB, ear infections, abscesses from broken teeth, malnutrition and resulting wounds, burns, arthritic pains, bilharzia, worms, eye infections, bleeding ulcers, and varied other skin diseases. We also saw about a dozen antenatal patients, and Sal even made a house call to the bush!

By the end of September, we had established a working relationship with both chemists in town and had negotiated a discount on medications. We had visited the district health office and told them of our plans. The old missionary had received a license years ago to open a "health post," and we were told we could start with that. We established clinic hours with Thursdays off for our shopping day in town.

Things were moving along nicely, but there were challenges.

First of all, I was not a world traveler and had never lived outside the United States. My entire experience with that kind of change was leaving the city of Pittsburgh and relocating to our small town in Maryland. So moving across the Atlantic Ocean to relocate to Zambia, Africa, was a life-changing event.

No question, there was fear! Some of that fear came from the thought of bugs, scorpions, and poisonous snakes. Some from the thought of running into wild animals roaming the bush. There was also the fear of people who were different from me—different language, dress, beliefs, customs, and lifestyles.

But probably the biggest fear was of failure—not being good enough, smart enough, strong enough, or young enough to carry out the very call

God had for me. Would I disappoint Him? I knew it said in the Word that He equips those He calls, and I already had eight years of His preparation, but I was still wrapped in flesh, and like it or not, there was fear.

I had tackled the first hurdle by saying goodbye to all that was familiar and getting on the plane. Once in my new surroundings, I needed to attempt to adjust to life in Zambia. I had already come to the decision that this would never be home.

It was my assignment, just a job to be done.

# Chapter 12

DAY BY DAY, THE JOURNEY CONTINUED. IN NOVEMBER, THE orphanage director went out to get a one-month-old set of twin boys whose mother, Susan, was very sick and unable to feed them. When she brought the babies back to the farm, she told Sal about the condition of the mother and asked if he would make a house call.

After clinic hours, Sal and the director headed out to one of the villages to see this woman. When Sal walked into the grass hut, Susan was lying on a bed, wrapped up in blankets. On initial assessment, Sal found her very diaphoretic with a fever of 103.5, having difficulty breathing, with a heart rate of 160 plus. She was emaciated, having had a large weight loss within two weeks after the babies were born.

Sal performed an HIV test. As he imagined, the test was positive. Our first HIV patient. Sal informed Susan of the results and immediately laid hands on her and prayed. After removing the mound of covers over her, he gave her two injections, one for fever and one for infection. He gave the family instructions to give her oral rehydration solution and keep her head elevated. He left the village that day and returned home.

That afternoon, we discovered that both of her babies had also tested positive for HIV.

Shaking his head, Sal looked nearly defeated. "I really wanted to bring her to the clinic, but she has to show me some fight."

I wanted to help, but all I could do was question. "What are you planning to do with her? Are you going to buy the antiretroviral medication? Are you going to take her to Livingstone to get on the free medication program if she qualifies?"

We both knew that once she started on that, she would need to commit to continuing the medicine. What if she couldn't get to town to receive it? What if she had to pay and couldn't afford it?

He let out a long breath, his shoulders hunched with the weight that I was only adding to.

His lack of response spurred me to continue. "We can't afford to pay for medication for everyone who needs it. How can we say yes to one person and no to another?"

In the middle of all my questions, Sal turned to me with tears in his eyes. "I don't know . . . all I can do is what is before me. That's all I know to do. I can't look at anything beyond that."

A few days later, he returned to the village to check on Susan. This time when he walked in, he found her sitting upright with a temperature of 100.8 and a pulse of 130. Her breathing was less labored, and she was not diaphoretic.

After discussion with her and her family, Sal brought Susan to the clinic to stay for a few days in order to give her IV medications and monitor her more closely. Her mother came with her.

In Zambia, whenever anyone goes to a medical clinic to stay for any length of time, a family member always accompanies them. They are responsible for meals and for giving any help the sick person may need, like assistance with bathing and walking to the bathroom.

The following morning, Susan was alert and more responsive, breathing easier with a temperature of ninety-seven and a heart rate of 110. She got up and, with the assistance of her mother, walked across the farm compound to go to the bathroom. With oral rehydration solution (ORS), IVs and IV medications for fever and infection, that night she was at ninety-seven with a heart rate of ninety. Very encouraging progress.

Susan had a dilemma that we feared was common to a lot of Zambians: What to do now?

To receive the free HIV medications from the government, she would have to travel to Livingstone for additional blood tests to determine whether she met the World Health Organization criteria. Then, the only way she would be able to get the medications would be to travel to

Livingstone once a month. Most Zambians with the greatest need for the medications do not live in the cities. They live in the bush and must travel long distances—in Susan's case, forty-five kilometers (around twenty-eight miles). Not only are these people sick, but their only travel options are to walk or get public transport, which is very expensive for someone living in the bush. Often, the expense of food is all they can handle.

I did not know the answer to this problem, but I firmly believed that God did not send us here to idly stand by and watch His people perish. I also realized that the problem was beyond anything I could do, so I watched God work it out as only He could.

After IV medications for a few days followed by oral medications and high energy protein supplement (HEPS) for a few more, along with the excellent care of her mother, Susan was ready for a short ride and some fresh air.

After her mama helped her dress in her Sunday clothes, we put her into a wheelchair and took her to the church on the farm. During prayer requests, we wheeled her up to the front of the church and read James 5:13–16. According to the Word of God, the elders of the church—along with her mother, her brother, Sal, and me—anointed her with oil and laid hands on her, praying in faith for total and complete healing.

Susan told Sal, "I want to live. I want to see my babies grow up."

We took Susan to see her babies in the orphanage before bringing her back to the clinic. She was tired and fell asleep almost as soon as she lay down.

During the week, as Susan gained strength, Sal and I received word that a man named Joseph was very sick and in need of care. Joseph's house was on the back four thousand acres, so driving there in the Land Rover was quite an adventure. No roads—we're talking about stony paths in the midst of a lot of bush, and even through a riverbed. The riverbed was dry. I guess in the rainy season, getting to Joseph's home would mean driving through water.

Once we managed to get there, we discovered that no one spoke any English, and we had no interpreter. In spite of this obstacle, Sal examined Joseph and found him to have malaria. We started him on antimalarial medicine and ORS.

On the way back to our apartment, Sal looked over at me. "Did you ever in your wildest imagination think we would be in Africa, driving through the bush, making house calls?"

We just smiled at each other. We both knew the answer.

On Saturday of the same week, a community health worker named Rona showed up, asking for a job. We decided to hire her to work Saturdays and overnight shifts and to go on house calls. She eagerly agreed to start that day.

I had just begun her orientation when the old missionary's wife showed up unexpectedly.

"There is an emergency . . ." Her eyes were wide as she caught her breath. "Joseph is very sick. He is spitting blood and having chest pain, and he can't get here."

Dropping everything, Sal took Rona, who could act as an interpreter, and headed out to get Joseph.

Upon exam, Sal found that Joseph's respirations were rapid and shallow, and he had no air movement on the right lower side. His chest pain was concentrated to the right side also. Sal suspected right lower lobe pneumonia.

By the time Sal and Rona got him to the farm, the power was out in the clinic, so we had to bring him to our apartment. After two nebulizer treatments, Joseph was able to breathe deeper. Air, although still decreased, was now heard over the right lung, and he was able to cough up some mucous, which was thick yellow with blood tinge.

When we finished the treatments, the power had been restored, so we took him back to the clinic. Since our only bed was taken by Susan, we put Joseph in the other room on the exam table. His temperature was 103.5, and he was starting to hallucinate. We started an IV, with an antibiotic and fever medicine. We sponged him down and continued to monitor his temperature.

It was not coming down past 102, so Sal called Zimba Hospital because there were Americans doctors there that we knew. After talking with the doctors, then to Joseph and his family, we decided to take him to the hospital. Thank God we had Rona, who would be able to stay with Susan to give her medicine and monitor her temperature in our absence.

While we were packing and getting someone to take Joseph's plow and chickens so thieves would not rob him while he was gone, two pastors came to visit Joseph. We asked them to pray with him, which they did. With the IV still intact and hanging from the sun visor, we left with Joseph and his wife, baby daughter, and brother. We also took an extra IV and his malaria medicine.

After the forty-five-minute drive to the hospital, Joseph's temperature was 98.9, and his pain was subsiding. The doctors there concurred with our suspected diagnosis and decided it would be a good idea to admit him. We helped get him into a bed, assured him we would come back to bring him home, then returned to the farm.

Looking back on this time at the clinic, I can see God's provision even before we knew to pray . . . before we knew what we would need. We'd purchased the bed for the clinic just a couple of weeks before Susan would need it. We had only just acquired the IVs before both Susan and Joseph needed them.

Also, Rona showed up and agreed to start work the day we needed her, not only to go into the bush to help with interpreting but then to stay late with Susan while we took Joseph to the hospital.

When Susan was finally discharged from the clinic, her health had greatly improved, but she still had a long way to go. Sal took her to Livingstone Hospital and had bloodwork done to see if she would qualify for the government program for HIV medication, and she indeed qualified. That was a blessing in one sense, but a person had to be pretty sick to qualify. That meant she was severe enough to warrant immediate treatment.

Without Sal going to get her to bring her to the clinic for treatment, she would have died in her hut because she was too sick for the family to walk or bicycle her out to get medical care. Without Sal transporting her to Livingstone for the bloodwork, picking up the results for her, taking her in to get on the antiretroviral therapy, and picking up her medication each month, she would have had no hope of living.

As for Joseph, he was doing much better. Sal went to Zimba Hospital and finally took him home. It was quite an adventure taking him to his hut in the bush, since by that time everything was muddy from the rains. Sal was a real stick-in-the-mud . . . or should I say, stuck-in-the-mud!

Still reeling from all the transport adventures, we made a discovery right on the farm. We found out that CARE International was feeding our children in the school. However, they were only feeding in one place, which was at the main location, about a fifteen-minute drive up on the hill. The majority of the four hundred schoolchildren were located in classrooms up there, but we also had seventy down on the farm proper. Those kids were permitted to go up the hill for the feeding, but it was a forty-five-minute walk, after they'd walked who knew how long to get to school.

We had already treated some students for malnutrition and related wounds, so Sal decided to feed these seventy children in their own location as a preventive measure. He purchased bowls and spoons and began providing a nutritious mealie meal grain mixture referred to as HEPS. He worked it out with the teachers to be responsible for the feeding and the cleanup.

Every day, the students ate, then went to the water tap next to our apartment to clean their bowls. You could hear them laughing and talking. The teachers on the farm reported better attention in class and less falling asleep, and the kids seemed to enjoy the supplement.

All glory to God. When we cried out, asking God what our purpose here was, He told us, *You are giving the people hope.*

## Chapter 13

BY DECEMBER, WE'D SEEN WELL OVER A THOUSAND PATIENTS IN the clinic. We came to eagerly anticipate Thursdays, because that was the day the clinic was closed and we took the day off. That became the day we went into town to get all our weekly errands done. We would usually eat at a restaurant before heading back to the farm.

One particular Thursday, Sal and I left at seven thirty in the morning to pick up Susan at her village. The previous Tuesday afternoon, we had taken her into Livingstone Hospital to get her started on the free government program for HIV meds. After registering at the outpatient department and walking over to the clinic for her to be seen, we found out she still needed bloodwork. We walked back up to the hospital, to the lab on the second floor, and found out that they only did these blood tests on Tuesday mornings and Wednesday afternoons.

I pleaded our case to the lab manager, and he agreed to draw Susan's blood. He told us we could pick up the results on Thursday. So our intention on that day was to pick up Susan's results and take her to be started on her antiretroviral drugs. Sounds easy, right?

But this was Africa...

When Sal and I showed up at Susan's home, her partner, Christopher, and brother Franksen were both with her. Christopher had also tested positive for HIV but did not qualify for the program because he was not sick enough. We decided he probably should be logged into their system for monitoring, so we agreed to take him in to be seen also.

Michael—one of the babies with cerebral palsy who went in for physical therapy once a week—and his mother, Miriam, were also waiting for

85

a ride into Livingstone to the hospital. Additionally, we had planned to talk with the occupational therapist about a clinic patient with half a foot who needed an elevator shoe made. The man in Livingstone who made the shoes had died before this patient was able to have his shoe made. He did not know where else to go, so he came to see us.

Sal, Susan, Christopher, Franksen, Miriam, Michael, a man named Howard—who had asked for a ride to town—and I set out for a quick trip to Livingstone. That was at nine fifteen.

By two o'clock, we had completed the entire hospital agenda. Michael had had therapy; Susan had been seen in the clinic and her lab results had been retrieved, then she was started on a two-week course of ARV therapy (HIV meds); Christopher had been entered into the system and ordered an antibiotic that the hospital didn't have (but we did); and the request for a specially made shoe had been left for the occupational therapist when he returned from a holiday. Oh, and Howard had been dropped off at his destination as well.

After taking everyone home, Sal and I decided to go back into town to finish the errands and have dinner. That was at two thirty.

At three, having just reached town, we received a phone call telling us that Alister—one of our OB patients—was in labor, and her husband, Graham, had come to the farm to get us. So we immediately turned around and drove back to the farm. We stopped at the clinic to pick up the packed medical bag and Graham, then headed to his hut in the bush.

Home visits are such an adventure; traveling alone is not for the weak of heart. Even though this couple lived on the farm, we still drove through uncharted territory, circumventing a lake made from the recent rains, driving through mud and heavy brush and over roads with craters as potholes. Then we had to walk across the railroad tracks to get to their hut.

Alister was indeed in labor, having contractions every twenty minutes that lasted about a minute. Graham told us she'd been in labor for two hours. Her water had broken but was only trickling, so Sal thought it best to take her back to the clinic to deliver the baby.

Graham remained at the hut with their other two children. He had declined to go to the clinic . . . he'd looked scared when we asked. Zambian men are not anywhere around when a woman is giving birth.

No way was I driving, so there I was in the back seat with Alister bouncing all around the back as Sal hurried over the rough terrain, as if he were in the States with lights and sirens blaring. I prayed the entire time that she would not deliver in the car!

Once she was comfortable in the clinic bed, she was examined and found to be six centimeters dilated, with contractions every three minutes, lasting fifty seconds. The fetal heart rate was 120 and strong. It was four thirty.

At about five forty-five, without one sound—just a wince on her face—Alister began to push. Sal was gloved up and ready to deliver. He looked down, only to see that it was not a head but a little butt presenting first. The baby proceeded to be delivered . . . butt, legs, arms, then head.

A baby girl! Praise the Lord for the little miracle.

Mom and baby continued doing well. Baby weighed seven pounds, had good color and bright eyes, and began sucking well. We made preparations for Alister and her baby to stay overnight for closer observation and to return home in the morning after being cleared for discharge. A female friend arrived to stay with her, and another woman came to visit, bringing *nshima* (a very thick porridge made from finely ground corn meal, called mealie meal) to eat.

After getting everyone settled, Sal and I returned home at eight thirty. We never did get dinner. But some things are worth missing meals for.

Since Alister lived on the farm, I wanted to help take her home the following day. On the way there, I asked, "What are you going to name your baby?"

Her answer surprised me.

"Oh no, the father will name her."

When Graham came out of the hut to welcome his wife and new baby, I asked him, "So what are you going to call your daughter?"

He looked at me and said, "What is your name?"

Confused, I answered, "Renee."

He smiled. "Her name will be Renee, after you."

I did not expect that answer. I was honored. She was our first baby delivered at the Sons of Thunder Clinic.

With the increase of inpatients, we soon needed the use of another room. There was a third vacant room in the same building, around the corner on the other end. We cleaned and furnished it with two more beds.

The added space necessitated the hiring of Janet. We decided to write an official position description for the staff, calling them clinical assistants.

Sal and I then took one more trip to Lusaka so that I could take the General Nursing Council of Zambia's nurse qualifying exam. I needed a Zambian RN license to continue functioning at the clinic.

The final accomplishment for 2005 was the establishment of Maternal Child Health with medications, equipment, immunizations, and proper government recordkeeping documents, all provided free from the district health office. That feat occurred only after two unsuccessful attempts and broken promises, causing us to file a formal complaint with the medical director in charge. That step finally got it done, but it came at great cost.

The Zambian people, especially where we were in the Southern Province, are for the most part nonconfrontational. When challenged, they display a passive-aggressive attitude. They might ignore you, make you wait longer than necessary, tell you to come back tomorrow, or go to lunch or tea before attending to you. They seem to be harder on their fellow citizens than on outsiders, probably due to all the free handouts and funding brought into Zambia by different "partner" countries.

Most do not keep time and forever break promises. If you schedule an event, the acceptable arrival time is two hours later. Life can be frustrating, to put it mildly.

It wasn't long into our time there that I got to experience this for myself.

We had decided to organize a Child Health Day at our clinic. I made two unsuccessful attempts to meet with the woman from the district health office to get immunizations and government recordkeeping documents required by them for pregnant women and children under five years old.

Finally, the woman told me to inform our area parents that on Monday, the day of our event, she would come out to the clinic with immunizations, needles, and paperwork to show us how the Under-Five Program worked.

So we had the Sons of Thunder pastors inform their churches on Sunday that parents could take their children to our clinic on Monday to receive immunizations.

The following morning, mothers started to arrive at eight. We weighed all the children, took their temperatures, and gave them their deworming pills while waiting for the woman from the district health office to arrive. She was supposed to give vitamin A to children six months to five years old, along with immunizations as needed.

At three p.m., we closed the clinic, sending all the mothers and fifty-two children home without immunizations, because the woman from the district had not shown up. She did not keep her commitment and showed little consideration for these mothers and their young children, who had walked very long distances to get there.

We told the mothers that Sal and I did not lie, that our word was good, and we were appalled at what had happened. We assured them that it would not happen again.

But everyone in Zambia, including these mothers, say, "Oh well, it's Africa," and excuse unprofessional, incompetent behavior. I guess Sal and I hadn't been there long enough, because for us there was no excuse for this lack of professionalism on the part of the health district.

Tuesday, after clinic hours, we drove to Livingstone Hospital to pick up some lab results. On our way home, we stopped at the district health office to file a complaint with the person in charge.

After a brief discussion, we were told to come in on the following Monday, and they would give us our start-up medications and paperwork to take with us to establish our program. Better late than never.

Thankfully, they came through, but throughout our journey, every step of the way, we always had to push.

I think we were eventually (after many years) included as one of their rural health centers just because we kept knocking at the door, refusing to quit, refusing to go away. We kept standing, advocating, and doing a good job until we were recognized by the provincial and national levels of the Ministry of Health.

Unfortunately, this attitude prevailed in all areas of health care. We found ourselves battling the lab and the hospitals. It was discouraging, to be sure, and it felt like an uphill battle all the time—too big for us alone. I got so frustrated with the medical care in Zambia—or lack of it. And it wasn't just that. It was the entire attitude. I didn't know how to change the attitude of a whole country—except one life at a time.

A prime example is the time I stopped to pick up some eye patients to take them to the hospital in Zimba. A mother had brought her very sick twenty-two-year-old daughter to the pickup point. She told me that her daughter, Netta, had HIV. She was so sick, I knew if she had shown up at our clinic, we would have transported her to the hospital for a higher level of care. So I agreed to take her with us.

At the hospital, they promised me they would start her on HIV meds, but they did not keep that promise. They didn't start her on them until she was too bad to swallow. She really needed IVs and antibiotics. She was a skeleton—totally out of it, in heart failure, septic, having seizures. Her poor mother was taking care of her, looking to me for hope.

I broke down in tears at the hospital as I questioned a clinical officer. We couldn't do anything but pray for her. We couldn't legally take her out and put her in our clinic, and frankly, there was nothing to do at that point.

Days passed, and I would wake up at two a.m. thinking of her . . . dreaming of her . . . praying for her. I'd read my Bible, trying to understand what the heck I was there for, because frankly, sometimes I just didn't know.

That hospital let a twenty-two-year-old woman die because . . . well, I really don't understand why. They only administered two IVs during her whole stay, right in the beginning. She couldn't swallow and hadn't eaten in the previous three days, but they did nothing.

If a clinic transfers a patient to a hospital, it's supposed to be for higher care. But they often end up dying because the hospital doesn't do anything except stick them in a bed and give some ineffective pills. Family takes care of the patient's hygiene needs and often their nutritional needs. We had put a TB patient into Livingstone Hospital the previous month, and she also just lay there for days without any TB drugs because she was too weak to produce a sputum specimen.

Of course, Sal and I both felt guilty for not just taking care of her at the clinic. In hindsight, she would have been better off with us. There was no doctor at Zimba. The one Zambian doctor they hired lasted one week, then went to Lusaka and called to say he wasn't coming back. So they just had clinical officers and nurses. There was not a lot of caring in the care they gave.

At times like this, I just wanted to go home, see my grandkids, and live life.

About the attitude that permeated the medical community—and maybe everyone else there—I don't think it was necessarily an "I don't care" attitude as much as "What's the use?" I think they didn't have the fight anymore . . . if they ever had it. You know that fight I'm talking about— that "try everything and don't give up" attitude we have in America. The "reason to live" attitude.

But in Zambia, death is the conqueror. The sting of death is still prevalent, still a reality there. You need the resources to fight, both physically and spiritually, and there is lack on both fronts. Medical resources are definitely lacking—technology and medications alike. Spiritually, however, I think they are also lacking.

I am reminded of 1 Corinthians 15:55–57: "Where, O death, is your victory? Where, O death, is your sting? The sting of death is sin, and the power of sin is the law. But thanks be to God! He gives us the victory through our Lord Jesus Christ."

As I was looking up this Scripture, I couldn't help but notice verse 58. God answers even when you are unaware. He says, "Therefore, my dear brothers (Sal and Renee), stand firm. Let nothing move you. Always give yourselves fully to the work of the Lord, because you know that your labor in the Lord is not in vain."

When I lived in Maryland, around family and friends, it was easy to pick up the phone and share joys, frustrations, and life in general as it was happening. But in Zambia, Sal and I found ourselves without family or friends, and without even the ability to vent to our fellow missionaries. We had no network for phone calls and could only send emails from the internet café in town once a week. As my blog gained readers, people eventually began sending words of encouragement and support. What kept us going, in addition to staying in right relationship with God in order to hear Him, was prayer coverage from faithful prayer warriors back home.

It was my desire to take my blog followers along with us on our walk with the Lord, but in order to do that, I had to be honest in my sharing. I wanted them to experience everything we were going through, including our breakthroughs, victories, sufferings, prayers, and emotions. There was no end of stories to share, many of them quite difficult.

We came to find out, however, that God was always with us. He was always *there*. Many, many times, encouragement and answers came from Him long before we ever got to share the story with another human, just like He reminded me by bringing 1 Corinthians 15:58 to my eyes that day.

Our labor in the Lord is not in vain.

## Chapter 14

LIVINGSTONE HOSPITAL WAS THE ONLY PLACE IN THE AREA TO GET the antiretroviral medications for HIV, and the system had been frustrating, to say the least. We had difficulty with many departments.

Problems with the outpatient department: clinical officers not showing up at all to see a whole roomful of patients; long queues (lines); and nurses with attitude.

Problems with the pharmacy: medications out of stock; long queues; and changing locations.

Problems with registration: we were charged a different amount each time we registered patients to be seen.

Problems with the lab: no reagents to do tests that had been paid for; lost blood samples, so patients had to have their blood redrawn and return in a week; and disorganization with finding results amid a sea of papers.

One time, I almost burst into tears of frustration with the inefficiency of the lab. I prophesied a full state-of-the-art lab at Sons of Thunder, with all properly working equipment and a never-ending supply of reagents. I told all the lab techs to get ready if they were tired of trying to do a good job with inadequate equipment and supplies, because we were going to be needing them!

One Thursday in January 2006, we had the Land Rover packed with seven HIV patients—five new and two reviews (follow-ups)—one family member, and one baby in a lap. This was the largest number of patients we had brought at one time, and we anticipated a long day.

But that day was different.

When Sal and I went to the lab to get results for our new patients, we expected a total of twenty pieces of paper scattered all over the room. But to our amazement, the tech greeted us with a smile and handed me five stapled packs of results. One patient's tests had not been completed because the blood had clotted, and they'd taped the tube on the pack to show us. I was impressed and thanked them for their organization and efficiency.

All the patients that day qualified for the drugs, except for the one who needed to have her blood redrawn. When we registered the new patients and went to pay the cashier, they told us there was no charge because they were HIV patients. For months, we had been paying ten thousand kwacha each for an OP registration card, so this was a blessing that saved us fifty thousand kwacha (about fifteen dollars).

The staff at the Fast-Track Clinic was taken aback with so many patients, even though I'd completed all the interviews and filled out their initial paperwork for them. The administrator came to see us and requested that we let them know next time how many we would be bringing. We promised to stop in on Tuesdays and inform them of the number they could expect the following Thursday. That seemed to ease the situation.

We were out of there by twelve thirty. *Thank You, God.*

The smiles on the faces of the patients as we walked back to the vehicle were worth more than gold. Clutching their medications, they had a new hope. They saw a reason to live.

Many would say, "But Jesus should be their hope." We agreed, but I think they saw Jesus through us. What they saw was that Jesus had sent us to show them He cared, that they were worth it, and that their life mattered. We showed them the love of Christ.

Just months or weeks before getting their medicine, they might have been dying in their huts, crying out to an Almighty God in despair and hopelessness. Now they knew that God answers prayer.

For a year prior to our leaving the US, Pastor Clark had us going out into the local community on Sunday afternoons, meeting physical needs, practicing servanthood, living the gospel, making a difference. I see now where our preparation was not only believing and sharing the gospel but actually showing the gospel in action!

God says, *If you are faithful in little things, you will be faithful in large ones.*

We were about to see exactly why God had prepared us with all those Sunday outings back home.

Susan, our first HIV patient, had become our poster child and was a walking testimony. God told Sal that her village was to be our first outreach.

Toward the end of January, we met with a headman, assistant headman, and council of her village, and they said it would be a privilege to have us come. Sal told them the privilege was ours.

We determined that the vision for the outreach was to show *unusual kindness* through fellowship, feeding, medical care, healing, and prayer—demonstrating the love of Jesus. After plans and promises had been made, we discovered that their territory included nine villages. We had envisioned one small village, but this was going to be nine!

We were a little shocked, and there was a fleeting thought of "Can we handle this?" But our God knows what He's doing, so we determined to trust Him.

We scheduled the outreach for Saturday, February 11, when a team of volunteers from North Carolina would be there. They had been in email contact with us, and although we had never met them, we felt that we were to plan the outreach when they could participate. They told us via email that they "just wanted to serve" and felt they were to do that with us somehow.

The team of five from North Carolina arrived on Wednesday the eighth: two women—Alma and T. B.—and three men—Pastor Billy, Greg, and Jim. Hearing Pastor Billy share the first night during a devotional time, I just knew God had put us together for such a time as this.

As I listened to Pastor Billy's heart for the Zambian people, I could hardly keep my own heart from pounding right out of my chest. The more we talked with the team, the more excited I got, anticipating the day and what God had planned.

Because of our caseload at the clinic, Sal and I hadn't had much time to plan, and God wasn't revealing much. However, despite the lack of a detailed plan, Sal and I were very much at peace.

I grew in anticipation when things started to heat up.

Late Wednesday night, Sal came down with conjunctivitis in his left eye. He wore a patch all day Thursday and some of Friday in the clinic, but when both eyes became infected, he had to remove the patch and just see patients with draining red eyes.

On Friday, the worship leader came down with malaria, as did one of the people we had designated as a cook. But even though it was the night before the Saturday outreach and we were still missing some answers, we trusted that God would light the stones as we needed them. We definitely wanted to leave room for God.

A while before, God had given me Matthew 9:35, which was the ministry of Jesus. Jesus went through all the towns and villages, teaching in their synagogues, preaching the good news of the kingdom, and healing every disease and sickness. Pastor Billy's Wednesday-night devotion had been from Matthew 9:9–13. So late Friday night, when I was seeking God and His direction, I decided to read all of Matthew 9. It became very clear to me that it held everything God wanted to say.

Late Friday night, the stones were lit. This outreach was to demonstrate the love of Christ through meeting both the physical and spiritual needs of the people through the enabling of the Holy Spirit, healing through medical care and prayer, and feeding of both food and the Word.

Sal and the orphanage director, who was also a nurse, would do medical; T. B. and Jim would take pictures; and Alma and Greg would cover prayer lines, joined by fellow missionaries Tim and Mary from Global Samaritan, a neighboring nongovernmental organization (NGO). Enoch was to have total control of the feeding program, cooking, collecting tickets, and rationing out food for everyone, with Doubt helping him. Lena, Beauty, Samson, and the other Doubt were the worship team members, and the rest were to be used as interpreters. I figured Pastor Billy and I would be the floaters.

Despite the obstacles being thrown at us, come Saturday morning, Sal and I started to load up the cars at six thirty, and the rest of our team began arriving at seven.

We had nine twenty-five-kilogram bags of mealie meal (for nshima). For the relish (the Zambian term for side dishes with their nshima), we had thirty heads of cabbage, with a large bag of onions and tomatoes and a very large bag of *kapenta* fish (tiny whole fish with eyes and all). We had packed three Rubbermaid containers with medical supplies and medications and also took tables, chairs, and twenty-five people in all.

After we had packed the vehicles, we met inside the apartment for prayer and last-minute directions. After encouragement that God was up to something good, we started out.

The sun was shining, and the sky was clear—something we had prayed for. The tarmac to Zimba, which had been filled with potholes when I'd last driven it, had since been fixed. God works out stuff even when you forget to ask Him.

When we got to the village, instead of the tiny Pilgrim Wesleyan Church, we were directed to the basic school. What a blessing! We were able to use three rooms: two for exams and one for gathering to share the Word and giving order to the day's events. The church across the way was to be used for food preparation and feeding.

After setting up, we gathered all the people into the meeting room, and I shared the Word. In Matthew 9, Jesus forgives sin, the lame walk, the blind see, the dead rise, the sick are healed, demons are cast out, and the mute speak.

Jesus eats with sinners, saying, "It is not the healthy who need a doctor, but the sick" (v. 12). He goes on to say, "But go and learn what this means: 'I desire mercy (that is, readiness to help those in trouble), not sacrifice.'" (v. 13).

All that in one chapter!

The praise team led worship, and the people were encouraged that Jesus is the same yesterday, today, and forever. They were reminded that Jesus said, "If you believe, you will receive whatever you ask for in prayer" (Matthew 21:22). The people were to get prayed for and anointed with oil prior to coming for any medical treatment. They were also to register and pick up their meal tickets.

The rest of the day was just as awesome and God-directed as the beginning. Over eight hundred people were fed nshima and relish; over three hundred people were seen medically, including two brought on oxcarts, or what we call "bush ambulances"; the children were played with; and the singing of praise and worship was heard sporadically throughout the day. The prayer lines continued all day, with twenty-five new salvations reported.

Most of all, His loving kindness was demonstrated to all. The team was great, the day was wonderful, and God was and is awesome!

As darkness fell, Pastor Billy had to encourage Sal to stop, and we arrived back at the farm around eight o'clock that night. After the ministry team joined hands to give thanks and glory to God, we all went our separate ways, feeling very tired.

But it was a good tired.

## Chapter 15

IN THE MIDST OF ALL THE MEDICAL WORK, WE ALSO HAD TO FOCUS our attention on the needs of the church. Sal taught the *Under Cover* series by John Bevere on spiritual authority during Sunday school at the church on the farm while also leading worship.

He met multiple times with the church board and selected a new treasurer. Together they developed a new church budget. As for preaching, many people took their turn as they felt led, including Sal and me.

I taught a series of lessons to the worship team on holiness, the sacrifice of praise, and the tabernacle as a pattern given for leading people into the presence of the Lord.

I also held "train the trainer" classes for the new group of Sunday-school teachers in the *Firm Foundations* course that we decided to begin in mid-February. We divided into four different age groups: adults, teens, school age, and tots.

By the time the classes started, we had been to Lusaka and purchased more Tonga Bibles. The hope was for a Bible to be in every pair of hands! After all, how can we know Jesus if we are not spending time in the Word? Feeding on Sundays only is just not enough. We need our daily bread.

Just as we started to feel that maybe we *hadn't* been called for more than we could handle after all, an unexpected challenge showed up at our door.

One Sunday morning at seven, we awoke to pounding on our front door. Sal opened it to a desperate-looking man who was carrying a young child.

"I think she has malaria," he blurted out.

Without hesitation, Sal rushed them over to the clinic and confirmed the diagnosis. He learned that the father was named Samson, and his four-year-old daughter was Jennifer.

After Sal administered treatment, Samson took Jennifer home, only to return later in the afternoon, still concerned about her. Although she had slept off and on, when she woke up, she would cry out with a crazed stare, and claw at the air as though fighting with something . . . almost like she was possessed.

Since darkness would soon be approaching, we told him they could spend the night, even though it was Sunday and our staff was not working. Sal was known to stay up through the night to monitor patients he was concerned about, but Jennifer was on her medications and had stable vital signs. At that point, she seemed to be sound asleep. Sal told Samson to come get him if he was needed for any reason.

With those instructions given at tuck-in time, Sal and I went to the apartment to get some sleep.

Early the next morning, Sal went to check on Jennifer, only to return to the apartment a few minutes later.

"Come quick," he called out. "She's dying!"

He raced back over to the clinic to start her on an IV while I quickly dressed. When I got to the clinic, Sal was not having success with the IV. Little Jennifer needed fluids desperately. How could this have happened in six hours with her dad present?

Praying *Lord, help us* and speaking "You will live and not die," I inserted an NG tube, and we started ORS.

Throughout this whole time, Samson never left her side. He had slept on a chair next to her bed. He sponged her down and helped whenever I wanted to turn or suction her. He assisted in every way he could. It was a very special thing for us to see a Zambian man so attentive to his child. Usually, all the nurturing is done by the mother and other women. We could definitely see how much love he had for his family.

Assessing her status, I saw that she was limp with a high fever. We administered IM medications (shots); one for the fever and one to protect the brain. Sal did an HIV test, which, thankfully, was negative. Her vital signs were not normal—her temperature was 101, her pulse 160, and her respirations at sixty. Her lungs were congested and sounded like a death rattle.

We got out the suction machine, and I stayed at her bedside. Reverend Mwiikisa, who taught Bible classes and lived on the farm, laid hands on her and prayed, anointing her with oil.

He told me, "There is a time to live and a time to die, and God knows the appointed time."

Sal sank into a chair, put his head in his hands, and sobbed.

The word of the seriousness of her condition got out somehow, and her mother and four siblings came, along with her grandmother, a couple of aunts, and friends of the parents. They all lifted up prayers.

As I was suctioning, I noticed that the NG tube had worked its way out of her nose. Not having much choice, I removed it completely. The short time it was in, we were able to get enough ORS into her to hydrate her, so her veins were visible. Sal was successful at starting an IV, which we were able to use for fluid and medications.

Not having much success getting her breathing under control, Sal told me to give a nebulizer treatment, holding the medication under her nose (despite her heart rate). I have to admit that as I was putting the equipment together, I lost it also, crying in between getting supplies and setting up the treatment. I desired to see God move in signs and wonders. I wanted to see miraculous healings before my eyes. I wanted with all my heart to see God be glorified.

But it did not happen the way I had hoped.

I prayed for another chance at a miracle. The whole time we were working on her, she never really woke up. Occasionally, she would open her eyes and moan, not focusing . . . almost like nobody was home.

But after the treatment, there seemed to be a change. Jennifer's breathing was easier, her respirations at forty, and her pulse at 130. A peace came over me, a feeling that the worst was over.

We continued to monitor her through the afternoon and evening. Her body temperature lowered to ninety-nine. She no longer needed suctioning; her lungs were clear; pulse and respirations were stable. She was incontinent of urine (we had put on a disposable diaper), so her kidneys were functioning. Everything looked like it was improving, but she still wasn't waking up. Sal even tried giving her a glucose IV to stimulate her and, hopefully, wake her up.

Unfortunately, nothing happened.

How much brain damage did she have from the high fever and cerebral malaria? Why wasn't she waking up? Would she ever?

At that point, we told the family we had done everything we knew to do. It was now in God's hands. We told them to keep praying.

Janet offered to work until midnight, so Sal and I went to the apartment.

When Sal returned to the clinic at midnight, there was still no change. Discouraged, he went to the adjoining exam room to spend the night working on charts, intending to check on her every hour.

At one a.m., no change. At two a.m., still no change.

Around three in the morning, he heard her crying in the next room. When he went to check on her, she was sitting up in the bed with her eyes open and focused. She was back!

As the night progressed, she continued to improve.

Sal woke me at five. "Come and see the little miracle!"

She was moving all extremities on her own. She recognized her parents. She told her dad she was hungry, then ate porridge and drank water.

There were tears of joy and dancing and leaping and praising God! I really think God gave us a miracle.

Reverend Mwiikisa said, "You get sick quickly, but healing is slow like a snail."

I'll take it however the miracle comes—immediately, over a couple days, or however God chooses to move. All I know is that Jennifer went home that day on her dad's back, with smiles galore and thanksgiving to God from everyone!

As I went into the apartment, I realized she woke up on the "morning of the third day," and I was reminded of the resurrection of Jesus!

## Chapter 16

OVER TIME, WITH GOD ALWAYS LIGHTING THE NEXT STONE, WE began a protocol for HIV patients: drawing their bloodwork on Tuesdays using our own forms and then transporting them to Livingstone Hospital on Thursdays for acceptance into the government program for free ARV medications.

When we saw that walking all the way to Sons of Thunder on Thursday mornings was a problem for many people, Sal began picking up patients in the Land Rover at designated stops along the tarmac, like a bus. We would then transport them to the Fast-Track Clinic at the hospital in town and pay for each one to be seen by the doctor administering the antiretroviral medications.

Fridays turned out to be our Zimba Hospital Day. The patient load at the clinic on Fridays often prevented Sal from leaving, so I was forced to drive, which was an adventure in and of itself. It wasn't just about staying to the left or the fact that I was operating a tank on wheels with a left-handed stick shift. The real difficulty was the road itself.

There was only one tarmac between Livingstone and Lusaka, making it the only option when driving to Zimba. It was poorly paved without any defined edges, and the rain left it peppered with potholes.

Sometimes there was not enough room for two vehicles. Imagine meeting a big truck coming from the opposite direction, with people walking on the side of the road, bicycles traveling both ways, and even the occasional baboon family. There were also street vendors waving large mushrooms or fish, trying to catch the attention of passing motorists. Not exactly the backdrop for a leisurely drive.

To date, we had admitted six patients there—two for TB, one for a high-risk delivery, one for pneumonia, one for surgical removal of a breast mass, and one infant with severe dehydration.

Joseph, the pneumonia patient, and Tito, a sixteen-year-old boy with TB, had been discharged. Joseph was healed and back to work on the farm, and Tito was on TB medications and a high-protein food supplement.

Belita, the other TB patient, was doing well but was still in the hospital. Jacqueline, the HIV-positive pregnant patient, was kept at Zimba until her delivery because she was high risk.

David, the infant with severe dehydration, died in the hospital.

Rona, one of our own clinical assistants, found a lump in her right breast and was admitted for surgical removal. Her surgery was performed by a visiting American OB-GYN physician. We received the report that the mass was cancerous and that she would need to go to Lusaka for further tests and management.

How our hearts sank when we received the news.

The weekly protocol was starting to become a routine until one Thursday morning in late February when God decided to add to the schedule. That day, we transported nine HIV patients to Livingstone District Hospital to be put on the free medications.

After registering them all into the outpatient department and picking up their lab results from the previous Tuesday's blood draw, we proceeded to radiology for chest x-rays to rule out TB.

With x-rays in hand, we headed to the Fast-Track Clinic, where they each saw the doctor who initiated the ARVs, then the pharmacist who dispensed them. When reviewing the lab results, we found that one of our patients—Elika—had a hemoglobin of 4.7. To put that into perspective, in the US, they transfuse blood when the hemoglobin is 8.0. In Zambia, they transfuse at 5.0. Elika's hemoglobin was 4.7, yet she was still walking around! She was admitted straight from the clinic to the hospital for transfusions.

After the other eight patients had their medications, we started back to our clinic, where we would dispense other miscellaneous medications that had been ordered, go over last-minute instructions, and remind them of their review dates.

While we were still in the vehicle driving back, God started working on me. These people—three men and five women, ranging in age from twenty-five to seventy-four, some married, some divorced or widowed—had all placed their hope in the little boxes of medications that they had hidden in their pockets or wrapped in their *chitenges* (a piece of cloth, two yards or meters in length, that Zambian women wrap around their body).

I felt like God was saying, *Their hope should be in Me.*

As I meditated on what I thought I was hearing, I realized these people would be on the drugs for the rest of their lives. How could Sal and I possibly continue doing this? The numbers were too great.

Each one of these nine people at least had a partner that either had HIV and died or was still walking around with it. That was eighteen. Then there were the children. One of these women had an infant on her back, who was probably also HIV positive. And what if there were multiple partners? You can see how quickly this multiplies.

Soon, our vehicle was not going to be big enough. We would need the lorry (truck). And when that wasn't big enough, then what?

But I knew we could not turn our backs and do nothing. God specifically told us to do whatever He put in front of us . . . so what would we do? We couldn't do anything without God. This was something that would require His intervention.

I was again reminded that all the HIV we had seen was a result of sexual sin. The patient had either been the victim of the sin or the perpetrator of the sin. Any way you sliced it, it was a consequence of sin! We discovered early on with HIV in Zambia—which still holds true even after more than eleven hundred people have been tested and placed on treatment—is that *every* case has some sexual immorality story: premarital sex, marital affairs, sex with a prostitute, incest (it had been taught at one time by witch doctors that sex with a virgin would cure HIV/AIDS and that it didn't matter the age of the virgin), sexual cleansing (traditional belief that after a husband dies, the brother of the deceased should have sex with his widow in order to "cleanse" her), or polygamy, which is still legal in Zambia.

Since we had come to Zambia to care for both physical and spiritual needs, it became apparent that we needed to minister to the whole person.

So we included God's Word and the truth of the Gospel in our HIV care at Sons of Thunder, in order for individual repentance and God's forgiveness to have their way in the healing process.

I was gently reminded that Jesus came so our sins would be forgiven. It says in 1 Peter 2:24–25, "'He himself bore our sins' in his body on the cross, so that we might die to sins and live for righteousness; 'by his wounds you have been healed.' For 'you were like sheep going astray, but now you have returned to the Shepherd and Overseer of your souls.'"

I felt God saying, *Tell them.*

So when we got to the farm, I gathered them all together in one exam room, and we had church! I shared with them what I felt the Holy Spirit quickened to me, and I felt led to hand out Bibles to those who didn't have one (which was seven of them). Some cried, some testified . . . but they all lingered in the room, not wanting to leave.

I told them they would be coming back in two weeks for review, and I wanted them to read Matthew chapter 9 and all the Scriptures on healing they could find. How can anyone believe for a healing if they've never heard what Jesus has done—what He has already purchased for us with His broken body and shed blood? How can we receive a gift if we don't even know one has been given to us? Someone must tell us that the package wrapped so beautifully is for us! We just have to pick it up . . . it's right there. Forgiveness of sin and healing are ours—all of ours, bought and paid for by Jesus Christ.

We all held hands and prayed before going our separate ways. I didn't know what God had planned for the next time this group got together, but I didn't want to miss it!

Sal had no idea that I was going to do what I did, and he missed most of what happened because he was busy evaluating and treating a stroke patient who had been dropped off at the clinic while we were in town.

By the way, Thursday was our day off!

That impromptu meeting, inspired by God speaking to me on the way home, led to weekly HIV meetings every Thursday following our day in town.

Either Sal or I had always been the driver using the Land Rover, but the numbers continued to grow, and soon we needed the lorry to accommodate everyone. It was during this time that God brought a wonderful man named Christopher to the door, and we hired him as our driver.

The plan that unfolded as a result of my simple obedience that day demonstrated to me that God *always* has the best plan. Sal and I were way too busy to sit down and formulate a plan. Most of what we did with HIV patients happened one step at a time with what He put in front of us or out of necessity or frustration.

Even with God's plan in place, taking the HIV patients to the hospital was seldom easy. Sometimes these very sick people would just lie on the waiting room floor because of their weakened conditions. After getting them their medications, we would give them a snack and drinks, then return them to the farm. While Sal completed their paperwork, I would share the Word and pray with the group. Then we'd take them back on the lorry to the designated stops on the tarmac, where they would be dropped off to walk the rest of the way home.

Once on the ARVs, vitamins, and other medicine as needed, they started to improve and get stronger.

When we came to Zambia, we wanted to show the love of Jesus to the people we were brought to serve. This is an excerpt I wrote for the February blog post:

> God is real and He is in this place. Through hearts that have been touched to give, we have been able to show:
>> Love and kindness to a people who aren't used to seeing it.
>> Hope to a people who have not known it.
>> Choice to a people who have never been given it.

It's all about showing that Someone cares. Through our hearts and hands linked across the Atlantic, we were showing these people this Someone—Jesus Christ. He cares!

## Chapter 17

ON A SUNDAY IN MARCH, WE WENT TO ZIMBA HOSPITAL TO VISIT the four patients we were currently treating. Jacqueline, our high-risk HIV-positive patient, had given birth to a baby boy during the night. She'd received her AVR cocktail, and the baby was due to get his medicine later in the evening. We would return the following day to take them home.

Our two TB patients, Elena and Headman, were on their meds and breathing easier. Big smiles appeared on their faces when they saw us.

Liz, the HIV-positive TB patient who'd had the four liters of pus drained off her lung, was not in her bed. The previous Friday when I had stopped in to see her by myself, the surgeon was removing a chest tube he had inserted. He looked at me, shook his head, and said her lung was not inflating. With her HIV status, he did not give her any hope. I had immediately laid hands on her and prayed with her.

Not seeing her in the bed, my heart sank.

I quickly tracked down a nurse. "Where's Lizzy?"

"Liz?" She waved a hand as if it were no big deal. "She went to the market."

The market was an open outdoor shopping area behind the hospital. It was quite a walk—about six blocks. It made little sense that a woman who, just two days before, had looked near death—frail, very skinny, in pain, having difficulty breathing . . . the whole nine yards—would have walked to the market.

I turned to Sal. "We have to find her. I can't believe she walked there."

As we entered the market area, we saw Liz coming toward us, beaming. She greeted us each with a strong hug. Her breathing was easy, not labored; her face looked healthy; and she told us she felt good.

We were witnessing another miracle. She wanted to know when she could start on the HIV medicines. This woman had a renewed hope.

Our God is amazing!

In April, a Zambian man, Kelly, brought his wife, Beauty, to the clinic because she was very sick. To be honest, I wasn't sure who looked worse.

They were both very thin, like skeletons, and drawn-looking. Beauty had a high fever and large lymph nodes in her neck. It was obvious she had some sort of infection and was very malnourished. She was weak and dirty and understandably had no interest in breastfeeding her baby. The baby, also dirty, just cried with hunger.

Kelly was malnourished and unkempt but showed concern about his family and his inability to provide for them. He had no clue what was wrong with any of them. He just knew he was too sick to work or make things better.

Both were found to be HIV positive, and unfortunately, so was their thirteen-month-old daughter. We kept Beauty in the clinic for three days on IVs and IV antibiotics while we drew their blood and took it into Livingstone for further testing. After discharging Beauty, we took her and Kelly into Livingstone Hospital to get them put on the HIV meds. We also gave them powdered milk for the baby with a couple of bottles, along with HEPS and a twenty-five-kilogram bag of mealie meal.

Kelly and Beauty had no family that could help them, and he had been too sick to plant and work his fields. There was not enough food to feed his family, which we found out also included a ten-year-old daughter and a four-year-old son. Kelly brought his ten-year-old into the clinic the following week to be HIV tested, and she was found positive also. He then brought in the four-year-old, but to our surprise, the son was negative. So four out of five in the family had HIV.

The ten-year-old, Gift, was covered with skin sores from head to foot. Even though her CD4 count was too high to qualify, they placed her on the medications due to her condition.

After a month, we took them into Livingstone for their review, and the change was just miraculous. I wish I'd taken pictures in the beginning for comparison, but it's hard when people are so sick and literally dying.

Kelly had gained weight and felt healthy. He was even sporting a little goatee. Beauty smiled and looked well, and Gift's skin had completely healed. They all had a hope in their eyes that hadn't been there a month before.

The smile on Gift's face alone was like looking into the face of Jesus. It reminded us of when He said, "When you did it for the least of these, you did it for Me."

The change in Kelly's family was a gift to us all.

At the end of our first nine months, it was time for a furlough. We took great pains to make sure the clinic would not close during our absence. We had already hired and trained staff, including the clinical officer, who would cover for us, working with our three clinical assistants. We had also hired Christopher by this time, and he would continue to take HIV patients to Livingstone Hospital on Thursdays and TB patients to Zimba Hospital on Fridays. We were pleased that we could leave things in an organized manner, not putting undue pressure on any of the other missionaries, who had their own areas of ministry. Things seemed to be coming together nicely.

We still had a couple more things to do. First, we needed to have a meeting with all the HIV patients in our care. The number now totaled over fifty on medications.

After months of individual meetings with the Thursday HIV patients, we had a gathering in the church with the entire group. This particular Thursday, instead of going into town to the hospital, we all met to share the Word, praise the Lord, have a time of prayer, eat a meal, and provide all necessary direction to be followed during our absence in order that they would continue to receive their medications.

The meeting was opened in prayer by Reverend Mwiikisa, and I shared the Word out of Romans regarding sin and its consequences. I started by sharing how until they were given the diagnosis of HIV, they were unaware that they needed a cure. They didn't know what was wrong. If you didn't know you had a disease, you wouldn't know that you needed a cure or a healing. The same is true of your spiritual state. Until you become aware that you are dead in your sin, you never know that you need a cure.

We talked about the wages of sin being death but the gift of God being eternal life. There is no one righteous, not even one. But Jesus offers a complete cure through His amazing grace. Once you know you are sick, it's there for the asking.

They were asked if they died that night—and many of them had been close to death—where would they go?

After the Word, there was an encouraging time of praise and worship and individual prayers of repentance for salvations or rededications. Thirty Tonga Bibles were distributed to those who did not have a Bible. It was sweet to see them hover over the Word, talking to one another. Once they had been given time to make their relationships right with God, they were encouraged to pray for their healings, and Sal and I agreed with them in prayer.

The informational portion of the meeting came next, beginning with introductions to Jha (the clinical officer), Christopher (the driver), Anna, Bertha, and Janet (the staff), and another Christopher (who helped us out when we were at Livingstone Hospital). They were each given a written personal schedule of medication collection and review dates.

The rest of the day was spent in fellowship as they shared a meal of nshima, cabbage, beans, and kapenta.

When it was over, hugs and goodbyes were exchanged before they loaded onto the lorry for Sal to take them home.

Once all the clinic responsibilities were covered, we turned to the church. Sunday-school curriculum was being taught by four teachers to the four different age groups, and those lessons on *Firm Foundations* would continue through all of 2006.

The church budget was being maintained, and the treasurer was keeping good records. The worship leader had been reinstated after his time of discipline, and he had participated in the classes taught to the worship team.

A new pastor had arrived to help Reverend Mwiikisa with Bible classes. The church board had decided to allow him to oversee the church while we were on our three-month furlough. It would serve as an orientation period. We would make a final decision upon our return about offering this pastor a permanent position.

The new pastor had already scheduled a baptism and baby dedication for April to correspond with a fellowship Sunday. It might have even been Easter Sunday, the day we were to leave for home.

Once all the preparations had been made for both the clinic and the church, the only thing left before getting on the plane was to inform the old missionary of all our plans.

Much to our surprise, that conversation did not go well.

# Chapter 18

BACK IN 2005, WHEN SAL AND I TOOK THE TWO-WEEK MEDICAL-MIS-sion-intensive course in preparation to come to Zambia, something stuck with us. The message to the group on the very first day was this: "The biggest enemy to a new missionary is an old missionary, because the old missionary has forgotten why he came and who sent him."

Everyone in the class chuckled that day, but once we were on the ground in Zambia, it didn't take long for Sal and me to realize just how true that statement was.

Looking back on our situation in Zambia, it is obvious that the old missionary had not been happy when he was informed that we were coming to start a clinic on the farm. The first thing he did was to postpone our arrival on the field for an entire year, telling us he wasn't ready for us. We found out later that he had already told the board he didn't think a clinic was needed, but he'd been outvoted. By making us wait another year, he hoped we would be discouraged and start questioning our actual call.

Granted, receiving the news that we would have to wait another year had been somewhat disheartening, especially after waiting a year due to Sal's diagnosis and treatment of non-Hodgkin's lymphoma.

Despite our reconfirmed call, however, the old missionary was still not happy or welcoming when we arrived. Thankfully, God had set some things in place to safeguard us that we were not aware of at the time.

The first thing was that He had set us up to be self-supporting missionaries. He had shown us the ministry of John the Baptist and how he was not financially beholden to anyone. That way, he was free to hear God and obey, giving allegiance to Him and saying what needed to be said to the Pharisees.

In our situation, we would continue to collect salaries from Associates in Emergency Care, the very business God had instructed us to start, thereby supporting ourselves. Being self-supporting also opened up the opportunity for us to share the story of Sons of Thunder, fundraising for the entire ministry instead of just ourselves, like most missionaries do.

Since the old missionary did not control our finances or those of the medical ministry, we were free to make decisions and set up the clinic on a firm foundation and under the proper authority, as God directed our steps. We had control of scheduling, staffing, and sourcing medications and supplies, as well as decision-making regarding anything medical.

We had been given one room to start and had medical supplies sent by our church. We also had purchased the Land Rover Defender, not only for our personal use but also for the medical ministry. Over time, we had added two more rooms, a team of medical staff, and a driver. The old missionary had control over every area of SOT except the medical ministry.

Of course, we recognized him as head of Sons of Thunder, Zambia, overall, abided by his rules, and sought his approval when we needed the lorry or had overall ministry issues. We informed him when we were instructed to do our large medical outreach and involve the mission team.

God had told both Sal and me, *Freely you have received, freely give.* So when the old missionary wanted us to charge patients, we had respectfully declined.

Another safeguard we had in place was, surprisingly enough, our blog.

Blogs were brand new when we first set it up. We documented life in Zambia as we experienced it, always including pictures. We just enjoyed sharing the story. Many people commented on how those stories made them feel like they were right there.

Looking back, it was definitely the Holy Spirit writing through me. I knew how much I enjoyed creating the posts and what a valuable tool this was for sharing, but we wouldn't realize till later what a godsend the blog actually was.

When we went to the main house to inform the old missionary and his wife of our plans, we expected them to be pleased with our efforts.

To our astonishment, the old missionary firmed his jaw and said, "We'll see."

Sal and I exchanged a puzzled glance.

Then Sal asked, "What does that mean, 'We'll see'?"

The man shrugged. "We have a phone call in to Pastor Jerry. So then, we'll see."

We returned to our apartment, still baffled. We called Pastor Jerry and asked him what was going on.

"Keep your heads down." We heard him pull in a breath. "And continue to do what you know to do. Stay away from the old missionary, and just get ready to come home for furlough."

So that was what we did. We left for furlough with our plans in place, eager to see our family and friends.

It was such a good feeling to touch ground on American soil. We couldn't wait to see our family. The scene at the airport was loud and crazy with squeals of excitement. Hugs and kisses all around. How I had missed them all.

Once we had recovered from jet lag and seen all our family, we met with Pastor Jerry to find out what was going on. We discovered that the old missionary had resigned. After ten years!

We were never told the full story, but we found out that he had told Pastor Jerry and the board that he did not want Sal and me back on the field. He made untrue statements and allegations of our neglect in prayer and ministry.

Our saving grace was the blog. Nine months' worth of stories of preaching, teaching, prayer, outreaches, healings, and so forth. At the time, I did not realize I was documenting what would later be evidence in our defense.

The old missionary and his wife had no knowledge of what we'd been writing. They and their family, friends, and supporters—including other missionaries in town—were not on our subscriber list. They had no idea that we'd been capturing our experiences in almost daily posts about individual patients, our frustrations and struggles, and opportunities for ministry.

We weren't the only reason for the old missionary's resignation, but we were definitely a large part.

Time at home was restful and restorative and filled with family and friends. We also made appointments for dental care and physical exams. Sal had a PET scan to follow up on his lymphoma. It showed two spots in the abdomen, which would require antibody treatments once a week for four weeks at a time, every six months for two years. That meant he would have treatments in March and September for the next two years.

Our furloughs were pretty well predetermined then, at least for a while. On the plus side, the treatments were not chemotherapy and didn't have the same side effects. We figured it was just God's way of giving us a much-needed break twice a year.

Of course, we were happy to have an excuse to see the grandchildren.

After three months, we returned to the farm to find the orphanage director and her husband in charge of everything. The Zambians reported that the old missionary and his wife had had a bonfire and burned pictures, clothes, and all sorts of things prior to their leaving. They were going to sell all the main-house furnishings until Pastor Jerry told them that Sons of Thunder would purchase it all.

During the first week of our return, one of the Zambian pastors came to Sal with allegations of the inappropriate behavior of the orphanage director's husband. In addition to that accusation, we discovered that he had tried to block the use of the medical vehicle by taking it for his own use. He had also unsuccessfully tried to access our personal computer to delete files. He had moved into the main house with his wife, and they had accepted a large number of orphans into the orphanage, none of them registered with social welfare.

Sal immediately called Pastor Jerry, who traveled to Zambia. He and Sal managed to verify the allegations of misconduct. The board decided to pull the orphanage director and her husband off the field, never to return, for conduct unbecoming a missionary.

The resignation of the original missionary and the subsequent removal of the orphanage director and her husband left us in a very unusual position. We were placed in leadership over all aspects of the ministry by default. God had already prepared us through our secular career paths, so we were not fearful or unfit for the challenge.

We hadn't heard the last of the old missionary. Whatever story he'd told our fellow missionaries throughout the region regarding his departure from SOT caused them to ostracize us. We found ourselves shunned. In order to make everyone more comfortable, we decided to stop going to the weekly missionary fellowships.

Later, we found out that the old missionary had started another mission organization right in Zambia, about ninety minutes north of us. We thought he had washed his hands of SOT and would put his attention on building and running the new ministry operation.

Unfortunately, that was not the case. He never took his hands entirely off Sons of Thunder. He called it "my baby" and told Pastor Jerry that he had stolen his baby. He continued to cause trouble for a while, not only for us but for all of Sons of Thunder.

All we could do was continue to concentrate on what God put before us and the people we had come to serve.

## Chapter 19

JUST AS THE DUST BEGAN TO SETTLE FROM OUR STAFF UPHEAVAL, literal dust and dirt appeared everywhere, due to the dry season.

The bright spot for us at this time was the birth of our fifth grandchild. Gabriel Josiah was born on September 25, 2006. Unfortunately, we were not there for his birth, but we knew we would be home again in November to meet him, because Sal would be speaking at a conference.

Soon we would experience mud from rainy season, as well as the inability to sleep due to the extreme heat of October with only a ceiling fan or stand fan. I reminded myself to be content and thankful in all situations.

Through all of this, I realized that being in Africa made the Bible come alive for me.

I didn't really understand the *washing of feet* until I went there. People were forever trying to keep their feet clean. It's too hot to wear shoes. Flip-flops—or "tropicals," as they are called in Zambia—are convenient and cool, but they get dusty in the dry season and muddy in the rainy season. After walking for any amount of time, both your shoes and your feet need to be washed.

It never made sense why Esther and the ladies had to take beauty treatments for an entire year, soaking in oils to make their skin soft, until I shook hands with some of the older women in the villages.

I didn't understand what it meant when Adam walked with God in the "cool of the morning" until I spent an October there without air conditioning. At around four or five in the morning, something "breaks," and you are finally relieved and able to fall asleep. It really is the cool of the morning.

The other thing I hate to admit not knowing but was schooled on by one of the American missionary doctors was that the sky and stars in Zambia are not the same as back in Pennsylvania and Maryland. There is no Big Dipper, but there *is* the Southern Cross.

Looking up at the nighttime sky and seeing the unhindered view of all the stars, I became a little more appreciative of what Abraham saw when God told him He was going to make his descendants more numerous than the stars. It's utterly breathtaking.

I understand a bit better about the plagues of Egypt also, thanks to the time Pastor Julius asked me to step outside. I did, only to see hundreds of baby frogs swarming the veranda of the main house and surrounding grass. He told me they were all heading to the dam.

Yes, definitely, the Bible came alive on that side of the globe!

One evening, Sal and I returned to the house, exhausted from yet another long shift at the clinic. Sal flicked on the light, and I let out a shriek.

"What's wrong?" He looked at me like I'd lost my mind.

Gasping for words, I pointed straight ahead of us. Scads of small black specks trailed down the walls like a curtain from out of the ceiling.

Being braver than me, or maybe because he was tired beyond the point of fear, Sal stepped forward to examine the specks more closely.

"Bugs," he announced. "I think they're stink bugs."

As off-putting as that name sounds, at least they don't bite. But they are very annoying! There were tens of thousands of them—small, *crunchy* bugs that stink when you kill them. It was like living on *Fear Factor*. The bugs came out of the ceiling and seams in the walls. They were in the shower and in the closets and in our *bed*. Really gross!

For the next several weeks, Sal and I spent a couple of hours every night cleaning them up with a shop vac. We still had them for a time, but thankfully they were winnowed down to about a hundred that we vacuumed up twice a day.

While cleaning them up one day, I noticed something black slip out from under the love seat. When I looked down, I saw a scorpion. I had seen them before, but they were nothing like this one. This one was as big as my cell phone.

Without even thinking, I removed my shoe and killed it.

When I recognized the fact that I was not scared or even startled when I found and killed that oversized scorpion, I came to the realization that all my fear was gone. I couldn't explain why. All I knew was that somewhere along the journey, God had removed *all fear*. I don't know how. I don't know when. I just know that was the defining moment for me. From that time on, I no longer walked in fear of anything.

Little did I know how important that would be as I went through the years ahead.

When we found ourselves in leadership, the first thing we did was move from the apartment to the main house. This was where mission teams stayed and where all operations of the entire farm were centered. We realized God had done it again. He had provided answers for us before we even knew we needed them.

A young, newly married couple named Jake and Jessi felt called to missions and had come to the farm just prior to our return from furlough. Sal called a meeting of the four of us, and we divided responsibilities and oversight of all four ministry areas: Sal would oversee the clinic, I would take on the school, Jake would take responsibility for the church, since that was what he'd trained for, and Jessi would be over the orphanage.

Jake's request to take the oversight of the church released Sal and me from any and all responsibilities there. Sal would review the last year with Jacob and be around for any assistance needed, but our time of being in charge of the church had come to an end.

Linah and Royce, the two orphanage supervisors who had been there from the beginning, would have to orient Jessi because Sal and I had no clue about the running of that ministry.

There were thirty-two families living on the farm at that time, all isolated along the borders living in huts made of grass—roofs and all. Fire was a problem with the grass houses, and there were a couple of heart-wrenching stories from those early years before Sal and I came. Each household had been required to have a garden with the same four vegetables: tomatoes, onions, cabbage, and rape—a spinach-like green—as well as a field for maize. They were given seed and fertilizer on credit and were expected to pay back at harvest time, which they were never able to do.

The only paying jobs on the farm at the time were the houseworker, who filled the water tanks; the ladies in the orphanage; and watchmen. Also, builders had been paid at certain times to add on to the school each year.

There were no water sources except on the farm proper. There was a dam and a small river, but clean water was only accessible where there were a couple of boreholes. Everyone had to walk long distances to source water and carry it back to their huts on their heads.

Sadly, the people overall were not clean or healthy. Most had no job and no shoes. A lot had malnutrition due to lack of food.

Besides meeting with the four of us, Sal also met with one of the Zambians, Alexander, chosen because he had recognizable leadership qualities, spoke English, and had been with Sons of Thunder from the beginning.

Sal got right to the point. "I want to move the people off the borders, where they are all alone, and shift them into groups or villages. Maybe four or five households together in one area so that they form a community." He paused as he considered. "Do you think you could find suitable land in different areas?"

Alexander knew the boundaries and all the land over the ten-thousand-acre farm. After all, herding cows had been his first job there.

"I can, Sal." He punctuated his response with a confident nod.

Sal continued. "Then after you do that, I need you to pick capable men to be leaders over each village. If there are seven villages, then you need to pick seven men to be headmen over them. Do you think you could select seven headmen?"

"Of course." Alexander nodded again. "I will do it right away." Alexander let his eyes drop, as though pondering whether to ask some lingering question.

"Listen." Sal firmed his tone. "I don't need a yes-man! I don't want someone who always tells me what they think I want to hear. I want someone who tells me the truth. You are no good to me unless you tell me what you think! So . . . what's on your mind?"

With a little shifting of his feet, Alexander met his gaze. "Well, I was just wondering about the borders. Remember all the trouble in the past with the squatters?"

"Good question." Sal took a slow breath. "I think we need a border patrol."

And that was how the first seven villages were created, and people excitedly shifted from the border to their assigned village. They began building their houses, but this time they upgraded to mud houses from the more dangerous grass. We gave out old iron sheets that were found stored in the tobacco barn to be used for roofs. So mud houses with iron sheets became the norm.

Seven men were selected to become headmen, and they, along with Alexander—our newly appointed village supervisor—formed the first Sons of Thunder headmen board. The board met every Tuesday to discuss problems, accept new families, and make decisions regarding village life. Sal led the meetings at first, teaching by example. He let the men know it was okay to have an opinion, even if it wasn't the same as his, and that it was okay to vote the way their heart directed.

Change is always difficult, but as decisions were made to improve life on the farm, things became a bit easier. People were starting to be happy.

## Chapter 20

IN THE MIDST OF ALL THE ONGOING DRAMA, PATIENTS STILL HAD to be seen and treated. People came to the Sons of Thunder Clinic looking for medicine, but they always left with a little more than they expected . . . they got Jesus!

Everyone got prayed for. The Word was spoken throughout the day, starting with a ten-minute message at eight a.m. by Pastor Julius, whom we had hired as our clinic chaplain. One-on-one sessions were common, resulting in salvations, healings, and just plain sharing the love of Jesus. It was no wonder people came from all over, walking many hours and many kilometers.

One man said it best: "We come because you care."

Sadly, in the weeks after our return from furlough, there were four deaths.

One patient was Nelson, a sixty-year-old man who came to the clinic on an oxcart, with extreme difficulty breathing. His family had walked for six or seven hours from deep in the bush.

His O2 saturation, which was supposed to be in the nineties, was in the fifties. His ankles were swollen with fluid, and his lung sounds were wet. He was literally drowning in his own fluids.

We put him in bed with his head elevated and started nebulizer treatments. We started an IV to give him Lasix and Aminophylline. After three treatments, his O2 saturation was still low, and he began foaming at the mouth. I suctioned him, as he was losing consciousness.

To make matters worse, there was no vehicle on the farm to use for transport. We called Tim, a missionary from Global Samaritan up on the hill, and asked him to transport us in his lorry to Livingstone Hospital. He agreed and came down.

Sal started bagging Nelson to assist with his breathing. This is a process of resuscitating a person using a bag valve mask. We got some men from the work team to help load him into the back of the lorry on a mattress. We took two team members with us, along with his wife; one team member held the IV, Sal bagged, I monitored his O2 saturation and level of consciousness, and the other team member comforted his wife. Everyone prayed.

What a sight we were in the back of the uncovered lorry, driving on the open road and through town to the hospital.

When we got there, Tim went to get a stretcher and came out with a canvas one like you see in the battlefield scenes of old war movies.

When we got inside and asked where we should put him, the only nurse around said, "Put him in the emergency room."

That sounded reasonable, but when she unlocked a twelve-by-twelve room, it was obvious that it was seldom used. One stretcher, drawers empty, some old equipment just thrown on top of counters. Sal was still bagging Nelson, who remained unconscious.

The nurse left, and no one else came. It turned out that the clinical officer was at lunch with no way to be reached, and this nurse was the only one covering the outpatient department.

We found an old oxygen tank and moved it closer, then we tried to find a mask. Sal had to rig up something that would work to deliver oxygen. We were then able to get his O2 saturation up into the nineties, and he responded to my voice if I were in his ear.

We waited for the clinical officer to arrive, then gave him our report and prayed. We left Nelson there, not knowing if they would do anything or if he was just going to die.

Days later, we were pleasantly surprised when we discovered he had been admitted to the male ward. We were even more encouraged when we found they had put him on Lasix, Digoxin, and Salbutamol.

When we went to visit, his wife hugged us for a long time. Nelson was discharged about a week and a half later.

As we were taking him home, we stopped at the clinic to get medications for him, since the hospital had given him only five pills of Digoxin and told him that was all he would need. While he and his family were in the vehicle, I was stirred to give him a Bible and talk to him about Jesus.

That day, we made sure he was saved and knew where he would spend his eternal life. The entire family—wife and grown children—witnessed this and professed their relationship with Jesus also.

Sal made a house call a few days later. When he returned, he looked grim. "He won't make it out of there again."

Just a couple of days after that, Nelson died at home. Saddened though I was for his wife and family, and sometimes frustrated at medical care in Zambia, I couldn't help but smile. I knew where Nelson had gone that day.

After Nelson passed, the headman of the village came to the clinic to ask us if we would come right before rainy season to provide medical care to his people in Matengu. Already telling God we would do whatever He put in front of us, Sal said yes and scheduled Saturday, October 28, 2006, as the date.

When the day arrived, we packed up all three vehicles with food, medications, and other supplies with a medical team of nine. In addition to the medical staff, there were eighteen volunteers from the farm to be part of the ministry team. We had no idea how many people were coming until that morning, and we were pleasantly surprised. As all twenty-seven of us gathered around the circle, I realized there was no mission team from America . . . this was to be an outreach of mainly Zambian leaders and ministers helping Zambians.

As I looked at the faces gathered, I heard God say that these people had been in prayer groups and Bible studies in their villages over the last few weeks, and they were as prepared as any work team to share Jesus. There were pastors, praise team members, and Sunday-school leaders, all with Bibles in hand. Pastor Julius led us in prayer, and after a few words of encouragement from Sal and me, we loaded into the vehicles.

We were, however, short one member—Jake. He stayed back on partial bedrest. He'd played in the Independence Day football tournament on October 24 and ended up with phlebitis in his right leg. Warm compresses, aspirin therapy, and rest had been the order of the last few days, and we determined it would be prudent for him to stay home this time.

Christopher drove the Land Rover, Sal the lorry, and Jessi tackled the Land Cruiser. It was an hour's drive deep in the bush, and when we finally arrived, people were already waiting for us. They opened in prayer and welcomed us with a song, a greeting, and a skit (which they call a sketch), then asked if we had anything to share. I shared the Word, and Sal and I both gave the plan and direction for the day.

Medically, we had a registration sign-in area, a station for temperatures, weights, and chief complaints, and three medical stations with Jha, Sal, and Joan—a volunteer RN from Zimba Mission—seeing patients. There was a separate room for HIV counseling and testing with our new HIV counselor, Vundakai.

Lonny, one of our teachers, took the children to the school playground, where he sang and danced with them and played football (soccer) and net ball. Obert and his team of five cooked nshima, cabbage, and kapenta for everyone. Jessi and the worship team led in praise and worship for a good part of the day.

The pastors and students who'd been taking Bible classes went in teams of two and prayed for people. They were pleased to report not just prayers for healing but salvations, deliverances, and even people asking questions and pouring over Scriptures from the Bible.

I was the coordinator putting order to things again—logistics. That seemed to be a lot of my role there in many different areas. I did get to have a teaching session with the mothers of infants about charms and their significance and why we cut them off their babies.

At the end of a very tiring but rewarding day, almost three hundred people had been seen medically and fed. Children and adults alike were ministered to and shown the love of Jesus.

We also discovered that Nelson had been the headman of the village. We never knew that. His brother Benson was now the headman, and the one who asked us to come. Nelson's wife gave both Sal and me a big hug when she saw us and another big hug when we were leaving.

We were very proud of all the ministry team that went with us that day. They represented Sons of Thunder and Jesus as well as any mission team could have done.

Just because we were following our calling to provide medical care and leadership in Zambia didn't mean our life back home was put on hold. Sal and I returned to the States on November 3 so Sal could teach at the Virginia EMS Symposium in Norfolk. His topic was EMS Missionaries: Spreading Hope.

The entire conference was a total of five days, from November 8 through 12. After it concluded, we went to a wedding on November 18, and Gabe was dedicated on November 19. Since Sal's parents were there and we were all gathered together, we had our Thanksgiving dinner also that day. Whew . . . what a whirlwind! Our return flight was scheduled for November 20, but I just couldn't do it.

The time home was too short. I couldn't pull myself away from the cutest little baby ever. Gabriel Josiah (*God is my strength and healing*) was a joy, and since we were staying with our son Shaun and his family (it was still our house), I got to spend time with Gabe and his sisters every day. Sal agreed that I should stay for Christmas, but he had to return to the farm to check on things and get back to the clinic.

Sal went back to the farm on November 20, 2006, to restart the projects he had left, most important of which was the repairing of one of the dams. They were working against the clock to try to accomplish it before rainy season.

I felt a little selfish about staying back, but it seemed right for some reason. I was where I was supposed to be. I planned to join Sal on New Year's Eve. We would begin a whole new year expectantly waiting to see God's continued vision unfold.

On Christmas Eve, with dinner on the table, Shaun and his wife, Rachel, had to take Gabe, who was just three months old, to the ER because he was vomiting. He was admitted to the local hospital at first but had to be transferred to Children's National Hospital in Washington, DC, because they discovered a problem with his lungs. Once it became clear that this was going to be a long-term condition and that he was stable, we decided

I should return to Zambia to be with Sal. Shaun worked out of the office in the house and took care of the girls. Rachel stayed full time with Gabe at the hospital. Occasionally, they would switch.

By spring of 2007, at almost six months old, Gabe was still an inpatient in Children's National Hospital in DC, in the Pediatric Intensive Care Unit (PICU). He had been diagnosed with a chronic lung problem after a lung biopsy and severe reflux, which required Nisin surgery. He was also diagnosed with SCIDS, which is a malfunctioning or absent immune system, like the "boy in the bubble." He was going to need a bone marrow transplant.

As daunting as all this was, God was faithful through it all, giving us a peace that passes all understanding.

Gabe did indeed have a successful bone marrow transplant, but while he was in the hospital for all those months, he had two critical events that deprived his brain of oxygen for too long, resulting in permanent damage. He was put on a ventilator, which he would remain on indefinitely.

After eight exhausting months, it was time to bring him home. His bed and all his medical supplies were set up in that loft right outside the master bedroom (remember the loft furniture God had me return). Nurses would spend the night shift giving care to him in that loft with his parents right on the other side of the wall, ready to answer at the first sound of an alarm or call if needed.

He has spent his life in the hands of loving and committed parents who take him everywhere and include him in all aspects of family life. Over the years he has had wonderful nursing care and support from nurses who have become like family members, even going on vacations in order that his life is as full as it can be.

Even through all these trials, our God remains faithful.

*Chapter 21*

ONCE I WAS BACK ON THE FARM WITH SAL, WE TURNED OUR FOCUS again to restructuring all areas of ministry at Sons of Thunder while also seeing patients. In order to do that, we had to start raising up Zambian leaders in all areas, increasing their responsibilities, creating jobs, and providing training. All while remembering our original call.

It was a very busy time. God had already told us to *Just do what I put in front of you*, and that was what we did. One day at a time, one problem at a time, one hurdle at a time. We kept our heads down and our eyes focused on Him, because if we were to lift our eyes, it would have been way too overwhelming. I believe that was why we had to go home on furlough in March and September. I know it was for Sal's treatment, but I also believe He knew we needed a break.

Every morning began before the sun came up, and by night it was early to bed exhausted, most of the time unsure of what had been accomplished that day. Things were always left unfinished as we crashed into bed with the hope that tomorrow would see it through.

Although we saw outpatients with all kinds of diagnoses, our main areas of care seemed to be HIV and maternal-child health. The number of HIV patients in our care continued to increase. We had approximately 150 on medications by this time and more than 200 waiting to be "bad enough" to qualify. We had a lorry full of patients being taken to Livingstone Hospital every Thursday that the Fast-Track Clinic could no longer handle.

When our numbers were too big at the hospital, I was called to the hospital administrator's office and told that we could no longer take our patients to Fast-Track—which was where we paid for each patient to see a doctor and get medications. We were told we had to go back to the lower-cost outpatient department with clinical officers who sometimes showed up and sometimes didn't. We had already had difficulties there, which was why we had ended up at Fast-Track in the first place.

Hearing the news, I broke down in tears.

Upon leaving the building, I ran into a man I did not know.

Obviously seeing my distress, he asked, "Madam, what's the problem?"

Through angry and frustrated tears, I poured out my heart to this stranger. That man—whose name I later came to know was Francis—turned out to be the government official in charge of HIV care for the district health office over the Sons of Thunder Clinic.

Because of that one encounter, the district medical director got involved and started making things happen. She pushed for Sal and Jha to get the training they needed for our clinic to become more self-sufficient. After two classes, one in Livingstone and one in Lusaka, and hands-on training with the health district, we had officially passed! We were now a recognized ART (Antiretroviral Treatment) center for HIV patients. We would now be given the free HIV medications from the government to distribute to patients without transporting them anywhere. We would still pick them up with the lorry along the tarmac, but testing and treatment would be done right at the clinic.

Staffing also changed during this time. Vundakai was let go after he went to Lusaka for two weeks without any notice, but God brought Chris to the door to replace him as our HIV counselor. Anna left to go to teachers' college in Livingstone, so Janet stepped up to the seniority position.

Rona was still recovering from her mastectomy at the time, so we hired Bridget for overnight patients. Rona never did come back to work and sadly passed away after a few weeks.

Bertha went to school, and we hired Namatama and Febby as clinical assistants. Jha was busy with his job in town and had been unable to work or cover during our furlough, so God provided Derrick, another clinical officer who worked at Livingstone Hospital but who was on leave until May. He covered patients in March when we went home for Sal's antibody treatment.

We were definitely growing!

In addition to HIV care, we saw an enormous need for good antenatal care and safe deliveries for pregnant women. There were a few different reasons for maternal deaths, HIV being only one.

We also saw a problem with transport. Imagine being in labor and trying to walk the long distances to reach a clinic and then, if complications arise, how to get to the hospital in town in time to save mom and baby. The paramedic in Sal just started answering the call the only way he knew how—by going out in the bush to handle the problem.

All the phone calls were about people dying in their huts from HIV or women in labor having difficulty. People saw that Sal always answered. It didn't matter time of day or night. He always went. Sometimes the delivery happened in the hut or on the side of the road, but most he was able to bring to the clinic.

It wasn't just families that called. Sometimes he was called by the professional staff in the other rural health centers requesting assistance when they had a problem delivery or needed transport to the hospital.

Night calls began happening more often, making us a round-the-clock facility. We never closed.

In the course of our HIV training, we were included in a two-week course offered to government health-care providers by Boston University, an NGO working in the country giving assistance and training for HIV-positive pregnant moms. The course was called Prevent Mother to Child Transmission of HIV and was very beneficial to our care of HIV-positive moms.

Over time, good antenatal care was promoted with increased education, routine scheduled wellness visits, mandatory HIV testing, malaria prophylaxis, and iron and vitamin supplements, all during the course of pregnancy.

Maternities continued to increase, with women from all over coming to deliver at Sons of Thunder. Proper protocols for HIV prophylaxis saw babies born to HIV-positive moms remain negative even after eighteen months of breastfeeding. It was working.

When the government decided to make us an ART center for HIV patients, we did not have adequate space. Since they were doing the on-site training, they required a room for counseling, an exam room, and a pharmacy. At that time, we had three rooms, but not together, and one was used for inpatients.

We remembered the tour we took through the door of our apartment that first day in Zambia. Since that time, no further work had been done on the building. It never did become a second orphanage, and the immediate need was for a clinic. God had already given us a glimpse of His plan way back then.

We waited for God to reveal that to our authorities, which He did. We excitedly moved the patients and all the furniture and equipment that we had from the three rooms into the new building. A lot of work was still needed to finish the building, but we were now able to comply with the government's space requirement.

We had previously been given a donation for the construction of a new clinic, so now we opted to use that donation to renovate this existing building. It needed windows with screens, covered patios front and back for a large waiting area as well as a sitting area for overnight patients, proper plumbing with a new water tank and septic system, new doors throughout, and flooring. God had said to *Raise the standard*, and that was exactly what we were trying to do.

We called the Zambian builder in Livingstone that we had met when we first arrived back in 2005 and met with him and his partner multiple times about the plans for the clinic renovation. It was to begin when we returned from furlough in April.

Once plans for renovation were agreed upon, all we needed was furniture—beds, overbed tables, and bedside stands for inpatient rooms; chairs for the indoor waiting room; exam tables, cabinets, desks, and chairs for exam rooms; file cabinets, shelving units, and more medical supplies—the list of needs was endless.

God works in ways that are not only mysterious but often quite roundabout. Case in point: how He made a dating-site "love connection" between Sons of Thunder and a nonprofit organization in the US.

It all started when a man came to Sons of Thunder on a mission team to utilize his computer knowledge to get some kind of networking set up between the main house and the clinic. He stayed for two weeks and was unable to complete his task, due to the lack of network availability in the country at the time.

He left with the group, a bit disheartened, and went home to Connecticut.

Once back to life in the US, he subscribed to an internet dating service and met a woman in California. While chatting online, he told her he'd just gotten back from Zambia. He went on to tell her all about Sons of Thunder, and she told him about her neighbor, who sent medical supplies all over the world.

The man ended up going to California to meet the woman in person and saw firsthand her neighbor's nonprofit, an organization called SAVE (Salvage All Valuable Equipment). He viewed her storage warehouses and equipment obtained from hospitals and doctors' offices. All equipment was usable and in excellent condition.

He told her about the medical clinic in Zambia, and within a few months, we received a forty-foot container of medical supplies, including hospital beds, exam tables, oxygen concentrators, wheelchairs, stretchers, and a host of other goods. The container had to be unpacked within twenty-four hours, so everyone came out to help. It was like Christmas.

The next time Sal and I went home on furlough, I traveled to California while Sal went to Connecticut. I went to SAVE and met the owner and all the people who worked with the organization. I was able to personally extend our gratitude.

Unfortunately, the man who joined the dating service did not end up with the woman he met online, but his endeavor sure had a great impact for the medical ministry here. You never know how God is going to use you. And we never know where His provision is going to come from. We just know it does!

## Chapter 22

IN AUGUST OF 2007, ANOTHER MISSIONARY COUPLE WAS SENT BY Pastor Jerry and the board in America to take over leadership of SOT. The woman had come on a short-term mission team and was very impacted.

Feeling called to hospitality, she went home and discussed a more long-term call on their life with her retired husband. They had been greeters at their church for years and had always talked of other opportunities, including possibly running a respite lodge for returning missionaries. They felt they were perfect to oversee mission teams on a long-term basis.

Pastor Jerry and the board agreed. But since the husband was a retired military officer, they believed it would be prudent to place him in charge of everything, thereby giving Sal and me opportunity to once again focus strictly on medical. Their church had also been included in the decision-making and had agreed to financially sponsor them on the field.

Our time in leadership of the whole ministry was coming to an end. Just prior to the couple's arrival, Sal and I moved back to the apartment, excited that night rounds and emergency calls would once again be just on the other side of the door.

It had been nine months since leadership had been entrusted to us. I heard God say, *Raise your head and look back over those months. What do you see?*

Those two teachings—*Under Cover* and *Firm Foundations*—came back to my mind. I realized for the first time why we had brought them. They weren't just for the church; they were for us. That was exactly what God had intended to do all along. He intended to put everything in all areas of Sons of Thunder "under cover," or under the proper authority, and on a "firm foundation." One of order and structure—something that could not be shaken.

There were now sixty families living on the farm in seven villages, all with a headman. Abson was made farm supervisor, and Alexander became the village supervisor. Headman meetings were held weekly at the guesthouse, with Sal training in leadership.

Village protocols were established. All villages were provided water sources for their fields and life in general. At first, water delivery was set up for those villages farthest away, and two boreholes were drilled at that time, one in a village and one at the new church construction site. Within a short period, each village had a borehole with a handpump for water access.

Every family was given land for a field and a garden. As we watched, the harvest of the fields of maize and the gardens of vegetables produced both a supply of food for the families and a profitable business for many.

All buildings were initially cleaned out. Believe it or not, the junk lying around was sold as God brought buyers to the door. Order was established with the storage of tools and supplies in their proper places.

Building projects on the farm included three apartments in the tobacco barn, originally for Reverend Mwiikisa; Pastor George, who would be returning soon from Bible college; and Janice, who was hired as supervisor at the main house.

Other projects included new latrines and garbage-burning pits. Repair of Dam One was started and two-thirds completed before rainy season came, and it held. The boundary fence between farms was strengthened.

We hired and trained a staff to work at the main house, which was given a thorough cleaning. They tore down the outside trellis to get rid of the bugs, snakes, and vermin and put up a new grass fence. We sold the lorry, Land Cruiser, and Nissan pickup truck and purchased a used lorry and two used Land Rover Game Viewers. After fixing the tractor and trailer, we hired drivers for all vehicles—Herod and Mwansa for the vehicles, and Marvin and Padmore for the tractor.

We discovered that district council fees and land assessments had not been paid, and we were three years behind in back taxes! All moneys owed were paid and taxes filed.

Up until this time, the people on the farm had to walk or bicycle for miles, carrying their maize to town to have it ground, then walk back, carrying bags of meal on their heads or bicycles.

One of our young men had been hit by a vehicle while returning from the grinding mill on his bicycle after dark. He suffered a serious concussion and was treated at the clinic for a week, where he fully recovered.

Realizing the problem, we bought a grinder so the people could have their maize ground on-site. We hired a worker to run the grinder and collect the small charge that was assessed, which was lower than anywhere else.

Godfrey established a workshop for carpentry and the construction of furniture in-house.

Two Sons of Thunder guys got sponsored for skills training: Terry for mechanics and Chanda for electrical. Terry had even been granted an internship in town with the Land Rover dealer. He was now our full-time mechanic and did all the maintenance and repairs on our vehicles.

A Sons of Thunder sign was posted on the roadside, welcoming people onto the grounds. The atmosphere became light, and the people seemed genuinely happy. We made a point of giving pay raises to all workers. There was now opportunity for open relationships with everybody.

Jake had taken responsibility for both the church and the Bible college, which was not really a college and held no accreditation as a school for pastors. Reverend Mwiikisa taught classes and tried to hold it all together with some kind of integrity and credibility but found it difficult. Jacob began teaching with Reverend Mwiikisa but found enrollment low and attendance almost nonexistent during planting season. The decision was made to shut it down.

After the Bible college closed, Reverend Mwiikisa retired to his home in Siachitema.

Pastor George arrived in December after graduating from Jembo Bible College and was ordained by the Pilgrim Wesleyan discipline. He was placed over the church, relieving Jake of his added responsibilities. Pastor George established a new church board and set up programs within the church, such as Sunday school, prayer meetings, evangelism, and outreach.

When it was discovered that six of the pastors of our nine outlying planted churches didn't even want to be pastors, the board closed seven. Winfred was still the pastor at Kasiya, and Gibson maintained his church in Sinde. These two men felt called to be pastors and wanted to keep their churches going.

Julius was the third man feeling called to be a pastor. He, however, was brought from an outlying church to be assistant pastor at Bethesda Tabernacle, the new name for the Wesleyan church on the grounds. He also maintained his position as full-time chaplain for the clinic.

People were brought to Sons of Thunder Church on the farm every Sunday by lorry runs. Village fellowship meetings, or "cell groups," were held weekly or more often in each village led by the headman. There was prayer, sharing of the Word, and praise and worship, along with an occasional meal. Mission teams had been invited to share in these times and found them filled with the presence of the Lord.

The small church building was never intended to be the final destination for the church. The new church location had been determined and building had begun. The new location was near the farm and close to the main tarmac, making it easily accessible to a lot of surrounding villages. All building was done by our own Sons of Thunder skilled workers and laborers.

The school was my responsibility. We were told our primary school was a community school, which we later found out was not the case. To be a community school, it must be on community land, and since we had never given land to the government, this was not the proper status. As a matter of fact, our school had no status at all, which meant we really didn't exist.

Upon investigation, we discovered that our options were *private*, where all moneys are paid by us; *community*, which was not an option unless we gave up land; or *grant-aided*, where the teachers' salaries would come from the government. Since the school had never totally been subsidized by donations alone, and since our numbers continued to grow—we had 402 students at that time—it seemed reasonable to pursue grant-aided status.

A primary school in Zambia encompasses grades one through seven. At the end of grade seven, the children sit for a national qualifying exam.

They must pass in order to continue on to basic school, which includes grades eight and nine. There is another national qualifying exam after grade nine that determines whether you move on to secondary school— grades ten through twelve. Successful completion of the final national exam after grade twelve results in a certificate.

Sons of Thunder primary school had four classrooms; four grades would go in the morning and three in the afternoon. Seventh grade had extended hours, since they were preparing for the exam. We decided at that time to move the children from classrooms on the farm to the main location at the primary school, so all the students were in one place.

While we were at it, we decided to pursue becoming a testing site for the seventh-grade test. Owen, the headmaster, and I had meetings with the Ministry of Education and turned in the proper paperwork.

Since an on-site inspection would occur before any decision was made, we scurried to complete work on the building and grounds. The bathroom plumbing was fixed, and a new soak-away was dug, fixing all drainage pipes. The windows—which, curiously, had never had glass in them—received glass, locks, and handles. We had the blackboards painted and broken desks fixed. Electrical wiring was repaired where needed. We had a cement patio extended along the school building and completed a roof covering. We even purchased a new flag.

Within two weeks, our construction team had built an office with an inside strong room to keep all testing paraphernalia secure. Painting began with the outside, as requested by the teachers. We waited for a second inspection by the district and approval for our status.

At the time of Jessi's being responsible for the orphanage, we had fifty-four children with a possible adoption looming on the horizon. The eighteen babies who had been received while we were on our earlier furlough were an overwhelming challenge for the staff. The babies were not gaining weight, and a couple were severely malnourished with intestinal infections.

After one baby died for no apparent reason other than failure to thrive, Jessi and I went into action. We took the two worst cases into our homes and began by treating their intestinal infections while putting them back on formula and a bottle. Their diets were changed to include mashed fruits and vegetables. Within a week, we began to see marked improvement and weight gain. After our test babies showed improvement, Jessi changed the diets of all the babies, placing any under one year old back on formula and bottles. The workers were taught how to mash sweet potatoes, carrots, bananas, and squash.

We found that twelve children had been placed on HIV medication, which had been privately purchased through a source in Livingstone. They were adult medicines and were diluted to be given to the orphans in varying amounts, depending on severity of illness. When we tested the twelve children in the clinic, some were found to be negative.

After consultation with organizations in the US, we decided not to remove any medications from the children until more conclusive testing could be done. At this point, someone literally walked up to the guesthouse from an orphanage in Monze and gave us the name of the clinic in Lusaka and the American who was being funded by a grant from Johns Hopkins to do DNA testing for HIV.

Jessi and I personally went to meet him on one of our trips to Lusaka and brought back the procedure and cards for specimen collection. Sal drew all the kids' blood samples, and Jessi took the completed cards back to Lusaka. We had results via email within a few weeks.

Seven of the twelve children were negative, and their medications stopped. The other five, who were true positive, were placed on free government pediatric ARVs through the clinic. All sick babies were now seen at the clinic for treatment in order to avoid improper diagnosing of illness and incorrect dosing of medications.

Linah and Royce—the two orphanage supervisors—held meetings on Fridays to discuss any issues. They handled all the hiring and firing, scheduling, and payroll for the orphanage workers, which totaled forty employees. They had also been doing all the weekly shopping. One of the drivers took them into Livingstone and escorted them all over town, picking up food and supplies.

We bought a new washer and dryer, and Godfrey made new orphanage furniture in the workshop at the farm. New mattresses were also purchased. The storage rooms had been cleaned out and organized, and new clothes and toys put into circulation for use. After a new porch had been added to the back of the orphanage building, one of the mission teams stepped in to paint it. One of their members was an artist and painted the back wall with a *Veggie Tales* theme. Little handprints in a variety of colors were sprinkled all over the short wall, with a corresponding name attached.

A new orphanage outdoor kitchen was constructed, expanding cooking capacity. Add to that a new freezer and a new hot-water tank.

Bright and Bruno, the twin boys of our first HIV patient, Susan, were found HIV negative, removed from their medications, and were able to go home with their now-married parents and their new baby sister, Cannister.

Most encouragingly, an orphan named Freda got adopted!

As planned, the clinic renovation began in April. By November, it was completed, with the final payment made to the Zambian construction company.

The freshly painted exterior of the clinic looked beautiful, with front and back covered verandas and gravel footpaths all around. There was wheelchair access on the side of the back veranda near the parking area. It also had concrete seating, making it a perfect outdoor waiting room and venue for the sharing of the Word every morning with Pastor Julius.

The old water tank was replaced and a new generator installed—the only two things Sal had demanded.

The inside looked as beautiful as the outside. First, we had the old wiring and plumbing replaced, then new security bars were welded in the windows and fly screens were added. Ceiling boards had to either be repaired or replaced, and all the rooms got painted. Doors were put in place where needed, either painted or varnished, and given new locks. In the bathrooms, we had doors placed on the stalls with handles and locks, ceramic tiling completed around the bathtubs and sink, and mirrors installed. A washer and dryer were added to the ladies' bathroom for clinic laundry. Ceiling fans were installed in the reception area as well as the surrounding rooms.

As for the floor plan—it was destined to be as I'd originally envisioned it. The very large reception area containing file cabinets filled with patient records also had an inside waiting area. There was a prayer-consultation room that served as Pastor Julius's office, a storage room for medications and medical supplies, an exam room, a lab, a maternity room, a female ward, and a male ward.

The maternity room was really the labor-delivery suite with only one bed. This room also had an exam table, so it doubled for Under-Five (Well Child visits and immunizations) once a month. Each of the wards had a capacity for three beds, comfortably. All in all, there was a capacity for seven: six inpatients and one maternity, but we could manage up to nine if needed.

Because the entire building had been renovated, all the upgrades were completed in our apartment as well, including new vinyl flooring through-out the apartment and a much-appreciated *air conditioner* for the bedroom!

As a culmination of those last nine months and all that had been accomplished, we had a Sons of Thunder celebration for all. The day was filled with thanksgiving and praise to God, feasting and fellowship with one another, and a time of testimony and healing from the past.

It was an awesome time of closure and a renewed hope and vision as we continued in the future direction for Sons of Thunder together.

*⌇❧*

# *Chapter 23*

AS THE CLINIC CONTINUED TO EXPAND, OUR NEEDS SEEMED TO expand right along with it.

One morning, I went in to work to find we had six inpatients in the clinic. There was Mary, an antenatal who was overdue. Since she lived very far away, Sal had decided to keep her until her delivery. She had three small children with her, because her husband wouldn't watch them at home.

Next was an HIV mom, Sheebo, who'd just had a baby boy and had stayed a few days. She was initially afraid to go home, for fear she would be beaten by her husband because he had forbidden her to be tested for HIV. After listening to Sal tell her about the benefit to her baby and the ARV prophylaxis that would be given once born, she'd agreed. We found that all mothers agreed to be tested once they knew it was for their baby's health.

When Sheebo's husband showed up one day, she asked Sal to speak with him, which of course he did. I could only imagine the conversation. Whatever was said, Sheebo thanked Sal and was no longer afraid to go home.

We also had Anna, who was in her first trimester and had come in bleeding. IVs and bedrest did not stop the progression, and she had a miscarriage. She would be going to the OB-GYN clinic at Livingstone Hospital for an exam and ultrasound to make sure everything was out.

Anna's husband stayed by her side the entire time. This was their second miscarriage. The first one had happened at seven months, and the baby had lived for four days. During her time with us, Anna found encouragement with the Bible story of Hannah, a woman of God who was unable to have a child until God heard her fervent prayers and gave her a son.

In the next ward, we had Christine and Juliet. Christine was an HIV patient who came to us near death with difficulty breathing, fever, and dehydration. We prescribed IVs, antibiotics, nebulizer treatments, and some medicines for breathing, along with her ARVs and prayer. We were also waiting for her TB test results. Her mother was with her.

Juliet had HIV also. She came by bus from Choma, which was two towns past Zimba and way out of our district. She had pain in her hip, and Choma Hospital and University Teaching Hospital in Lusaka had not helped. She'd heard of our clinic and decided to come here.

Sometimes I had to chuckle and ask God what He was doing! It took her three hours to get from the road to the clinic with her one crutch. She was on bedrest for a few days with Prednisone and prayer.

The last patient was Agnes, who came to us near death. We diagnosed her with HIV and TB. After a week of IVs, antibiotics, TB medicine with nebulizer treatments, breathing medicine, and prayer, she had seen great improvement.

I stopped in one morning and asked Agnes if she wanted anything. She gave me a shy smile. "Coca-Cola."

So every day I took over a Coke with ice. Her smile grew as she sat up to drink it. Such a small thing, yet it meant so much. It was our link.

With all these patients, it became clear that we needed a cook. If we were going to feed patients, it would be cost effective to grow our own vegetables for relish. Answering another lighted stone, we hired Enoch and his wife, Winifridah, to be in charge of food production and preparation at the clinic.

The three of us went to the Maramba market the following Monday and bought supplies and food. We had a great time!

Soon, the garden was plowed and seeds planted, and the patients were being served three nutritious meals a day.

God just kept moving forward. We never seemed to be static. He obviously had plans for the clinic, and our job seemed to be just keeping up with Him.

While things were hopping at the clinic, He also began to stir us to start going out.

Twenty-five kilometers (almost sixteen miles) from the farm was a settlement of seven hundred people called Kasiya. It had a brand-new government clinic that had stood empty since construction was completed two years before. It was right beside one of our planted churches, where Winfred was the pastor.

We'd been getting a lot of patients from that village, walking the long distance. Groups of moms had been coming to our Under-Five Clinic, and three of our last few deliveries were from there. Sal had driven out in the middle of the night to get them, because it was so far away.

God began stirring us to set up a clinic one day a week over at the unused building. Sal and I talked with the settlement council and Winfred to see if the doors were open and if people would be receptive.

Later that same day, a woman came for her ARVs and asked to speak to me. It turned out that she lived so deep in the bush that it took her two days of walking just to reach the main road where the lorry picked her up. She'd only had sweet beer (a nonalcoholic drink made with roots) to drink for the last two days and no food.

The whole time she was speaking to me about her journey to the clinic, the thought kept popping up in my head about our company in the States, Associates in Emergency Care, and how we took training to people and corporations at their places of business.

I said a silent prayer. *Are we supposed to take the ART clinic to different locations, Lord?*

Before this woman set off for her trip home, I gave her some buns and a packet of drink, along with some money. Together, we asked Sal to give her enough medicine for two months.

I went about my business, awaiting God's answer, having no shortage of things to focus on as I waited.

Life on the mission field is all about taking the bad with the good, the sad with the joyful. Many died, young and old alike. Often, the only things we could do were to make our best attempt at medical care, pray for God's miraculous intervention, share the gospel message of salvation, and show the love of Jesus.

The most discouraging experiences with death were when it was unfounded and involved little ones.

One such time involved Caleb, the two-year-old son of Janice and the grandson of Reverend Mwiikisa. He was always with Janice at the main house, and he had the brightest little smile. He would wave and throw me a kiss whenever he left to go home. He reminded me a lot of my own little grandsons.

The mosquito spraying patrol came to the farm to spray all our buildings, one of which was Janice's home. She took a lot of things out of her house so they could spray, then had to wait two hours before returning inside.

While everything was outside, Caleb picked up a bottle of Betadine mouthwash, which is used in Zambia for toothaches and mouth sores. He drank some of the solution, then chucked the bottle over his head because the liquid had such a bitter taste. Janice immediately checked him out to make sure he was okay. Little Caleb was behaving normally, so not much was made of it.

But around midnight, Sal and I heard that familiar pounding on our door that is never followed by anything good. It was Janice and her husband, Albert. They had brought Caleb to the clinic because he was having a bad reaction. He must have aspirated some of the mouthwash into his lungs because he was foaming at the mouth and couldn't breathe.

Despite our prayers, medication to reduce the pulmonary edema, and best efforts at suctioning, we were unable to stabilize him. We called ahead to the American doctor at Zimba Mission Hospital, who got up and waited for us to arrive. We were five minutes too late in reaching the hospital. Caleb died in Janice's arms in the back seat of the vehicle.

Caleb's little body was placed in the morgue at Zimba Mission Hospital until a small wooden coffin could be purchased. Family was contacted and the burial planned. He was bathed, wrapped in white cloth, and placed in the coffin. A group of ladies carried the coffin to the family home they were staying at in Zimba, singing all the way.

The burial took place the next day in Zimba, with many people present. Three vehicles carried our Sons of Thunder families so they could give support. A message was given by Pastor Julius, and people were able to process in front of the coffin and view the body one last time.

The ladies picked up the coffin, and we all walked to the place of burial, again with singing all the way. The men dug a grave in an isolated area, and prayers and more messages were shared by many different pastors. The men took turns shoveling dirt on top of the coffin until a small mound was made. The ladies sang and packed the dirt with their hands. Flowers in small bags were handed out to different people to place on the grave as memorials. People were allowed to speak, including the parents, and then we walked back to the village.

I will not forget the faith of Albert and Janice. This was not the first child they had lost. The other child, a girl, was the very same age as Caleb, yet they continued to stand firm in their faith and praise and worship the Lord.

## Chapter 24

SINCE IT IS OUR FAMILY TRADITION TO CELEBRATE CHRISTMAS Eve, Sal and I decided to have a one-night getaway—just the two of us.

December 24, 2007, started with Sal seeing twenty-five patients at the clinic, giving instructions to the on-call staff, then walking out the door at noon. All the inpatients had been discharged.

The sun was shining when we left for the Chrismar Hotel in Livingstone, so we hoped to spend the afternoon at the pool relaxing and reading. However, as soon as we checked in, we heard thunder. Before we knew it, the downpour came. The sky got dark and dreary, and the rain continued.

Thankfully, the electricity stayed on, so the air conditioning, TV, and teapot were all working. I took a nap while Sal tried to watch NFL football. I say "tried" because the satellite connection kept going in and out on that station.

Eventually, the rain quit, but the sun never came back. We watched a movie, then got ready for dinner. The hotel had a very nice buffet, so we didn't have to go anywhere.

We had just returned to our room when Sal's phone rang. It was Janet, one of the clinical assistants, who had just started labor pains with her first child. Needless to say, my caring husband with paramedic blood filling his veins couldn't refuse to help. He made me stay, promising he would be back soon. His plan was to examine her, admit her to the clinic, then leave her there with the on-call person until morning.

No sooner had he left than I received another phone call from the husband of a three-month pregnant woman, Doricah, who was bleeding. Sal would have to meet them halfway and bring her to the clinic along with him.

There I was, alone on Christmas Eve . . . and I decided to check my email.

I opened one from my daughter-in-law Rachel and cried when I read the struggles of my children. It was the previous Christmas Eve when all the problems had started with Gabe. Ironically, they had to take him to the ER again this Christmas Eve. Praise the Lord that he was able to return home and didn't need to be admitted.

Shaun tried so hard to keep the family traditions. He had planned on having the rest of our family over to the house for dinner and the traditional Marini Christmas celebration. But my other grandsons, Daniel and Finn, were sick and couldn't be around Gabe. Rachel didn't want to leave Gabe to go to Scott's house nor did Shaun think it wise to take the girls over to where they could get sick and bring it back to Gabe.

I didn't know what Mark's plans were.

So it looked like all the Marinis would be having a "by themselves" Christmas Eve. How I wished I could be there to make a meal . . . make the nut roll . . . make some cookies . . . hold Gabe . . . kiss my grandchildren . . . pray . . . give hugs . . . and just be Mom. But I couldn't. I was on the other side of the world, where God had me planted.

As I sat alone that Christmas Eve, I prayed that we would all receive a revelation of the true meaning of Christmas and the extent of God's love for each one of us.

At around eleven, Sal called to let me know that he had picked up Doricah, who was bleeding heavily. She needed to be admitted and have a drip started. That was what they called an IV in Zambia. Janet had reached the clinic in the beginning stages of labor, so he had two patients admitted.

Since it was late, I decided to go to sleep. So much for spending our Christmas Eve together.

When I awoke at six, Sal wasn't back yet, so I called him for a status report. He told me that Doricah's bleeding had stopped and her vital signs were returning to normal. Janet was going to deliver at any minute. Once she did, he planned to drive back and meet me for the breakfast buffet.

The buffet was only open till ten thirty, so at nine thirty, I called again for a report.

"Things are not going as quickly as I thought." Sal's voice was raspy with fatigue. "You better eat without me."

So I went to the buffet alone.

After breakfast, I asked for a late checkout, around noon. I found out the hotel was having a Christmas luncheon buffet with turkey, cranberry sauce, and all the fixings at twelve thirty, so I thought maybe Sal could at least make it for that.

I sat in the room, talking with the maid and clicking TV channels. At noon, I called the porter to help me with my bags, then went to the lobby. I proceeded to check out, then plopped onto one of the couches in the lobby to read a book while I waited for Sal.

By two, Janet still had not had her any-minute-now baby. There was no one else to come and rescue me. All the other missionaries had gone to spend Christmas Day with friends. Herod and Mwanza, our two drivers, were celebrating Christmas at the church with their families. Mwanza was even in charge of skits. So being the problem solver that I am, I decided to take a taxi back to the farm.

Once there, I went in to see Janet, who looked relieved when I walked in. I later confirmed with Sal that she had only allowed two people in— older bush women who were friends. Her family was not with her nor would she let the other workers in. I decided to stay with her for the duration, since she was a scared first-time mom who needed support and encouragement.

At last, at seven forty-five p.m., out came a healthy baby boy—3.3 kilograms (7.3 pounds). So our first Sons of Thunder Christmas baby was born!

The clinic was active as ever in 2008, and we found ourselves always in need of more. More time. More supplies. More medicines. More beds. More rooms. More staff. More help. More prayers, and more money.

But most importantly . . . more God!

It was hard trying to serve and minister to a different culture, and it took a while before the local traditions and beliefs began to unfold. Foreigners were not made privy to traditional practices until the barrier of judgment was removed and there was a development of mutual trust and friendship.

Secret things were hidden from outsiders. There was witchcraft and the occasional rumors of body mutilations and sacrifices. The Tonga beliefs and traditions were slowly diminishing, thanks to education and a growth in Christian beliefs, but they still existed, especially in the rural communities we served. Giving medical care and Jesus became somewhat interesting and challenging at times.

We discovered the hard way why we had some really difficult labors and profuse bleeding with mothers.

When we took one of the mothers to the hospital one night, the ultrasound tech commented nonchalantly, "She told me her mother gave her *elephant pups.*"

Having never heard of such a thing, I frowned. "What's that?"

His brow rose in apparent surprise that I didn't know. "We call it African oxytocin. It is a root that helps to bring on labor when the mother is full-term. Sometimes they take it before it's time and it causes the uterus to contract, but the cervix doesn't dilate. The uterus then ruptures, and the woman can die."

We had all kinds of problems with this until we were made aware of the practice and educated our mothers and the older village women to stop using the root because of the dire consequences.

Many of the traditions, superstitions, and beliefs were grounded in fear. Young mothers were told that if they cried out in labor, their babies would die. During childbirth, there was not a sound uttered by most women. You could only tell what was going on by the grimace on the mother's face. It was amazing, especially since it was all-natural childbirth.

Lots of teaching accompanied the medical care given at Sons of Thunder. As we showed the love of Jesus in our actions, combined with God's Word, we hoped to see these myths and superstitions dissipate.

Kasiya was inundated with such superstition and tradition. This was where we had felt directed to go, to provide weekly full-service medical clinics.

Finally, the doors were open in April 2008. This settlement was under a different district, which was why it took so long for us to get approval.

About a week prior to our getting started, a man by the name of Alick showed up at the Sons of Thunder Clinic on the farm, asking for a job. He just happened to be from Kasiya and was an HIV counselor. Mind you, he knew nothing of our plans regarding Kasiya. I just smiled once again at God's provision and His next step.

We decided to visit Kasiya on Wednesdays and made sure the settlement was notified.

The morning of the first Wednesday, we packed the vehicle with an old bookshelf, a folding table, and four chairs.

We arrived at eight a.m. and began to unload. Alick and four other volunteers showed up to offer assistance. We discovered that Livingstone District had furnished the clinic with two exam tables, a privacy screen, a desk, and four old chairs. There were also two large boxes of medicines and supplies and a Coleman container for water, since there was no water or electricity there.

When patients were not coming by nine, we began to get concerned. Our fears were alleviated, however, when people started coming at ten and didn't stop. By dusk, we had seen 118 patients.

The people of Kasiya were needy, both physically and spiritually. They were poor, with no shoes and tattered, dirty clothes. The rains that year had been so heavy that the maize crop had not produced a good harvest, so they were hungry or would be soon. The lack of water seemed to add to their poor health and dirty appearance.

Spiritually, they were in need of Jesus. Covered in charms, they showed lots of evidence of traditional healing methods by witch doctors. Since Pastor Winfred was a local pastor and well known to the people, it only made sense to make him part of our Wednesday team. He preached the Word and prayed with people. He cut off charms and taught the Truth. He counseled those in need and spoke words of hope and encouragement . . . all similar to Pastor Julius back at the Sons of Thunder Clinic.

It was a tiring day—seeing all those patients, unpacking and repacking—but when we placed our heads on our pillows that night, there was no question in our minds that we had heard God!

*Chapter 25*

THE COLOR YELLOW TOOK ON A WHOLE NEW CONNOTATION FOR me in those days. In the past, whenever I thought of yellow, I immediately thought of the sun or maybe a flower. But at that time, it made me think of urine.

Pretty weird, I know, but here's why . . .

Steven was a thirty-six-year-old married man with children, one of them an eighteen-month-old daughter. The little girl was afraid of Sal and me because we were white skinned. She would hide under her mom's chitenge whenever we came around. It was very cute!

We admitted Steven to the clinic, as he was very sick with a high fever. He had a dazed look and appeared dehydrated. He had been treated for malaria at another center just days before. Surprisingly, his HIV test was negative. A malaria test was also negative but was expected to be so since he'd already been treated. IVs, broad-spectrum antibiotics, and fever control were the order of the day.

On his second day at our clinic, his fever was still up and down. I was making my rounds, greeting patients and families, and praying. When I entered his room, I noticed his urinal on the floor with something in it that clearly wasn't urine. It was black! Not tea-colored. Not dark amber. Not blood-tinged. Just black.

We immediately ran tests. His urinalysis was abnormal, with protein and ketones and bilirubin. It turned out that Steven had blackwater fever, a very serious form of malaria. We immediately started him on quinine.

A couple of days later, we started a urinary antibiotic, which we had (coincidentally?) just received for the first time from the district.

Despite the new treatment regimes, things were not looking hopeful, so Sal went in to talk with Steven and his family about the probable outcome. He wanted to give them the option of taking Steven home to die or staying at the clinic with a high probability of the same result.

Pastor Julius accompanied Sal to talk with the family. After the talk, they all prayed together before Sal left to tend to other patients. Pastor Julius remained with the family to pray and offer support.

Steven and his family decided they would spend another night at the clinic and go home in the morning. His brother agreed to stay at his bedside all night.

In the middle of the night, Sal was called out to pick up a woman in labor, so I got up and went over to the clinic.

When I walked in, I saw Steven's brother bringing out his urinal to empty it. I had to chase him into the men's room, because my Chetonga was not that great and neither was his English. I had to make sure the urine was Steven's, because it was clear yellow.

Just a few hours before, it had been black . . . with no change, despite all our efforts . . . until we had given up and prayed! As quickly as possible, I tested his urine. It showed all normal results!

After Sal arrived and got the pregnant woman settled, I showed him the urine and the test results.

He looked at me, awestruck, with tears in his eyes. He went to Steven and the family and told them we had all just witnessed a miracle. He gave God all the glory.

The family did take Steven home the next day and continued the course of medicines. The outcome we expected was changed that night.

We continued to serve a God of miracles.

As of June 6, 2008 and every Friday thereafter, Sal and I, along with Alick and Pastor Winfred, would be taking ART clinics out to surrounding villages. No longer would we send out the lorry on Thursdays to pick up two loads of HIV patients to bring them to Sons of Thunder. Instead, we would see them in their communities, where they could be linked to other support services. We decided on four areas: Kabuyu on the first Friday of the month, Katapazi on the second, Sinde the third, and Siakasipa on the fourth.

Every Friday, we packed up the vehicle and went to the respective community. Utilizing the rural health center in that area, we saw our Sons of Thunder HIV clients, giving them their ARV medications as well as treating any other ailment they presented with.

Our God-directed idea proved so successful that when a Japanese organization called JICA came to partner with Zambia to provide HIV services years later, they modeled the SOT program throughout Zambia and called it Mobile ART.

God was building an intricate network of care, involving a widespread area and many facets. Stigma and discrimination, which had been preventing people from seeking help, would not have the strong hold they once had. Only when people came forth physically could we hope to help them spiritually.

However, I felt something was missing. I couldn't put my finger on it, but I knew it had something to do with these new outreach areas of HIV care. So much was needed.

Everywhere I turned at that time, I kept hearing the word *community*—in my devotionals, in conversations not only with Sal but also with the district health office. A *community* health worker even came up to us when we were at Kasiya asking if she could help us whenever we were there. Now we were *in the community*. I was confused and still waiting on God to give direction and clarification.

In the meantime, we continued seeing patients one day at a time. After a particularly traumatic and emotional baby delivery, an answer to prayer arrived on a container from the US: an old-model ultrasound machine that had been donated specifically for use with maternity patients. We wanted to be able to check for a fetal heartbeat, estimate the gestational age, and most importantly, verify correct positioning.

Knowing nothing about ultrasound, I tried to self-teach, but I still had questions. After a few days of trying and failing, an answer came to me.

An older American woman knocked on the front door and requested to use the bathroom. She was part of a mission team from Zimba Hospital, about forty-five minutes north of us, and they were on their way to Livingstone for a tourist day. She was unable to make it the thirty minutes to town, and the driver knew about Sons of Thunder, so they'd stopped.

As she used the facilities, I invited the rest of the group into the main house for refreshments and a chat. The woman's husband, Ken, told me he was a vascular surgeon. While volunteering, he was performing general surgeries at the mission hospital in Zimba under Pilgrim Wesleyan Church. His wife, Marie, was doing some ultrasound teaching with their technician.

"What?" My jaw dropped. "She is an ultrasound tech?"

I could hardly wait for her to come out of the bathroom. When she did, I rattled off my questions. "Could you possibly spare just fifteen minutes to come to the clinic and teach me fetal heartbeat, gestational age, and correct positioning?" I added that one of our workers was pregnant, so getting a patient wouldn't be a problem.

Thankfully, she agreed to look at the machine, and her team agreed to wait for her. She taught me what I needed to know and answered my questions.

When we joined the team once again at the main house, Ken said to me, "Did Marie tell you where she's going?"

"No." My interest piqued, I turned to Marie. "Where *are* you going?"

"Swaziland." Her eyes shone with enthusiasm. "I am going to teach a one-week course on community health evangelism."

I stood there, stunned, digesting those three words.

*Community*, which I had been feeling stirred with. *Health*, which was what I'd worked with my whole life. And *Evangelism*, which was what all of us were supposed to do as Christians.

My mind raced. We had already accomplished so much here. We'd been working with HIV patients—stigma was still a problem, but people were slowly coming out of hiding. Our clinic had been made an antiretroviral treatment center. We had started Mobile ART in four different locations, but I felt there was still something missing. Maybe this was God's answer.

I stood speechless for a few seconds, then uttered, "I think I'm supposed to go and take your class. Do you think there's room for me? Will they let me in? Is there a place for me to stay?"

Long story short, Marie and I left for Swaziland two days later. I stayed with her for one week in an apartment and took her course. The training there provided me with the information I needed for the next step with our HIV patients.

Meeting Marie was definitely a God-ordained encounter. We still do ultrasounds on all our antenatal patients. Only now, we have a portable ultrasound, provided by Marie, for ease with all our outreach areas. Meeting Marie that day started a friendship that has lasted more than a decade. She and Ken have continued to impact the ministry at Sons of Thunder.

## Chapter 26

FOLLOWING MY TRIP TO SWAZILAND TO LEARN COMMUNITY health evangelism (CHE), we sent seven people living with HIV to a workshop in town to become treatment supporters under a program sponsored by AIDS Alliance. We also established a group of people from among Sons of Thunder residents to form a home-based-care group.

I began teaching weekly classes with both the treatment supporters and the home-based-care group together. We started with team building and covered the CHE classes, targeting HIV and all its ramifications. HIV-positive and HIV-negative people found that working together ministered to our group of HIV clients, which by that time numbered over five hundred.

In those classes, we covered topics such as What is HIV; transmission, prevention, and treatment; consequences of sex outside of marriage; God's plan for marriage; requirements of marriage partners; emotions, such as denial, fear, worry, guilt, anger, bitterness, forgiveness, and unforgiveness; and counseling, compassion, and caring for the whole person.

We spent weeks discussing tradition, customs, and culture, contrasted with what it says in God's Word.

Class was on Thursday mornings. On Friday, the group would travel with Sal to an outreach site. We had three pastors in the group. Two of them always went to the outreach areas with us.

Whatever God had the group discussing over the month, we would use to develop a drama, which we performed at each outreach site. Included with the drama would be corresponding Scripture.

While Sal saw the HIV patients, the treatment supporters talked with individuals about adherence to medications, answered questions concerning living with HIV, taught lessons on nutrition or some other relevant subject, and counseled and prayed with individuals.

In addition to going on the outreaches, the treatment supporters and home-based-care group visited homes in the areas that had been designated as needing house calls; perhaps a patient was too sick to make it to the clinic or for whatever reason refused to go get help.

The treatment supporters took over certain areas of responsibility: Lena at Sons of Thunder; Abel at Katapazi; Kenneth at Sinde and Siakasipa; Sally at Kabuyu; and Charles as secretary, keeping written records of all the activity.

Over the months, it became apparent to me that each community where we offered HIV care needed a support group. It also became apparent that a leader's group was developing in each area. The treatment supporter overseeing the area would be instrumental in helping a support group form from among HIV-positive patients. A leader's group of both HIV-positive and HIV-negative people would be crucial to carrying out home visits.

At a certain point, I felt God tell me that my time of teaching Thursday mornings at Sons of Thunder was finished and that I was to turn the lessons over to someone in the group to carry on. Precious, one of the treatment supporters, was selected, and she led the class with the CHE lesson she selected to facilitate. The class reported that it went well and that they didn't have to translate. They could just use Chetonga.

When teaching CHE at Sons of Thunder was over, it was just starting in all the other areas as the leaders' groups formed. The same classes I'd taught for the previous nine months (how appropriate) were to be taught in the outreach communities.

Sally, one of the treatment supporters, had already begun teaching the CHE classes to her group in Kabuyu. Precious continued the teaching at Sons of Thunder. God was growing this effective web of ministry, reaching people physically and spiritually. We spoke truth right from God's Word. We didn't sugarcoat the message or tickle ears. These people were already faced with their own physical death. They needed and wanted to hear the truth. Their eternal lives were at stake.

Some of the leaders on the farm were in the CHE classes and were so impacted that they asked me to teach some of the classes to the married couples on the farm. With so much in front of us, Sal and I would not do a thing just to *do* it. We watched and prayed until we saw what direction God wanted us to follow.

After a period of waiting, God brought confirmation through many different ways and people, so I agreed to teach the classes.

We had the classes, and people were convicted. The lessons opened eyes and minds to the Truth of God's Word.

The CHE classes started with HIV clients but ended up being marriage classes for all the residents of SOT and anyone else who wanted to come.

As always, many were blessed by God's perfect planning.

Zambia was a country riddled with HIV and AIDS and their devastating effects, not just on the patient but on the family as well. It takes a toll physically, emotionally, and spiritually on everyone. Death was sometimes a relief for all.

Ngandu was a man in his late twenties, married with a very sweet three-year-old daughter. They lived in Ndola, in the Western Province of Zambia, a train ride away. His family was from Kabuyu, and when they heard he was very sick in Ndola, his brothers went to get him and transport him here for medical care.

When we first saw Ngandu, he was indeed very sick. In fact, he was dying. When he was carried in, we saw a man who was very thin, wasted, and incredibly weak. He had a high fever, diarrhea, and shortness of breath. After some testing, we discovered he was HIV positive and was dying of AIDS. With the respiratory symptoms, we suspected TB also.

IVs, antibiotics, and a heart-to-heart talk not only with his wife and brothers but also with him was in order. An honest discussion of his condition and probable impending death led Ngandu to pray and ask Jesus into his heart as his Lord and Savior that night.

Sometimes I wonder about those "back against the wall" prayers, but then I remember the thief on the cross next to Jesus. It's all about the heart.

The next few days, Ngandu spiraled downhill. He stopped responding coherently, became incontinent and had to wear diapers, and was only able to tolerate liquids. We had never had anyone on a clear liquid diet before, so I introduced the family and the clinic cook to Jell-O.

It was hard for me watching this man worsen and his attentive wife hold back the tears.

TB tests came back negative, but his lungs started to fill with fluid. As a matter of fact, there were no lung sounds audible on the right side. Sal added medication to his regime to try to pull the fluid off the lung. One of the two oxygen concentrators from the medical container had been retrieved from storage, and we'd used it since his arrival to provide oxygen through a nasal cannula. Frequent positioning and changing bed linens were carried out in an effort to keep him comfortable. It reminded me of hospice care.

One day I walked in to his room to witness his brother holding a basin while Ngandu was coughing or vomiting (it was hard to tell which) blood, with very large clots coming from both his nose and mouth. I was sure this was going to be the end. What an awful way to watch your loved one die. Feeling very helpless and small, Sal and I just stood in the hall outside the room.

I started to walk away, then suddenly turned back. "What about vitamin K?"

After it was out of my mouth, I realized it had not popped into my mind from any knowledge or experience I had ever had. I had never given vitamin K in all my nursing career, nor do I remember ever having a patient that had received it. Sal and I just looked at each other, knowing in our hearts it had been divinely given.

Sal smiled. "We have that. I just picked it up from the district health office last week."

I returned the smile. God always provided what we needed right when we needed it.

After reading about the administration and dosage of vitamin K, we gave it to Ngandu. The bleeding stopped, but his condition continued to plummet. He was no longer able to swallow pills, which meant he wasn't getting his ARTs (HIV medications).

So we waited. Family came in waves to say their goodbyes. Each night we expected a knock at our bedroom window to wake us up and tell us it was over. But instead, each morning proved to be a new day dawning.

His brothers got him in a wheelchair and took him to the shower. He started eating again—first liquids and then, when we were sure there was no more vomiting, soft foods. Soon he was able to take his oral medicines again.

His IV was no longer needed. His lungs sounded clearer, and there were breath sounds in all quadrants. He no longer needed oxygen. Each day, he was taken outside in a wheelchair. He was continent again and didn't need diapers. He still needed to gain strength and couldn't stand on his own, but we knew he was a walking miracle! He was a testimony to the power of God.

Sal and I will both proclaim that he is alive only because of God.

Ngandu's wife and daughter were also both HIV positive. His wife was still healthy and didn't qualify for the medicines yet, but his daughter was put on pediatric ARVs because her CD4 count was low. I don't know the ending of this story, but a lot of people were witness to the awesome healing power of God. There can be no denying it: Jesus is our only source of hope.

Because of this particular patient, Sal felt God say, *Work the other end.* Instead of focusing all our attention on treatment, Sal felt directed to start incorporating prevention into the mix.

He felt stirred to put together a PowerPoint and call it "Choices." With God's help, I wrote a drama presentation. We presented the program twice, once for a youth group in Livingstone at a church called Potter's House and once on the farm to our Sons of Thunder families. Both presentations were successful, leaving people talking and thinking. The presentation in town was strictly in English and also included a DVD on sexually transmitted infections. The one on the farm was translated into Chetonga, and we omitted the DVD.

Owen, our headmaster, and the teachers came to evaluate the program's level of effectiveness for the seventh graders in primary, basic, and secondary level students. After a positive review from them, we planned to give the presentation to our seventh graders next and then take it out to schools from there.

HIV patients continued to increase as people came out of hiding. They were definitely our special group and one we felt God wanted us to focus on.

We are all going to die, but when you are told you are HIV positive, your death becomes very real, and you start to evaluate your life. It can open a door to repentance and salvation. It can be a turning point—a turning to Jesus.

We saw many decisions for Christ and changed lives—people who, after coming to Christ for forgiveness of sin, wanted to make a difference in the time they had left. It was this group that I felt compelled to make sure had Bibles.

There were so many more miracles.

Costa was a forty-eight-year-old married man whom we had met in 2005. He was on the council at Kabuyu, from whom we sought permission for our first medical outreach. He was skeptical of the white missionaries, very demanding, and frankly, quite rude that day. Even the other council members told him to be quiet.

We came to find out that he had been inebriated that day, and was . . . I won't say an *alcoholic* but a rather heavy drinker.

Costa was HIV positive and became one of our patients. We diagnosed both him and his wife back in 2006, and they were put on antiretroviral medications.

By 2008, we had built quite a relationship. I'd had lots of opportunities to talk with and minister to him and to share the Gospel and pray with him, as well as hold his hand on what we thought was his deathbed.

He was diagnosed with TB and, at that point, was in his fifth month of treatment. He had been an inpatient three times during that year, the last time on oxygen and very close to death. He lost a lot of weight and was unable to work or even garden. There was no food in his home and no family to help. Sons of Thunder Medical Ministries had assisted him with money for food every month and had provided him with a Tonga Bible, rich in God's Word and promises. Food for the body and food for the soul . . . feeding Zambia physically and spiritually.

Costa was a fitter by trade, and since he could no longer work, he wanted to file for early NAPSA (like our Social Security). He wanted to get his money at that time instead of at the usual age of fifty-five.

It's a procedure to apply for early NAPSA, starting with a medical letter from us and a review in front of a medical board in Livingstone, then a trip to Lusaka—all on borrowed money. But it was important to him to receive that money to leave to his son, because Costa had tasted death and felt his own mortality.

The saddest part was that his whole savings for his entire life of forty-eight years was three million kwacha—not even a thousand dollars. But it was a lot of money to him. He'd probably never had that much at one time.

We let him stay at the clinic overnight so he could ride into town early in the morning for his medical review. The night he was here, I sat down beside him to chat, and we reminisced about the day we first met.

Looking me in the eyes, he got very serious. "I was a drinker then, but I have changed"—he lifted his Bible from his lap—"because I fear this. I want to be clean, and when"—swallowing tears, he never said the words *I die*, but that was clearly what he meant—"I want to be in heaven."

I gave his hand a squeeze. "I thank God that He brought you here."

Costa continued, clearly on a roll. "You have done so much for me. Every Sunday, I am in church, and the pastor has been to my house every week to visit and pray for me. I want to live right."

I was humbled when I listened to this changed man's heart. I know it was the Holy Spirit that drew him to repentance and that every life touched is for the glory of God. But to think that God would use me as His instrument to bring about a change in a heart is just mind boggling to me.

I am nothing special, but it lets me know that God can use anybody. We all make a difference in this life for someone.

## Chapter 27

ONE SATURDAY NIGHT, WE ATE DINNER AT THE MAIN HOUSE WITH a small team of volunteers. During dinner, Sal got a call for a woman in labor at Kasiya. After he left, I spent a short time in additional fellowship, then decided to head back to our apartment.

Armed with my usual small flashlight, I exited the house and proceeded along the path toward our building. The moon was shining pretty bright. I almost didn't need the flashlight—or "torch," as it is called in Zambia. I started thinking of an earlier conversation I'd had with one of the ladies on the mission team. She had told me of her fear of snakes and asked if I was afraid living here.

I'd honestly told her, "No . . . I really am not fearful of anything. It's like, one morning I woke up and realized that all fear was gone."

As I reflected, I rounded the corner of the building and began to unlock the door. Suddenly, I heard a *hssst*.

I looked down. Not more than a foot and a half away was a coiled-up cobra, looking right at me!

I very quickly backed out of its range and circled wide to the front door of the clinic. I had to do something because Sal was on his way home, and I didn't want him coming up to the door.

I darted inside, where Collin was working the weekend shift.

"Collin, there's a snake!"

He glanced up. "Where?"

"Outside my apartment."

He immediately came outside, and together we went to where I had seen the snake. Collin picked a few rocks and pitched them, each with careful aim, leaving the snake paralyzed.

The cobra had hidden himself in the rocks used to decorate around the outside of the building, so Collin found a large stick to move the rocks. After using the stick to lift the snake onto the road, then giving it a few additional hits to the head, Collin had succeeded in killing the snake.

After releasing a jittery breath, I asked, "Have you ever done that before?"

He answered in a calm voice, "Many times."

As we further examined the corpse, Sal pulled up in the Land Rover. Collin and I relayed the story and showed him the snake. What an exciting night!

After we went into the apartment and closed the door, I realized just how fortunate I was. That snake had been close enough to bite me. Although having a profound respect for the seriousness of the situation, I can honestly say that I was not scared. I thanked God more than once for being my protector.

Over the years, there have been a few more run-ins with snakes. There was the one that came through the front door of the main house, when a disabled man had left it open. The man was seated in the foyer and his back was to the door, so he did not see the snake. Since I was the only other person in the house at the time, and I knew that he could not move fast enough to get away quickly, I stood up to get the "snake stick."

Yes, we kept a few strategically placed, just in case!

As I was about to meet the challenge, another man approached the front door. Motioning in sign language and mouthing *Snake*, he entered and finished the deed.

Another close call happened when Sal and I were getting ready to go to town for some shopping. The roof had been leaking in different places throughout the rainy season, and there was a hole in the ceiling tile in our bathroom. I went to use the bathroom before our journey and closed the door. When I was finished, I came out and told Sal it was his turn.

No sooner had he gone in than he came right back out. "Get the snake stick!"

I hurried to get him the stick, but by the time I did, the snake had found its way into the bedroom. I called outside to where Alexander and

Padmore—the tractor driver—were sitting. They followed me into the bedroom, and the three men found and killed the snake.

There was one question I couldn't shake. Where was that snake when I was in the bathroom?

Every time we thought we had God figured out, there was another level, another step, another piece in the puzzle. And for us at that time, He began moving so fast, we were running to keep up.

All our weekends started to feel like "EMS weekends." I mean, really. "Call 9-1-1" in America, translated to "Call S-A-L" in Zambia.

Calls to houses in the bush and to other clinics . . . emergency transports to Livingstone Hospital . . . yikes! Day and night. Sal's phone number must have been on everyone's speed dial!

*What are You saying, God?*

On one particular Friday in September 2008, the alarm clock went off, as it always did at five a.m. By five fifteen, Sal's first cup of coffee was ready. He completed his quiet time by six and went to the clinic to check on our pregnant HIV patient, who had gone into labor the night before. After that, he got ready to go to Kabuyu for our Mobile ART clinic.

Geoffrey—a newly graduated clinical officer we had recently hired—arrived a few minutes before seven and checked on the expectant mother and the other six inpatients.

Sal set off with a small staff for Kabuyu in the Game Viewer. They arrived by eight, set up, and saw over thirty HIV patients.

Meanwhile, back at the clinic, Geoffrey delivered a baby girl and prepared to see patients.

By one o'clock, Sal had just seen the last HIV patient. I called to tell him that a woman in another village had gone into labor at only seven months, with moderate bleeding.

Sal left the staff and supplies at Kabuyu and took the Game Viewer to Bwiketo Village (fifteen minutes away), where he found the thirty-eight-year-old woman in obvious discomfort, still in her hut. On exam, he saw that she was fully dilated and delivery was imminent. He reviewed her prenatal card, since she was not one of our patients, and saw nothing to cause concern.

He called and asked me to send someone in the Land Rover to go to Kabuyu to pick up the staff, since he was obviously going to deliver this baby in the hut.

Thirty minutes later, her water broke and out came a baby boy that maybe weighed one pound. Sal attempted to resuscitate him for about thirty minutes without success. At seven months' gestation, this baby's lungs were not developed enough.

During the attempted resuscitation, he looked at the mom and saw that there had been no change in her abdomen size. He handed the baby to the grandma and quickly taught her how to continue with resuscitation so he could focus on the mom, who was bleeding profusely.

By the time he turned around, a second bag of water had broken. Great—*twins*! The prenatal card didn't mention that fact.

Meanwhile, the staff had returned to the clinic. Sal called and asked me to send them to him, because he needed the Land Rover. After about an hour, they had the mom in the clinic with IV lines running. We all prayed that the second baby would come out on its own.

Another hour passed. Sal decided to take her to Livingstone Hospital for a C-section to remove the second baby, who was clearly already dead. During preparation for transport, a call came in from Kasiya about another woman in labor. Geoffrey and Mwanza headed to Kasiya while Sal went to the hospital, and I stayed to cover the clinic.

Two hours later, Sal returned to find that Geoffrey had just delivered his second baby girl of the day. It was ten p.m., and we headed to our apartment to call it a night, although Sal remained on call.

At ten forty-five, he received a call from Katapazi Clinic for an HIV patient in labor. He rushed over there and ended up doing the delivery at their clinic. He started the baby on the protocol of a prophylactic short course of HIV meds. He arrived back at the apartment at one thirty, changed IVs on the patients in the clinic who needed them, and was in bed by two.

The alarm went off at five on Saturday morning, and we started again.

On this particular day, he left in the Land Rover at seven fifteen to go into Livingstone to do some shopping for medicines, office supplies, and food.

Traveling the back bush road had become the norm, to avoid the huge potholes in the tarmac. While on the gravel road, he came across an accident scene. A truck had overturned, throwing people from the open back in all different directions. Sal never ever passes up an accident scene, and this accident on a dirt road in the African bush was no exception. He had his medical bag in the back of the vehicle, like a true paramedic.

After checking about ten or twelve people, all with minor injuries like abrasions, he said his goodbyes, with many voicing their thanks, and proceeded on into Livingstone.

On the way back to the clinic, Sal received a call from Siandazya about a woman in labor. He went to pick up the patient and bring her back to the clinic.

At around one, another call came from Siakasipa about an eighteen-year-old girl in labor, so Sal went to her. Upon arrival, he found that this first-time mom was too far along to move. Her baby was delivered in the hut. Everything was fine.

He arrived back at Sons of Thunder at five and made his rounds on all the inpatients twice before going to bed, still on call. Twice during the night, he awoke to check on the pregnant patients. All was well.

Sunday morning, Geoffrey agreed to cover the clinic while we went to church in town. One of the missionary couples who had been there for six years was returning to the States, and this was his last sermon.

After having lunch, we returned from town, only to find that Emeldah, one of our AIDS inpatients, had suffered a stroke and was close to death. Pastor Julius had already been called, and family was around her bed.

About thirty minutes later, Emeldah died.

After the usual washing and wrapping of the body, we took the family and Emeldah back to her village for burial.

On Sunday night, Sal was still on call for five inpatients and knew that the alarm would sound at five on Monday morning.

How was *your* weekend?

Times like this proved that God had truly raised up Sal with that "paramedic instinct." My husband not only gets up and goes when others would stay home or stay in bed, but he also recognizes a need and stops when others would just keep on going!

God has a way of using circumstances to bring people into our lives.

One October afternoon, Sal was in town, and Geoffrey was on call.

Anna came to our door and said, "There is an *emergency*. Can you come?"

I immediately followed her to the clinic to find a sixty-eight-year-old white man lying in the bed with a concerned wife standing at his side and a son at the foot of the bed, very eager to start telling me the story.

As I listened to his words, I observed the surroundings to find that Geoffrey had already attached the transformer to raise the head of the hospital bed and then to the oxygen concentrator, which he had brought out of the supply room.

I was a little confused when I saw the wife squeezing an Ambu bag over her husband's face. He had a nasal cannula in place, but not in his nostrils. As I looked closer, I realized he was conscious and breathing on his own. So why the Ambu?

She was obviously distraught.

Listening to the son tell the story, I surmised that his father, Iain, had a history of high blood pressure. He'd also had an episode of bronchitis in the past month.

With what seemed like an overload of adrenaline running through his veins, the son went on. "This morning, while we were eating breakfast, he went out a couple of times and stopped breathing. I had to stimulate him to come to."

The wife, Fiona, chimed in. "We put him in the car and started to speed off toward Livingstone to take him to see the doctor in town, but you can't speed anywhere in this place nowadays because of all the craters in the road." Her voice shook with frustration.

The son chimed in. "We were right near your farm when he went out again, and we remembered there was a clinic here, so we decided to stop."

As I asked a few questions and listened, I slowly and calmly walked over to Iain's wife and took the Ambu bag out of her hand, checked the oxygen concentrator, and placed the cannula in his nose. During a brief break in the conversation, I took vital signs and then proceeded to call Sal. After hearing the report and assessment of Iain's condition, Sal decided to head back to the clinic.

I found out later that—with Janice and her children in the car—Sal did indeed race back to the clinic in the Land Rover on one of the back roads, at a speed that delighted the kids and sent Janice into a white-knuckled panic.

While waiting for Sal, Geoffrey started an IV, and we made Iain comfortable. Iain began to regain color and was able to answer questions. He even began to crack jokes, which I discovered was part of his sarcastic personality.

Once Sal arrived, he dug out the monitor-defibrillator and the pads. Using the machine as a heart monitor, we were able to see a very rough picture of the heart rhythm. Sal diagnosed him as having had a heart attack, administered appropriate medication, and started to prepare the Land Rover for transport into Livingstone.

With the back of the Rover padded with a mattress and multiple pillows for propping, Sal and I transported Iain and his wife to the private physician in town. We gave verbal and written reports to the doctor, helped get Iain transferred to a patient room, and placed him on oxygen again (we'd been unable to run $O_2$ during transport). After multiple thank-yous and goodbyes, we headed back to the clinic.

Talking to the doctor the next day, we found out that Iain had been sent on a commercial airline to South Africa for continued treatment. He was our first cardiac patient and the first real EMS system in operation—the first time when we could actually see transfer of care to a higher level. It was a good feeling.

Through this process, Sal and I came to know Fiona and Iain and were pleased when they moved into a small cottage on a farm just north of us. Iain loved to cook for people and was exceptional at it. That was what gave him purpose and enjoyment, when he was otherwise disabled and not in the best health. Their cottage had a very small kitchen, where Iain would sit on a stool and cook. He could turn from one side to the other and reach everything.

At this point in my life, I desperately needed a place of respite and a friend to confide in, so Saturdays became my day to get together with Fiona. I would go over in the morning and stay for whatever lunch Iain prepared. We'd sit at the table in the outside shelter, talking, laughing, and sharing stories.

There was a game park across the drive, and we would often see eland, impala (two types of African antelopes), and zebras at different times. The time together proved to be beneficial to all of us.

Sadly, Iain would pass away in January of 2019 from osteosarcoma, but Fiona and I would continue our Saturday tradition.

# Chapter 28

LIFE IN ZAMBIA WAS DRAMATICALLY DIFFERENT THAN IN THE US, and we were frequently reminded of that fact.

After living there for more than three years, we had kind of adjusted to the dry season and the rainy season. We had even gotten used to the bugs and lizards, the occasional bush fire, electricity outages, and the like. But every now and then, we became keenly aware of just where we were.

One such reminder happened to me one evening on the way home from town. It was just after dark, and I was driving the Land Rover on the back bush road, because the main tarmac had enormous potholes and was almost impassable.

I rounded a corner only to find an ominous black silhouette staring at me from a small knoll on the side of the road. I could not make out its face or features because of the way the moon was shining, but I distinctly saw the large ears and enormous stature. It towered over the vehicle, standing very still . . . almost challenging me to try something.

I stared in disbelief at what was clearly a very huge elephant!

I had become much more knowledgeable about these creatures than I ever hoped to be. They are not the delightful animals that entertain us at the zoo or the circus, nor are they adorable little Dumbos. They are very dangerous critters, inducing a lot of fear among the nationals. Imagine living in a grass hut and seeing one or more of those creatures right outside your door! Or waking up in the morning to find your fields destroyed by their passing through the night before.

A couple years before this, a mother with a baby on her back was killed right in Livingstone by a rogue elephant. And a few weeks before, a few of them were spotted on the farm proper, trying to drink water out of the cistern that was approximately forty yards from the main house, the clinic, and the orphanage.

That night on the road, I quickly prayed as I kept driving. I had no desire to stop and look for a camera. By the time I reached our apartment, my heart was back in my chest, and I thanked God for being my protector.

I remember Dorothy in *The Wizard of Oz* saying, "Toto . . . I have a feeling we're not in Kansas anymore." Believe me, that night, I became intensely aware of exactly where I was.

That sighting was just the beginning of our experience with the elephants. At one point, those four-legged creatures terrorized our villages and ravaged our fields and gardens. I am serious! We had literally hundreds of elephants on the farm.

Zimbabwe, the country just across the southern border of Zambia, was in such a state, facing starvation, that even the military suffered from hunger. They started shooting elephants for food. The elephants, understandably, ran for their lives.

Since the Zambezi River, which forms the border between Zambia and Zimbabwe, was crossable, they began migrating north into Zambia. Our farm was only twenty-five kilometers (roughly sixteen miles) outside Livingstone—which is near the river—surrounded by forest and has lots of orchards, gardens, and maize fields. So . . . plenty of food!

Consequently, there were herds in the farm villages and even on the farm proper.

Elephants disappear during the day—to where, I don't know—and come out under the cover of night. They are big, *big* animals that can't be seen right in front of you because they are black as pitch.

One night, when they were out in force, I went out on the front porch and heard them on both sides of the main house. They were on the left—in the small orchard and garden area—and on the right—where the main gardens were. I felt helpless. After all, what do you do to get rid of an elephant in your garden?

The only solution was to call ZAWA.

The Zambian Agriculture and Wildlife Authority came out with firecrackers to help scare off the animals. They even stayed on the farm for ten days, answering calls about nighttime sightings. We also brought in people to work with our farmers in growing chili peppers around their gardens to keep the elephants away. It seems the elephants don't like spicy food!

But our fields and gardens continued to be destroyed. Nothing was working, and the number of elephants was, in fact, increasing. So it was decided that an elephant would have to be killed. This would be an indication to the herd that this area was not safe for them.

One night, a lone bull elephant was spotted in the garden by the house. To our dismay, ZAWA sent out a novice with an AK-47. After three shots—and three misses—the elephant charged. He chased the shooter and Alexander into the building we referred to as "the dairy."

The next plan was to send two elephant hunters with high-powered weaponry to the farm. About three days later, word came that they had killed an elephant. People from the farm were called to come collect the meat.

After that, the herds started migrating farther north. Thankfully, they have never returned.

It's like they say, "an elephant never forgets."

With the elephants out of our hair, we moved on to other concerns.

On the day we left for another furlough and Sal's final treatment in 2008, the couple that had been in charge for a year and a half took us to breakfast in town. They chatted sweetly, telling us to have a good rest. After breakfast, they drove us to the airport and told us they would see us when we returned in six weeks.

A few days after our arrival in the US, Pastor Jerry called and asked to meet with us. During the meeting, we found out that there was a conspiracy between the missionaries and their church to have us removed from the field. Talk about being blindsided!

The missionary couple was on the payroll of their church and held mission positions on the board, so they gave the ultimatum to Pastor Jerry that it was either us or them—that we could not both remain on the field.

Sal and I had done nothing to the couple except offer help when needed. We hadn't even had any dealings with their church, so this came as a big shock.

But Pastor Jerry was determined that we would indeed be returning to Zambia once our furlough was over.

As I reflected on the situation, I felt like maybe there had been some mistakes made when placing the short-term leaders in the field. First, they were selected because the man was a retired military officer and it was felt in man's eyes that he would be a good leader. Second, he was being paid by his church, which meant he had two allegiances, one with his church and one with Sons of Thunder. I couldn't help but remember where it says in God's Word, "'No one can serve two masters'" (Matthew 6:24), and "'No purpose of yours (God's) can be thwarted'" (Job 42:2).

These assaults on God's call and our integrity were not easy to walk through, but we weren't there because of or for man. We were there at God's direction and because He had chosen us.

We also knew that if we were going to be obedient servants, we were going to run into obstacles and persecution. We just hadn't expected it to come from inside the family of God. We were determined to "stand firm and see the deliverance of the Lord."

I wish that persecution was all we had to deal with and overcome, but unfortunately, it was not. There were many other blows that occurred over the years from all kinds of places.

But thankfully, in the middle of all the drama once again, Sal finished his antibody treatments, and praise God, he had another clean medical review, just as he'd had every time we'd gone home on furlough.

When we arrived back in Zambia on December 10, we were given the news that the other missionaries overseeing everything else besides the medical ministry would be leaving Sons of Thunder on December 17, a mere week after our return.

The couple was being sent by their church to Kenya on another assignment. That church was a very large contributor to the SOT orphanage, so when Pastor Jerry told them he'd made the decision to keep Sal and me on the field, they pulled their funding. They told Pastor Jerry that he had made the wrong decision and that the ministry would fail within three years.

To once again guard our hearts, we kept our eyes fixed on what was ahead. We knew that forgiving was the only way to keep our hearts clean, without bitterness and without holding grudges. I can honestly say that our hearts were free; forgiveness was there.

That didn't mean we wanted to keep in contact or be friends with the couple, but we wished them no harm and prayed for God to bless their future. It says in the Word, "Bless those who persecute you" (Romans 12:14).

No longer surprised by God, for His plans are not our plans (Isaiah 55:8), we buckled down to once again resume the oversight of all the ministries. That meant moving back into the main house, which we did on December 18. Next, we tackled the end-of-the-year financials, getting a handle on all the budgets. We reviewed all areas with regard to operation, personnel, and maintenance issues.

Then, of course, there was Christmas and the orphanage children. There were no plans in the works, but because God is our provider and always there for us, a woman in town called. She had just finished making shoeboxes for the children in town and had thought of SOT orphanage.

She sweetly asked, "Would you like shoeboxes filled with goodies for all the children?"

I didn't hesitate. "Oh my, absolutely. That would be wonderful!"

I could practically hear her smile as she continued. "My husband and I love to wrap packages for the kids. Could you give me a list of all their names with their sex and age?"

I was thrilled! God, You are good!

Because of her kindness, every child got their own present on Christmas morning.

We had two volunteers from Travelers Worldwide who had been working in the children's home all month. They wanted to spend their last day, which was Christmas, with the children handing out presents, playing games, singing songs, and presenting the story of Jesus's birth. Linah and Royce had bought extra goodies for a Christmas meal like rice, beef, and cake. It was a nice time.

But that was not where God's provision ended. The day after Christmas, the children were once again blessed by a lodge in town. The owner and staff of David Livingstone Safari Lodge arrived at the children's home in vans with their chefs, repairmen, and cleaning staff, all armed with the supplies of their trade. Not only did they come prepared to do work, but they came to celebrate as well. They brought a small Christmas tree and decorated the front room. They brought balloons and sweets with bananas and drinks. "Father Christmas," as they called him, came with a red suit and a pillowcase for a beard. He sat the children one by one on his lap and gave each a present.

Every child got a new T-shirt to wear!

All this was quite a surprise, but they also brought a camera crew and newspaper reporters. The provincial minister himself arrived and gave a speech. Sal and I, caught off guard, were also interviewed (in our scrub shirts, of course). The next day, SOT Children's Home was on the local news—and so were we.

We did not know that would be the last Christmas the children would be with us.

But God knew.

## Chapter 29

THE CLINIC WAS BURSTING AT THE SEAMS. ON ONE OCCASION, WE had twelve patients admitted in a clinic that held nine if stretched. We needed a mothers' shelter. We needed more wards.

We needed more skilled staff and the money to pay them. We needed staff housing. We needed another vehicle. We needed Tonga Bibles.

Our monthly budget was $2,500, but we realistically needed five thousand just to meet our operating expenses—things like salaries, medications, inpatient food, lab reagents, office and cleaning supplies, and diesel. And that didn't include repair and maintenance for either the vehicles or the building.

It says in His Word that His plan will not be thwarted. God was making a difference. Each and every day, we saw His hand, and if we looked hard enough, we saw His face.

It was at that time of increase that we were back in leadership over all of Sons of Thunder in Zambia. I was led away from medical and more toward administration, logistics, accounts, and frankly, overseeing everything else. Geoffrey got posted to a government rural health center at the end of December. That left Sal as the only licensed professional in a clinic that kept getting busier and busier. The workload was increasing and should have been overwhelming, but I watched my husband work day and night, doing whatever was needed without complaining. I became very aware that God indeed equips those He calls. God is good, and He provided all Sal needed.

After Geoffrey left, we had four groups of nursing students, each scheduled over a three-week period. No fewer than fourteen students were on the farm at any one time. They stayed in the tobacco barn and rotated between the clinic, orphanage, and school—a week at each site. They covered night shifts and helped with emergencies, and we got to teach them some skills and theory. The director of the school liked the experience and training they got here so much that she asked Sal to teach some lectures at their school in Livingstone starting in August.

Just when the nursing students from Western School of Nursing had left, a midwife named Ethalinda came to us seeking a position at the clinic. She and her husband, Phillip, had spent the last twenty or so years working in Botswana. They had decided to come back to Zambia to retire and were looking to supplement their income.

We hired Ethalinda, as maternity cases were increasing, but we received a bonus. Phillip held a degree in education and had been a headmaster during his time in Botswana. At the time, we had applied for grant-aided status for our primary school in order to get assistance with finances, since school donations had been dwindling. Under grant-aided status however, teachers' salaries would be paid by the government, giving us the relief that we needed.

The only hinderance was that we had to find a headmaster with at least a bachelor's degree. God had provided not only a midwife for the clinic but also a headmaster who fit our requirements. God brought two answers right to the door!

As I reflect back over the years, God always brought people to the door at precisely the right time, starting with our first driver, Christopher. He arrived just in time when we needed to shift from the Land Rover to the lorry.

Clinical officers like Jha and Derek, who were looking to supplement their income and work during their off time, came just when we needed coverage during furloughs so that we didn't have to close the clinic.

Geoffrey had been here as a clinical officer student. When he graduated, he came to seek employment prior to getting posted by the government. He helped Sal and me tremendously while he was here, and I am sure he gained a lot of experience that has continued to benefit him.

Other Zambian health professionals like Ephraim, Watson, Liboma, Dora, and Benjamin came for short stints to fill their time while waiting for their next career moves.

God even provided assistance from other countries. Serena was a physician from the UK who came on a short-term mission trip with Travelers Worldwide.

Three Americans came to SOT at different times and spent a year of their lives answering their calls.

Carrie was a chemist who came to teach at the school, or so she thought. She ended up being the headmistress for that year and mentored Anna, the now-Zambian head who, at the time, was a newly graduated teacher working at the school, waiting to be posted by the government.

Jaime came from the US to Zambia for a year in 2008 before going on to law school. She worked as an administrator at the orphanage that entire year, putting things in order and getting everything under authority and on a firm foundation. During that year, all the children were finally registered with social welfare.

Cristy was retired, having worked on different assignments as a military doctor. Since she could not work as such in the civilian world, she decided to volunteer with Samaritan's Purse. They had been sending medical volunteers to us for short-term missions, and Cristy was one of the first. After her mission with us, she decided to volunteer for a year working at the clinic.

The commitment of Samaritan's Purse to send medical volunteers to Sons of Thunder lasted only a year and ended at just the time when the district health office decided to post our first government-paid RN.

Even Jake and Jessi had been there at just the right time. Jake had covered the church until Pastor George came, and Jessi had covered the orphanage until Jaime came. Now they were feeling called to another ministry organization they had come to know in Livingstone. They are still with that organization today.

And when we had gaps, God provided nursing students and midwifery students on their three-week rural health clinical rotations—students from five different schools.

God showed Himself over and over again as our provider, in every area of need.

When I first met Marie and spent that week with her in Swaziland, we did a lot of talking. During one of our conversations, she told me of a type of farming that she hoped would be taught to the local farmers in Zimba, a town in southern Zambia, where she and her husband had been involved in ministry for years. This type of farming was called Farming God's Way and was a type of conservation farming that did not require plowing. One of its features was something called God's blanket, like mulching, which would hold water in the soil longer.

I politely listened during that time, because I was still trying to figure out what God was telling me about HIV and "community." Having gone to Zambia for medical and not having any knowledge of or interest in farming, I didn't pay much mind.

Months later, a man who was coming to Zambia from South Africa to teach the farmers in Zimba about Farming God's Way found himself stranded at the airport. There were no rental cars, like he thought he would find, and no one meeting him at the airport. The only phone number he had was mine at Sons of Thunder, because someone had given it to him at the last minute and he'd put it in his pocket. They had told him we might be a good contact to hear about Farming God's Way and that we were near Zimba.

So not knowing what else to do, he called me. He introduced himself—his name was Patrick—and told me of his dilemma. We sent Terry, one of our drivers, to pick him up at the airport. We told him he was welcome to lodge at the farm and that we would provide transport and a driver for his FGW classes in Zimba, all without cost. No problem!

The next day, when Terry arrived at the farm to pick up Patrick for his first class with the Zimba farmers, Alexander unexpectedly hopped into the car. God had a plan and a purpose.

That day, Alexander learned Farming God's Way and was hooked. He and Patrick developed a friendship, and Patrick ended up teaching a three-day workshop to SOT farmers on that trip to Zambia. He would continue to come twice a year for the next two years, teaching, training, and mentoring FGW principles and farming methods, as well as composting.

Alexander ended up traveling to Zimbabwe and South Africa and completed the training and testing, becoming a certified national Farming God's Way trainer.

From that point forward, Sons of Thunder has been a FGW farm. There is no plowing or burning of the land. We use what we have in our hand—the *jamba*, or hoe. We make sure that planting is on time. We plant in order, with accurate, straight-line measurements. We take out the weeds. We make sure there is no wastage, and we cover our fields with God's blanket. God has prospered and blessed the farming at SOT, even during periods of drought.

And it all started because of a piece of paper in a man's pocket!

In June of 2009, a retired American home-economics teacher named Sue came to hold sewing classes for the Sons of Thunder ladies. She taught four classes a day, and the ladies made chitenge outfits for themselves and stuffed elephants and Tonga-lady dolls to sell.

While she was there, Sue purchased four hand-crank sewing machines in town to leave with the ladies. One of the more advanced students, Eunice, had already taken some tailoring classes and had a machine of her own. She agreed to head up a sewing center and continue teaching the ladies on the farm as needed.

Initially, we set up one of the rooms in the main house until a separate room could be found. The classes continued with little boys' shorts and little girls' chitenge skirts or dresses. The first ones went to the children in the orphanage.

Since its inception, the sewing center has been a ladies' gathering area, and individual lessons and assistance have been given, as well as classes taught to newcomers as they arrive on the farm. Eunice has had six classes so far. She has made uniforms for cleaners and workers in different areas, as well as curtains and covers for furniture. She does repairs and mending as needed. She makes school uniforms, chitenge outfits, and purses to be sold at the shop or as requested. She also makes Tonga-lady dolls for sale in one of the local tourist shops in town, as well as in Lusaka and at the airport.

The sewing center has been very beneficial to the ladies as well as the farm, providing a much-needed service. However, the one who I think has benefited the most and received God's love and provision has been Eunice. She has become quite the businesswoman.

Also in June, the main road was finally being paved by China-Geo, a Chinese company, which had been awarded the government contract. They slated our little road to be the detour, so for an entire year, all vehicles—including buses and trucks—traveling between Livingstone and Zimba passed by our front gate and right by some of our residents' homes.

Abson—farm supervisor, tour guide, and driver for volunteers—put up speed humps in order to slow the big trucks and thereby keep the children safe. Unfortunately, when a truck slowed down, it created an opportunity for hijackers and thieves to lie in wait and steal from their cargoes.

It was quite an eventful time. Driving on the tarmac had been difficult for years, due to crater-size potholes and no proper lines on the road. During construction, things were slow moving, and dust flew everywhere. People were forced to close their windows whenever cars on opposite sides passed each other. A trip to town for shopping took hours, and a shower was needed when you got back home.

When September rolled around, Sal continued to be forever busy seeing outpatients, not only at Sons of Thunder but also at Kasiya and the four Mobile ART sites.

Weekly outreach to Kasiya was going strong. People were waiting every Wednesday morning as the Land Rover pulled in, filled with staff, and packed with supplies and medicine. We had been averaging over one hundred regular patients every week, and when we added Under-Five week or Child Health week, we topped two hundred. A relationship was being built as we provided care. Traditions, myths, and misconceptions had to be met head-on with education and the Truth of God's Word.

Two more communities were asking us to provide medical services in their areas. Both Siandazya and Siamasimbbi were approximately thirty kilometers (around eighteen to twenty miles) away from Sons of Thunder, and we were the nearest medical facility. The villagers of Siandazya built a grass hut for us to use as a clinic building and came to the farm with the headman to present their petition.

Knowing that we were supposed to do what God put in front of us, we planned to start in October, providing full services to them twice a month.

Along with outpatients, we had a full inpatient ward most of the time, caring for predominantly HIV/AIDS patients and obstetrics.

It was well known that Sal answered calls twenty-four hours a day as well.

One of the widows on the farm said to him, "I know what your gift is. You never get tired. You are always working in God's strength."

I believed that to be very true.

I, on the other hand, had been busy administrating for the rest of the ministries—children's home, primary school, farm, piecework, sewing, vehicles, taxes, budgets, and payroll—as well as hosting traveler volunteers, student nurses, and visiting teams from the States.

I know that sounds like a long list, but the only reason I could do it all was because the Zambian leaders in each area did a fantastic job. We had Linah and Royce with the children; Phillip and then Carrie as heads of the school, along with excellent teachers; Alexander and Abson in leadership over the villages and farm; Pastor George over the church; Terry with the vehicles; Eunice with the sewing classes; and Janice, who was training Advent at the guesthouse.

Sometimes, however, I did get pulled back to the clinic. I still conducted Under-Five and did statistics, both on a monthly basis, but occasionally I was called down for wound care.

One weekend, Abson borrowed his brother Terry's taxi to drive a couple named Peter and Linda to Choma for a wedding. Upon returning, he had a problem with the fuel pump. Someone from the village offered to take a look at it, and of course, Abson helped.

I wasn't sure of the details, but there was a spark close to gasoline, and Abson's left forearm, hand, and leg received second-degree burns.

Taken immediately to Choma hospital, he was told to "go sleep outside and wait for the doctor to arrive at eight o'clock in the morning."

After about seven hours of waiting outside the hospital, Abson called me and said he wanted to be treated at the clinic.

I can only guess the pain he must have been in. Imagine being told by a hospital to go sleep outside! They didn't even offer him water or Tylenol, let alone look at his wounds.

Terry started off on a bus to go get him and check out the vehicle. But our "bush man," Abson, got on a minibus alone, leaving Peter and Linda with the vehicle to wait for Terry.

He arrived at the clinic feverish, dehydrated, weak, and in pain. We immediately put him in bed and evaluated his condition. An IV was started to rehydrate, medication given for pain and fever, antibiotics started, and wound care given for his burns.

His wife, Harriet, arrived, bursting into tears as she saw his condition. Thankfully, all his joints were unaffected—knuckles, wrists, elbows, knees, and ankles were all free of trauma and able to actively move.

Three days of treatment and many, many visitors later, Abson was recovering well. He had no more fever, his IV had been discontinued, he was eating well, and his burns were healing nicely. Burns take a long time to heal, so he would be in the clinic for a while. But he was thankful to be receiving care and feeling loved.

## Chapter 30

IN THE BEGINNING OF SONS OF THUNDER, MOTHERS WERE DYING in their huts during childbirth due to poor conditions, the use of traditional herbs, no help if complications arose, and of course, undetected HIV. The consequences of the large number of maternal deaths were large numbers of babies left without anyone to breastfeed and families not financially able to buy formula. Not knowing what else to do, orphanages were started, including the infant orphanage at Sons of Thunder.

The orphanage on the farm had been in operation since 2000. Many of the newborns placed there still had grandparents and relatives in the area. Some even had dads.

As medical people, our goal was to provide good antenatal care, transport during labor, in-clinic deliveries, and proper protocols for HIV-positive mothers and newborns with the hope of no more maternal deaths and therefore no more orphan crises. We even had HIV-positive moms giving birth safely and breastfeeding for two years. The kids remain negative, thanks to proper care and protocols.

Back in December of 2008, when the church in the US told us their decision to stop financially supporting the orphanage, they planned to cut to half in June and gave us until completion of one year before withdrawing the other half. Looking with man's eyes, circumstances made it necessary to decrease the numbers in the orphanage, but as time went on, it became apparent that God had a slightly different idea.

It was during this time that the old missionary—the one who had resigned from the ministry during our first year there—came back into the picture. We learned that he had gone to all the churches in the surrounding communities to preach. From the pulpit, he told the people that SOT was closing the orphanage and sending the kids far away.

That unsubstantiated message had put fear into the hearts of the families of the orphans. So one by one, they started arriving at the orphanage and social welfare, requesting their children. It was that very misinformation that caused social welfare to find placements for all the children without any direction from SOT.

This also happened to be when the new orphanage was being built right in Livingstone with the providential name SOS.

God's plan was obviously to close the orphanage entirely, because as the months went on, provision for placement of each and every child was made known.

Sons of Thunder Orphanage closed its doors officially on the thirtieth of October 2009. Nine children went to Global Samaritan Children's Home to be with siblings and attend Sons of Thunder Primary School. They would be guaranteed further education at Global Samaritan Basic School, then proceed to secondary schools sponsored by Global.

Thirteen children went home with their fathers, two with their grandmothers, and one with his aunt, after home evaluations by the Ministry of Social Welfare. The remaining thirty-one went to the newly opened SOS Orphanage in order to stay close to their home villages and families for visiting. They also were guaranteed both primary and secondary education.

As we took the last children to SOS, we were left with mixed emotions. This Scripture came to mind: "'For my thoughts are not your thoughts, neither are your ways my ways,' declares the Lord. 'As the heavens are higher than the earth, so are my ways higher than your ways and my thoughts than your thoughts'" (Isaiah 55:8–9).

It became very clear to me that God had orchestrated the whole thing. You know that Scripture—what the enemy meant for evil, God turns to good. Well, that was exactly what we saw happen.

But life in Africa was never easy.

It was November 2009, and it was my birthday. I'd had a rough couple of months, with the closing of the orphanage, the loss of three of the teachers in the primary school, and taking time to train nursing students who had come to the clinic for three weeks. Not to mention the ongoing projects, such as the church and day-to-day operations of farming and piecework and payroll—all with menopause raging! And to top it off, my back hurt. The day before, I had lifted a patient from a chair to a wheelchair.

Mwanza drove me to town in the lorry that day, and I was jarred the whole way on the bumpy road. At one point, I even had to lift myself off the seat to minimize the stabbing pain.

When I got to town, I had a lot of places to go, which meant getting into and out of the vehicle multiple times. I had Mwanza drop me off at the first stop—the Department of Lands. I verified the new budget increase for land rent of 80 percent for next year—everyone was going to love hearing that.

When I left the office, a taxi driver named Fines was standing there. He glanced my way and removed his hat. "Renee . . . do you need a ride?"

I thought about how much easier it would be getting into and out of a taxi than the lorry. I knew that God had provided for me, so I said, "Yes, please."

He took me to my next stop—the post office. I had sent Terry on Friday to pick up a package—there were limited hours when customs was involved—but the man behind the counter had refused to give Terry the package, stating that I had to come and sign.

With the clinic hours and outreaches, it was impossible for either Sal or me to pick up packages, so I needed to see the postmaster. He was in his office and very nice. We came to an agreement that as long as the person I sent carried my ID, they could retrieve any packages.

From there, I went to talk with the man at the counter, and we also came to an amiable agreement. While I was picking up the package, he asked me to collect six small packages for Global Samaritan, which I agreed to do. Funny, but Mirriam—one of the leaders at GS—didn't have to sign in order for *me* to pick up *her* parcels.

Once again, there was Fines, standing there to carry the packages.

After the post office, it was off to Immigration to check for Sal's work permit. I'd collected mine about a month before, but they were playing games in Lusaka with Sal's—not sending it to Livingstone and asking for five thousand kwacha to "make sure it gets in the pile to be sent."

We had never paid bribes, nor would we ever, so I had told them, "We will just wait."

Lo and behold, at the very bottom of the page that I had checked just days before, there was an added name in a different-color ink—Sal's! Somehow, by the grace of God, it had arrived, and without any added kwacha.

By then, it was ten o'clock, and the woman who worked in accounts where you pick up the permits had not arrived yet. Ugh.

As I left the building, a woman in uniform was getting out of a taxi, so I waited. Sure enough, it was the woman from accounts, and I was able to collect Sal's permit.

Three stops completed. Next, I was off to see about some graphic design work—we needed business cards for the sewing ladies. One shop owner in Livingstone had agreed to try to sell their Tonga-lady dolls but had suggested we make them even more personable by attaching a card with a photo of the seamstress on it.

"It would be a very profitable marketing tool for tourists," she had advised.

The graphic designer was friendly and seemed knowledgeable. She told me she would make a sample page and call me. Number four done— off to the next stop.

I needed to go to the two vehicle-hire (car rental) places to get estimates for a group of Farming God's Way men who were coming from South Africa. They would be staying with us from November 28 through December 8 while they visited sites in Choma, Zimba, and Kalomo. They would spend some time with our farmers, seeing their progress and reinforcing FGW techniques.

With estimates from both places in hand and my back screaming, I proceeded to the Spar shopping center. Shopping in Livingstone was definitely not like going to the mall. It was not fun at all . . . it was work!

I sat down with all my packages to have an iced coffee. It was very hot out—at least a hundred degrees. Fines put all my packages on the table for me as I waited for Mwanza and the lorry.

Once I had been picked up by Mwanza, we came across Terry in the Land Rover. He had brought Nixon, the eighteen-year-old brother of

Thelma—one of the ladies who worked in the main house—to the hospital. He had been attacked by an elephant on the road to the school!

Sal had seen him at the clinic and diagnosed him with at least two broken ribs. Sal had not liked his breathing, so he'd sent him for x-rays and further evaluation. Terry said that the x-ray was all right, just soft-tissue injuries, and he was breathing better, but they had admitted him.

So I hopped into the Rover to ride home with Terry. Well, I didn't exactly "hop" in; I slowly pulled myself up into the Rover, knowing that the ride over the dirt road would be easier on my back in this vehicle than in the lorry.

Upon returning home, I found that the electricity had gone out at ten o'clock in the morning and had not yet returned. Sal asked if I wanted to go back into town for a birthday dinner, but I couldn't even think of it with the way my back felt.

At dinnertime, still without electricity, we had ham sandwiches and watched a DVD of Jack Bauer on *24* on the computer.

In the middle of the second episode, Bridget called from the clinic, asking Sal to come quickly. Terry also called to ask where the key for the generator was. Obviously, something was going on over at the clinic.

It turned out that when one of our expectant moms had been sitting outside with the other patients, she'd said, "I think I need to go lie down."

She went inside to lie down, and almost immediately, out came the baby!

Once things were handled at the clinic, Sal returned and resumed our *24* marathon. Three episodes in, the battery on the computer was finished, and we still had no electricity.

At about nine, the electricity returned. After putting on the bedroom air conditioner and taking some Tylenol, I went to sleep.

Sal's plan was to get up at three thirty and watch the Steelers play football. I awoke at four thirty in a sweat, only to discover that the electricity was out again. When I went to the living room, there was Sal lying on the couch. He told me he had watched the first quarter before the power went out. Needless to say, he was disappointed.

This was my day—extreme heat, dusty roads, a vehicle we couldn't shut off because it needed a new starter that we didn't have enough money for, distrust and corruption in federal offices, an elephant attack right on our property, no electricity for over twelve hours, and a baby delivered in the dark—all to get up the next day and start over.

I giggled to myself when I read all my birthday greetings from home. Most talked about "rest and relaxation." Rest and relaxation in the US would have meant lunch at Panera, then an afternoon at the day spa or reading a book poolside somewhere or going to dinner and a movie. But for me, the meaning of those words had changed.

I guess I was able to "relax" with Fines lifting and carrying my packages and driving me around town to do my errands instead of getting bounced up and down in the lorry.

I "relaxed" when the postmaster worked out a plan for me to receive future packages without difficulty.

I "relaxed" when I saw Sal's name on the list at Immigration and when the woman from accounts arrived just when I needed her. And when I held Sal's work permit in my hand.

I guess I "rested" as I cooled off and eased the pain in my back sitting at the outdoor restaurant, sipping a refreshing iced coffee while waiting for Mwanza.

I "relaxed" eating a ham sandwich with Sal by candlelight and watching our favorite show on the computer.

I "relaxed" when I found out that Nixon had survived the elephant attack and was going to be okay. Then when the mom and baby, who had been delivered in the dark, were both healthy and happy.

I guess I "rested" for those five hours when the electricity was working as I slept in the comfort of air conditioning.

It's all a matter of perspective, isn't it?

*Thank You, God, for allowing me to see You in the midst of my day and in how You provided for me.*

## Chapter 31

AFTER THE ORPHANAGE CLOSED, PASTOR JERRY GAVE STRICT instructions not to use the building for anything permanent until the Lord showed us the plan. Walking into the empty orphanage building, I was left with the thought, *Now what, God?*

As I made my way through the main room toward the back door, I saw the two smaller rooms on each side of the hallway and the painted wall with brightly colored safari animals. I thought about all the Sons of Thunder families, over fifty at that time, and their small children. I thought about Christine, who had been the teacher for the children at the orphanage and was now out of a job. Then it occurred to me, if it was important to have preschool classes for the orphans, why not preschool classes for Sons of Thunder kids?

After speaking to a very excited Christine, I began planning for a preschool program for ages three to six for SOT residents only. We hired Alexander's wife, Agatha, as an assistant, small tables and chairs were made, and school supplies were purchased, as well as food for daily snacks.

In January 2010, the preschool began in those two rooms inside the old orphanage building. We knew this would only be a temporary location until we found a more permanent place, but the walls were decorated so nicely for kids, and the back covered veranda was a good place for outdoor play.

Preschool helped prepare the children for first grade, as well as giving them a head start with English. The headmistress at the primary school said she really saw a difference in the children after attending preschool versus the ones from the surrounding villages who did not have the opportunity.

The kids themselves loved to go to preschool with their friends. They even wore little school uniforms.

After some time, we had a few different people asking us if we had a place to hold meetings. CARE International wanted to train community health workers under the Ministry of Health. We also had nursing students we had previously put in rooms in the tobacco barn, but we had been limited on the number we could house.

Looking over the orphanage building, I noted that it had a sizable sitting room that could accommodate large conference tables and chairs. There were electrical outlets for projectors and equipment to show PowerPoint presentations. There were two sides to the building, each with bedrooms, toilets, and showers. Clearly one side could be used for women participants and one side for men. Laundry facilities were already in place. The back veranda would be a good area to serve food. There was even a smaller room that could be used for a second classroom or overflow.

After discussion with Pastor Jerry, we received approval to move forward. We began by having conference tables and chairs made to accommodate a meeting capacity of thirty participants. We had additional bunk beds and picnic tables made too.

An outside water tap with a kitchen sink was put in on one end of the veranda, as well as a wood-burning cooking area. The existing furniture in the inside kitchen storage area could be used for serving food on the back veranda.

Linah was put in charge, and a full staff was selected and trained, raising them up to feed and accommodate guests as in the hospitality industry.

I shopped for pillows, sheets, and blankets, along with dishes, cups, and pots to furnish the new conference center. The final touches were painting the walls and making uniforms for all the workers.

Over the years, the Ministry of Health, both District Health Offices in the area, Livingstone Hospital, and the province have all held meetings and workshops at the conference center. Adjustments were made to include more furnishings and supplies to accommodate more people. Currently, a conference of fifty participants can be adequately managed.

Student groups have utilized Sons of Thunder for their rural health clinical rotations, including registered nurses from five different nursing schools in the Southern Province, one clinical officer school from Lusaka, and now midwifery students from Livingstone. The conference center has also been used for wedding receptions, workshops for Farming God's Way training, teacher conferences, Bible studies, and monthly meetings for the Sons of Thunder men's and women's ministries, as well as some accommodations for overnight guests, visitors to Livingstone, or overflow mission teams from America. We have even had visitors from France and Malawi stay with us for a few days.

God always has a plan. Sometimes all it takes is for us to move out and take a step of faith.

One morning, Sal and I were going about our business in the main house when a trilling noise gave us both a start. There was an old rotary phone in one corner of the main house that we never used. Immediately realizing that was where the noise was coming from, I looked back at Sal.

"The house phone never rings." Curious, I crossed the room. "Who would be calling us?"

When I answered, I was greeted by a woman named Olive, who told me she was from Victoria Falls University, a new college in Livingstone.

I was a little taken back by a university calling us. They probably just wanted money. But when she said she wanted to come out and talk to us about "business," I immediately relented.

God had recently been speaking to me about businesses. People had been coming to me individually over the past couple of weeks, sharing their dreams about starting businesses. Abson had talked about wanting to start a poultry business. Alexander and Tyson—our lorry driver—had mentioned a desire to do commercial farming. Graham—our clinic driver—had told me he wanted to start a business of dried maize.

And of course, we already had Eunice, who was making dolls to sell, and Pastor George, who, in addition to pastoring, was running the tack shop. This was a little store where necessities were sold—a convenience shop of sorts.

Godfrey—our head bricklayer and carpenter—had told me he wanted to make furniture, and our driver, Terry, had dreams of opening a garage.

So when Olive said "business," I felt God had something for us. We made an appointment for her to come to Sons of Thunder.

When she arrived, I asked what had made her call us. She informed me that Victoria Falls is known as the "Smoke That Thunders." When she found us in the directory as "Sons of Thunder," she was immediately taken with the parallel wording. As the discussion ensued, it became clear that she was indeed there to ask for a donation to help the new university get started with an entrepreneur workshop.

After listening to her request, I told her that she might have thought she was coming to ask for a donation, but I knew exactly why she had come. I had about eight people to put in her workshop. Eight people who had come to me with a dream of starting a business!

Approximately four weeks later, while I was in the United States on furlough, Alexander, Tyson, Abson, Graham, Godfrey, Terry, Pastor George, and Eunice went together on the lorry truck to attend a three-day workshop on entrepreneurship. They all received certificates at the completion of the course.

After I returned to Zambia, God said, *Take the first step.*

I called them all together, told them what I had felt God say, and asked each of them to think and pray and tell me what their first step would be.

Godfrey told me that he needed a wall between the grinding mill and the workshop to prevent the mealie meal dust from getting all over his working space and products.

Terry needed a ramp to raise up vehicles so he could work underneath them.

Abson had to find a place for his poultry. He selected an area at the main building where he already worked overseeing supplies and workers. The area had old, unused cattle pens demarcated out of cement. He could just finish the building using those as his base. His next step would be for us to persuade the Sons of Thunder builders to help him finish the poultry building without immediate pay, then wait until his first sale of chickens to collect any moneys due.

Graham needed to locate and prepare a field, digging holes using Farming God's Way.

Eunice wanted to find a market to sell the dolls she had already been making and hire employees.

Tyson and Alexander needed to source seeds in Lusaka, so they would have to save money for transport and for the merchandise.

Pastor George sought to expand his shop with different products.

Godfrey built the wall and even put electricity into his workshop to accommodate power tools. He made furniture for people as well as the farm, but being a bricklayer at heart, he took other outside jobs. Unfortunately, Godfrey left Sons of Thunder to stay with his mother and help her manage their family property and cattle.

Terry built that ramp and used it to get underneath vehicles for a lot of oil changes and car repairs. He left Sons of Thunder to try to open a garage in the town of Kalomo but never did. Nowadays, he drives and fixes cars from his home. He did, however, train a hardworking man named Japhet as his assistant, so he took over at the SOT garage, using the ramp for oil changes and ease of vehicle repair.

Abson procured and sold chickens until he gave the business to his brother Ocrist in order to pursue truck driving. Abson upgraded his trucking license to include double trailer and dangerous goods and took outside jobs, even crossing borders into South Africa and the Democratic Republic of the Congo while still maintaining his home at Sons of Thunder.

Ocrist operated the poultry business for years, until the operation was taken over by Sons of Thunder for village chickens.

Graham found the field, planted maize for a few years in a row, and made a profit every year with the harvest. He then oversaw the planting of maize on the farm for a year while continuing to work as a driver for the clinic.

Tyson and Alexander went to Lusaka and bought seeds. They planted large vegetable gardens and made profits for years. Tyson's first year of butternuts made him enough profit that he purchased a used vehicle. Seeing his example, a lot of people became serious with their gardens and expanded their crops to the more high-end vegetables.

Alexander always had beautiful gardens and maize fields. He made profits for years, supplementing his SOT income, until he decided to give up his area of land to increase SOT farming. His role as director of Sons of Thunder has increased his responsibilities, and his focus is now more on SOT farming than his own endeavors.

Pastor George ran his tack shop for years, until things started going downhill. Quantities of supplies were dwindling as well as the variety of products. It was suggested that Sons of Thunder take over the shop. Building a new shop was not a problem, since we already had our own team of builders, but I did not have any desire to run the shop or keep inventory and sales records.

After some time in prayer, an idea came to me. "Why can't everyone have an opportunity to make a little bit of money by supplying something for the shop?"

When I proposed the idea, it was received well. Someone supplied the biscuits, someone else the cooking oil, someone else the sugar, and so forth. Pastor George was happy to just be one of the suppliers. Sons of Thunder agreed to hire and pay workers to sell the products and help keep inventory records. Once a week, all suppliers received their profits, minus a small percentage for SOT. Inventory was maintained, the shop kept orderly and clean, sales were managed, and proceeds paid out to suppliers. All in all, everyone was happy.

Eunice was our golden girl! We helped her find a market for her dolls at a curio shop in town with branches at the airport and in Lusaka. She is still making dolls and profiting from sales to this day. She also expanded her business to making school uniforms, purses, and chitenge outfits. She operated the sewing center on the farm and taught sewing and tailoring classes to all the newcomers. She made uniforms for conference and child-care workers, as well as cleaners at the clinic. She also made curtains and recovered cushions for furniture at the main house.

Olive still works at Victoria Falls University in Livingstone, and we talk from time to time.

God is good!

When I began this journey in 2005, I felt that Zambia would never be home. It was just a place where we had come on assignment, to do a job which had to be done. But somewhere along the journey, my attitude changed.

One of my favorite movies when I was a child was *The Wizard of Oz*. I remember liking the moment when Dorothy clicked her ruby slippers together, saying, "There's no place like home. There's no place like home."

I agreed with her wholeheartedly. There's a feeling you get when you've been away for a long time and you're almost home. That was the feeling I had at the beginning of my furlough in September 2010 as the airplane circled the Baltimore airport and I knew my son would be there to meet me. I had it again when we pulled into the neighborhood, and when I walked into the house and hugged my grandchildren. It was the feeling I had when I cuddled up under the covers of my own bed that night.

The difference with this trip was that I found myself just as eagerly waiting to return home to Zambia. I felt excited when the airplane circled the Livingstone Airport, and I knew Alexander, my Zambian "son," would be waiting to pick me up. I had that same "coming home" feeling that I had on arrival in America. It came over me as we pulled into the Sons of Thunder gate and headed up the driveway.

I felt myself feeling at home when I got out of the vehicle and greeted all my Zambian family. I felt at home walking into the house, and I slept like a baby in my bed there, cuddled up under the comforter.

The question I continued to ask myself was, "Where is home?"

Ultimately, those of us who know Jesus as our Lord and Savior can rest in the knowledge that our ultimate home is with Him.

Speaking of movies I loved as a child, there's a scene in *Mary Poppins* when the admiral fires the cannon at a certain time every day, causing his wife, the maid, and the cook to take their places in the house. That scene came to mind whenever it rained in Zambia.

At the first hint of rain, I'd get the buckets, Advent would get the towels, and we would proceed to our "battle stations" in the main house. We put down towels, moved furniture, and positioned our buckets in just the right spots to collect water from the leaking roof. Thankfully, the bedrooms had been spared, at least so far. The bad spots were the front foyer, the bathroom, and the kitchen. However, every rain required a walking inspection, because new places of leakage surfaced each time, depending on which way the wind was blowing.

Unfortunately, the main house was not the only building affected. Earlier, in November, the wind came one day like a little tornado and blew iron sheets off the clinic roof. The back porch, which served as the outside waiting area, was mostly affected.

Godfrey and the guys put the iron sheets back in place, but there were some areas where rain was able to get in. After the last two rains, the entire back porch was flooded, and one of the ceiling tiles was sagging significantly on the already low ceiling porch.

That repair took top priority, in order to avoid injuries to the waiting patients. The last thing we wanted was for the ceiling tile to completely cave in! Once the repairs were completed, we had to concentrate on the main house, but we were waiting on the go-ahead from the US.

By 2011, we were given the funds to repair the roof on the main house, which desperately needed it by then. We felt an urgency to get the job done.

Because of the size of the building, it was quite the endeavor. We had to wait until all the visitors had left, so in September, Godfrey, Pathias—another SOT bricklayer—and the guys started taking off the old roof and putting on the new.

The main house is quite huge, and in the middle was a glass dome over a fountain area. The glass had already been replaced once, but it continued to be a major source of leakage. The guys carefully removed the glass from the dome but unfortunately had to wait until the next day to place the new roof. Meaning that, for the night, this area would be open to the sky.

"No problem," I said. "We'll be okay. We'll be able to see the stars!"

The first thing that happened was a bat flew in. After a jaunt or two around the main areas of the house with Sal and me scurrying to find something to help chase it out, it found its way back into the open sky.

Later that night, Sal got called down to the clinic for a maternity call, so I was alone in the house, with the open roof. Wouldn't you know . . . we had our first early rain!

I didn't know what to do. Much of the water went into the fountain, but there was a large area around the fountain that was uncovered. What a mess! I got towels and started to cry. I called the watchmen for help, and we all tried to contain the flood.

Sal felt bad for me. "Why don't you go home until the roof is done?"

He didn't have to tell me twice! I was on the next flight out to the States and didn't return until word came that the roof was on.

Over the years, there were other obstacles to overcome. Times when fear should have permeated my being, but because God had removed all fear, I met each challenge as it presented itself. I can honestly say I have been in most government offices in Zambia at district, provincial, and/or national levels for all sorts of issues. Each issue had to be met head-on, some requiring trips to the capital city of Lusaka, some handled right there in Livingstone. Some required legal counsel, but most were handled without.

I have introduced Alexander to most of these offices, both in Livingstone and Lusaka, and I can say that he also has learned how to stand and overcome with Jesus holding his hand. God is always there—He never leaves you nor forsakes you. His promises are yes and amen. He is faithful, and you can trust Him.

It says in a song I heard Dolly Parton sing: "All the miles of my journey have proved my Lord true, and He is so precious to me."

Other frustrations and sources of discouragement were when we thought we were raising up people to be in certain positions, spending years of training and teaching them, giving them our trust and added responsibilities, only to have them disappoint us, either by leaving abruptly and without reason or demonstrating behavior not expected—like alcohol abuse, sexual immorality, or stealing money or equipment. It is disheartening, especially when we thought of all the time and trust invested in them.

And then, of course, there is the daunting thought of starting over with someone else.

All the stories I have shared of frustration and discouragement are just some examples throughout the years. These were all issues that needed to be handled while insurmountable needs of drought, hunger, and lack continued coming to the door. People wanting food, people asking for jobs, people asking for money for school fees. And the list goes on.

When I felt depleted and at the end of myself, with limited resources, I would say to Sal, "I'm so tired!" and I didn't mean sleepy. I meant just plain tired. Tired of fighting, tired of standing, and of starting over. Tired of sin, corruption, "I don't care" attitudes, not enough money. Tired of electricity outages, borehole issues, termite infestations, and leaky roofs. Tired of everything!

One day, when I felt so helpless, unable to meet the needs of whoever it was at the door, I went inside with tears starting to come. All of a sudden, I heard God say, *Renee, you are not the Savior! There is only one, and it is not you!*

I stopped and just stood there. I cannot express how much of the burden He removed from me as I heard those words in my spirit.

Throughout the rest of that year, He continued to encourage me with the message *Don't quit!* He showed me I wasn't burned out. I was "drained out," and He called me to enter His rest. It took determination to stay the course, but I'm really glad I did!

## Chapter 32

THANKFULLY, IT WASN'T ALL OBSTACLES, FRUSTRATION, AND discouragement. Interspersed in between the hardships were God-given opportunities seen as a "new day dawning," just waiting for us to seize them.

One such opportunity presented itself during a midday phone call.

"I'm sorry . . ." I said into the phone, my attention divided between the call and the task I had in front of me. "Who did you say you're with?"

"I'm calling from the Zambia National AIDS Network." Patience permeated the caller's tone, in spite of my asking her to repeat herself. "I wanted to suggest you apply for a grant."

Now she had my attention. I stopped what I was doing and gave her my full focus. "But . . . why Sons of Thunder?"

She told me she had recently been hired by ZNAN, but prior to her new position, she had worked with the district health office in Kazungula and had been to the clinic and had seen our work with HIV patients.

"If anyone deserves the grant, Sons of Thunder does," she said.

I told her I would be happy to apply, but I was afraid I did not know how. She promised to email me an application. I was to fill it out and send it back to her, and she would take care of the rest.

Imagine, someone from the grant office had actually called and *asked* us to apply. It was an amazing confirmation that God saw our needs.

Sure enough, we were awarded a grant from the Zambia National AIDS Network under the Global Fund. We went to Lusaka to accept the grant and were given a brand-new Nissan Hard Body vehicle to use for five years. We were also awarded funds to build a freestanding laboratory, as well as acquire a CD4 machine and a very large-capacity generator to handle all the main areas of the farm. Funds were also given to cover salaries, diesel, and other operating costs.

God is amazing!

But as always, with provision came continued needs.

It was obvious that our citrus orchard, or what was left of it, was coming to an end. The fruit was souring, the harvest amount dwindling, and people in town were complaining. We contacted the Department of Agriculture and were told that an orchard's life span is about twenty-five years, which was what he estimated our trees to be.

In the past year, Professor—who ran the orchard—had gone back to school and lessened his attention to the orchard, requiring us to look for a replacement. We found that Passmore—an SOT farmer—had experience and loved taking care of the trees, so he became our orchard caretaker. We had discussions about what to do with the orchard, but without funds, we were limited. Although we talked, no decisions were made nor directions given.

One day, Passmore came to the house and asked to speak to me. "I cleared land for the new orchard, and we must plant by August."

He said it very matter-of-factly, clearly assuming that I knew what land he was talking about. But we had never discussed moving the orchard, and I had no idea where to buy new trees. We didn't have money for trees anyway.

"Okay, Passmore." Not wanting to squash his enterprising spirit, I smiled and nodded. "Good job!"

Looking pleased at having delivered his message, he headed back to work.

I closed the door behind him and blurted out, "God, what are You doing? If You want a new orchard, then You are going to have to show me where to get trees."

Having gotten that out of my system, I went back to business as usual.

The very next day—literally, the *very* next day—a man came to the farm to speak with us. His introduced himself as Derek and explained that he was South African and worked in Lusaka for an organization called International Development Enterprises (IDE).

"I have a meeting with the farmers behind your farm," he explained. "I wanted to pass through your property as a shortcut, but I was told to stop at the main house and seek permission first."

Since we'd had some difficulties with people using our farm as a shortcut road, we appreciated Derek's consideration. On his way up the drive, he had passed the Farming God's Way maize fields and gardens, so he asked me about Sons of Thunder and our agriculture.

After a ten-minute conversation, he went on to his meeting.

Three hours later, he again knocked at the door and told me he had never made it to his meeting. "We took the wrong turn and got stuck in the mud. It took us all this time to get unstuck."

I hadn't realized there were more guys in the vehicle when he first came to the door, so I was surprised when he asked if they could come in and talk with me. There were three of them, Derek from IDE and two from an organization called Greenpop. The three men were all South African; Derek was in Zambia to work, and Misha and Jeremy were here to organize an NGO project.

Greenpop's mission was reforestation, or planting trees, and after doing research, they found that Zambia has the second-highest rate of deforestation in the world. Their project was called Trees for Zambia. They told me their plan was to plant a total of five thousand trees in Zambia—at Dambwa Forest, Victoria Falls Heritage Site, twenty different preselected schools, and on five hectares of maize fields with subsistence farmers.

They also had some fruit trees to plant. That was what they were hoping to meet the farmers behind us about.

I caught my breath. Fruit trees?

Since they never made their meeting and they had seen that we already were an organized and well-structured group of farmers using conservation methods, they wanted to know if we would be interested in the tree-planting proposal. Oh, God is good. This was my answer and His plan all along!

The trees they would be planting on the maize fields were called Acacia albida trees, the only tree that loses its leaves during the rainy season, when the maize needs direct sunlight. The leaves cause the land to become more fertile, thus reducing the need for fertilizer. I also saw the advantage of natural God's blanket or mulch without any labor. So yes indeed, I was interested. I felt this was God's next step. He was lighting the next stone for us.

I also told them about our existing orchard, the plan for the new one, and that we didn't know where we were going to get trees. They were an answer to prayer.

The meeting was maybe an hour in length, and they left with the promise to be in touch. That was the beginning of May.

Greenpop's plan was to plant Acacia albida trees on five hectares (approximately twelve acres) on the maize fields of subsistence farmers. That was the area they had already determined and planned for before meeting us.

In the middle of June, Derek came back to Zambia and met with Alexander and me. He measured the ground we had available to plant the maize fields. It measured *exactly* five hectares.

He asked if we would be willing to plant all five hectares. We said yes. We weren't really sure *how*, but we didn't want to miss God's gift. It wasn't just a coincidence to me that it measured exactly five hectares.

We had less than two weeks to prepare. We had to cut down all the dead guava trees, remove the stumps, cut all the grass by hand with slashers, then pile up the grass into heaps around the fields. It took about three days and quite a few men to cut the trees down with axes. Then it took Abson about three days of bulldozer work to uproot and help remove all the trees and stumps. While he was bulldozing, the rest of the men began slashing. That tedious job took about seven straight days with up to seventeen men each day to clear that land.

Besides planting the five hectares of maize land, we also had to plan, purchase, and install an irrigation system for the new citrus orchard. First, Ocrist—who was working as our plumber—and Alexander went to farms around Livingstone to get an idea of different irrigating techniques for the orchards and the new gardens, especially fresh maize gardens.

After that, Ocrist drew up plans, then went to Livingstone to purchase supplies for phase one of the plan—poly pipes and gate valves to install the irrigation system to the new orchard.

It took one day to dig the trenches with the help of Abson and the bulldozer, one day to lay the pipe, and the third day to cover everything with dirt. That was on a Thursday, just six days before the tree planting was to begin.

Friday brought disaster. Four fires were deliberately set at different locations around the farm. One right after the other was ignited by . . . I guess you would call them arsonists . . . and raged so that it was impossible for us to put them all out.

The first one started behind the clinic on the way from the dam coming around the back of the main house and ending at the garden belonging to one of our farm workers, a man named Arnold.

Once that one was under control, someone shouted, "The orchard!"

Everyone ran to the existing orchard, only to discover an already hot and consuming fire. The entire orchard was burned.

We hadn't had time to grieve when someone else shouted, "Behind the tobacco barn!"

Once again, everyone ran to the tobacco barn area to put out the blazes that were threatening Airport Village.

But then someone cried out that there was a blaze at the church. Everyone took off for the church, men and women alike, with all sorts of fire-extinguishing tools—wet bath towels, large "beater" branches, back-pack water sprayers, buckets, containers, bowls, and anything else they could find.

The area near the church that burned was the new orchard and the place where we had just put in the new irrigation system. Thankfully, the pipes had been covered with dirt the day before, and no homes were damaged. We had already decided to let the old orchard go, and only a corner of one garden was damaged. Praise God, no one was hurt!

After all four fires were extinguished to smoldering ash, everyone was exhausted and dismayed. Who had done this, and why? Questions that only God knows the answers to.

No plan of God can be thwarted, so the following Tuesday, Derek arrived with a man from the Conservation Farming Unit of Zambia and gave lessons on the importance of trees and the reason for the reforestation project in the country. He gave practical demonstrations on building a tree nursery and made albida seedlings. It was decided that he did not have to discuss conservation farming or composting, since our farmers were already using those methods.

Early Wednesday morning, compost arrived in truckloads, and midmorning eighty international volunteers arrived. They planted a hundred lemon trees in the new orchard and two hundred albida trees in the maize field areas. Eight of our farmers worked alongside the volunteers, and we provided a cooked Zambian traditional meal of nshima, rice, potatoes, chicken, cabbage, rape, and *mazoe* (an orange drink). What a day!

The planting of trees by the volunteers from Greenpop occurred on three consecutive Wednesdays. By the time they left to return to South Africa, we had three hundred fruit trees, five hundred albida trees, a nursery of thirty albidas to be used as replacements if needed, two hundred seedlings of moringa trees, and a bag of a thousand moringa seeds.

Greenpop came every year for the next six years and planted food forests in different locations. First at the main house, then in all six villages (we had reduced from the original seven to six), and finally at the primary school. They also planted more citrus trees, expanding the orchard. Their initiation to moringa has led to a field of over five thousand moringa trees at our southern corner.

Greenpop loved coming to work with us, bringing international volunteers to our farm. We loved to have them, not only as an opportunity for planting trees but for us to tell them about, and show them, the love of Jesus.

But God wasn't finished showing us tree miracles.

I looked up from my work one day to see a properly dressed gentleman approaching the main house. I asked him to enter and take a seat in the foyer.

Once he was settled and I had gotten him a cold drink, he stated he was from ASNAPP (Agribusiness in Sustainable Natural African Plant Products) and was there to ask if we would like two thousand banana trees free of charge. All we had to do was to go to the area near the Zambezi River and transplant them from there to our farm.

Since our citrus orchard had just been relocated and the land cleared with the arson fire, we had the land available for the bananas, which of course was not a coincidence!

My answer was a resounding "Yes."

We organized a workforce the very next day. Half of the farm dug holes in the new banana plantation, making ready the dirt with manure. The other half went to Livingstone near the river armed with shovels to dig up what turned out to be twelve hundred viable trees and transport them back to Sons of Thunder for transplantation. Two trips with the Hino, and the entire job was completed in a day.

At the end of the day, every family was blessed with a banana tree for their home, and over eleven hundred stood in the new plantation.

Not long after, a man came to the clinic and, seeing the new bananas, introduced himself to Alexander. His name was Roger, and he had worked for years with a company just outside Livingstone that was sponsored from an international source to raise, market, and sell bananas. Everyone knew where their farm was because of the massive irrigation setup seen from one of the main roads. Roger volunteered to help us with our new endeavor, giving instruction to our guys in the raising and cultivating of bananas.

Here's an interesting fact: bananas are not yellow. They are green. But no one will buy green bananas. So we had to learn how to turn the green bananas into the yellow fruit you see in grocery stores. We also had to learn how they grow and reproduce in their planting stations, how to thin the suckers, how and when to fertilize and water.

It was a new learning process, and God had not only provided the source (ASNAPP) but also the teacher (Roger). God is amazing!

## Chapter 33

BESIDES SAL'S DIAGNOSIS AND TREATMENT AND GABE'S ISSUES, WE also had the declining health of Sal's dad to contend with. He had suffered for three years with Parkinson's disease, affecting both his physical and mental capabilities. He progressively went downhill.

In September of 2012, we decided we'd better head back to the States if we wanted to see him again. We were on the plane on a Thursday, arrived in Maryland on Friday night, then drove to Pittsburgh on Saturday. We reached their house at twelve thirty p.m., and he passed at four. God is good.

Family time and the burial happened on Tuesday. The military service at the gravesite was touching.

Wednesday at three a.m., we rushed to the hospital. Sal's only niece had gone into premature labor and delivered a four-pound, four-ounce baby girl four weeks early.

On the way back to Sal's mom's house, we heard that Gabe had turned gray and needed to be resuscitated. He was life-flighted to Children's Hospital, where he spent three days in ICU for tests. The doctors found everything normal and sent him home.

We spent the rest of Thursday and Friday taking Sal's mom to the doctor and doing things for her around the house. Then we went back to Maryland so we could spend Saturday seeing all the grandkids at whatever activity they were in: flag football at nine a.m., gymnastics at ten, football at eleven, and soccer at two. It was fun!

We visited Mark Saturday night at his house. On Sunday, we attended church and spent the afternoon with my best friend, Roberta, who told me that another friend was looking to rent a house.

Monday, we met with that friend for coffee. She and her husband were eager to rent our house (which hadn't sold, after being on the market for one year after Shaun and his family had moved into a house of their own). Monday night, we had dinner out with Scott and his family. Tuesday, we packed and collected last-minute things to take back. We went to dinner with Pastor Jerry and Cheryl, who then took us to the airport.

We got back to Zambia on Thursday in time for outreach on Friday. *Whew.*

God was in control for us to get so much done in such a short time. Talk about a whirlwind trip!

While we were gone, Janet had moved into the clinic apartment and stayed the entire time. Collin screened patients. Janet, Bridget, Dorica, and Precious delivered seventeen babies!

Alexander went to South Africa to start certification as a national trainer for Farming God's Way, so Abson took the reins. Linah had two CARE International five-day conferences at the conference center. The preschool went on a field trip to the airport on a Saturday in the lorry and went for ice cream afterward.

The schoolteachers had to go to Senkobo to a one-day workshop and swearing-in for the upcoming seventh-grade exams, which would be held at SOT later that month, since we were made a testing site. Terry serviced and repaired our vehicles, and Advent and the ladies scrubbed the floors in the main house.

So, in our absence, God was in control in Zambia as well.

Upon our return, I had much to pray about. I am not a theologian or an expert on God. What I share is strictly from my own experience, my own walk with God.

He says in His Word, "My sheep hear my voice" (John 10:27 ESV).

I am merely one of His sheep, knowing my shepherd and hearing His voice.

In spite of all the progress we were making, some people back home still had a hard time understanding our mission. Wanting a very close relative to understand, I explained, "God told us to start a clinic on the farm in Zambia, Africa."

Her response disappointed me greatly. "If you never say that again," she said curtly, "I think we will get along much better."

I was shattered. Didn't she believe me? Wasn't she interested?

I asked God, "Why did she have that reaction? Why is it that I still can't talk about what we are doing here at Sons of Thunder with some family members?"

God led me to John 8:47, which says, "Whoever belongs to God hears what God says. The reason you do not hear is that you do not belong to God."

Wow! God had answered, and I understood. The prerequisite to hearing God is to belong to Him, to be one of His sheep. The way to do that is easy. You just have to ask Him to come into your heart and be Lord of your life.

It says in the Bible in Romans 10:9–10, "If you declare with your mouth, 'Jesus is Lord,' and believe in your heart that God raised Him from the dead, you will be saved. For it is with your heart that you believe and are justified, and it is with your mouth that you profess your faith and are saved."

Praise God!

One of the things we never had was a plan of our own. People, especially funders, would ask what our five-year plan was. Without a detailed five-year plan, some organizations, even Christian ones, will not give funding or financial support. We always laughed to ourselves because we had a hard time just doing what He put in front of us each day. We were always so busy, and I think God made it that way so that we wouldn't have time to make a plan.

Another thing we discovered, mostly from mission teams, was that the ones who came to SOT with their own plan usually failed. Revival meetings would be sparsely attended or rained out. Building projects would remain unfinished due to lack of supplies in town. Computer gurus would end up burning up the computer because they were not used to 220-volt electricity.

But the ones who came prayed up and ready to serve, doing whatever was needed or open to whatever God had in store for them, would be blessed and succeed.

A perfect example was a mission team who came to us. The two women already had in mind to do Bible studies, one with the women and one with the grade-seven girls. The three men, however, said they would do anything we needed. They were just coming to serve. The whole team had spent many days of prayer and preparation prior to their departure from the US.

Before they arrived at SOT, we received a box of Sunday-school material from one of our church supporters in the States. In the box was a teaching for adults on spiritual authority and men as heads of their household. I felt God say, *This is for the SOT men*, but I knew I was not the one to teach them.

Sal was way too busy at the clinic, and he wasn't feeling stirred to teach. So when the team arrived, I asked the leader to look over the study with his team of men and see if they felt like doing a teaching with the guys.

After discussion and seeking God, they said they would do it. It ended up being a blessing for all. The Americans taught the lessons over a week and included a foot-washing and an ice cream night. The men at Sons of Thunder belong to different denominations and attend different churches, but they thoroughly enjoyed being together as SOT men, worshipping, praying, testifying, and learning God's Word together.

The ladies had a wonderful time, as ladies always do. Their lessons included crafts, and they made their own T-shirts. The schoolgirls learned about abstinence and had an overnight at the school. They all enjoyed and were blessed. But the Americans were also amazingly impacted and blessed at how God showed up when someone is willing to be used and comes without their own plan.

After the mission team left for the States, the Zambian men at SOT started their own men's group and not only met together monthly, but also started going out in ministry, sharing the Word in surrounding communities. Those meetings are still ongoing today.

I was in the office one afternoon working on the computer when the houseworker—who fills the water tanks and works outside—came to the door, a little out of breath. "Come quick; there are visitors."

Instantly switching gears, I followed him out to the veranda and saw that there was a family of four in the driveway with three bicycles. Not your usual bicycles, but three heavy-duty ones with what looked like mule sacks on the sides for carrying things. Both of the parents and the girl—who appeared to be around ten years of age—had their own bicycles. A boy of around seven rode on the front of Mom's bike in a carrier seat.

As I went down to join them in the driveway, the woman gave me a bright smile.

"Bonjour!" She continued in very broken English and with a distinct French accent. "We are looking for a place to stay the night. We asked people when we were on the road, and they directed us here."

It took a while to get the story, but they had traveled on bicycles all the way from France. Really! They had taken the children out of school for a year and had been traveling by bicycle, staying in local villages with headmen or at different missions, eating local foods, bathing in rivers or other bodies of water. Talk about the ultimate camping trip! The mom had been doing a bit of homeschooling along the way, and wherever they went, they learned about life and culture and nature and people.

Needless to say, we put them up in our conference center. Finding Sons of Thunder to be a varied and interesting place, they stayed for a couple of weeks and became involved. The children, Zoe and Yan, went to school with the local friends they had made. Mom and Dad, Nathalie and Jean Marie, helped with farming and tree planting, as their stay coincided with that of the Greenpop volunteers.

They were very well received by all of us at Sons of Thunder, and it was a sad day when they decided to continue on their way. With bags packed and the bicycles at the door, they came to the main house to say goodbye. Jean Marie told me he had a mapped-out plan to continue on the other side of Zambia to see more waterfalls, but if the way was blocked or he ran into any difficulty, they would come back here if that was okay. I said that of course, this would not be a problem.

As Jean Marie took Zoe and Yan to get situated on their bikes, Nathalie lingered and asked to talk with me. We went back into the house and sat down, and I waited patiently for her to formulate her words, hoping I would be able to understand and converse with her.

Finally, she looked me in the eye and carefully voiced her thought. "Renee, I want what you have."

In my heart, I knew she was not talking about anything material. She was asking for Jesus.

Oh my! I prayed silently, asking the Holy Spirit to help me, especially with the language barrier. In the next fifteen minutes, as the rest of the family waited outside, I walked her through the good news and salvation prayer in the best broken English-French conversation possible. I wanted to give her a Bible to take with her, but all I had was an English New Testament. I gave it to her and told her God would make a way for her to understand. And she left.

After waving goodbye and watching them pedal off down the driveway, I returned to the house alone and started talking to God. "I didn't have a French Bible for her. Please open her eyes to see and understand and her heart to receive." That was all I prayed.

About an hour later, the houseworker once again came to the door and told me there were more visitors. When I went outside, I saw a Land Rover filled with four Americans, three men and a woman. They were part of an NGO and explained that they had driven past the Sons of Thunder sign on the main road. After they had gotten a couple of kilometers north toward Lusaka, the driver had pulled over off the road.

He said, "I'm sorry, guys, but I have to turn around and go back to that sign that said Sons of Thunder. I think God has something for us there, and I have to go find out."

So there they were at the door, and we started talking. I answered their questions about SOT and even gave them a quick tour. When we got back to the house, they still did not know why they had come. It was my turn to ask them some questions. I asked them to tell us about themselves, which they did.

Then I asked, "Where are you going?"

They told me they were on their way to the Congo. I remembered that they speak French in the Congo, so I asked if they by any chance had any French Bibles with them.

Looking a bit confused, one of them nodded. "Yes, as a matter of fact we do."

I smiled, my heart filling with understanding. "Oh my, I know why you are here." And I told them about Nathalie and the French family.

The Bibles were packed in the back of their vehicle, but they happily unloaded it to get to them. They handed me a French Bible, and we all prayed.

After farewell hugs and thanks, they were on their way. The driver had told me that he felt good that he had indeed heard God say *Turn around and go back to Sons of Thunder. There is something there for you.*

When I was alone once again and closed the door behind me, I glanced upward. "Thank You, God!" My heart was full. I knew the French family would be returning.

Sure enough, a week later, the family showed up on the doorstep once again, and they ended up staying for a month right there at the main house, because the conference center was in use. I could not wait to tell Nathalie how much God loves her! I couldn't wait to tell her the story about how Americans in a vehicle on their way to the Congo had passed the sign, turned around not knowing why, and came back to Sons of Thunder. And the reason God brought them back was because He had heard her hunger for Him. He was making sure she had a French Bible so she could read His Word and get to know Him more.

Over the years, God's wonders would never cease.

When Alexander and I were asked to do a presentation at an FGW training in 2014, we felt like we had more than enough experience to draw on.

Our PowerPoint presentation showed the history of farming at Sons of Thunder and how things had improved immensely with Farming God's Way. We also spoke and showed pictures of all the challenges we had faced over the years. Crops had been destroyed by the neighbor's cows, by elephants, by bush pigs, twice by arson fires, and even by *frost*, which Alexander had never seen before in Zambia.

We also told them about the one thing we hadn't done . . .

We hadn't quit! We just picked ourselves up and started again.

It was a well-received encouragement to all the farmers in the training that day. Our hope was that they would remember Sons of Thunder and its example whenever discouragement hit.

For our part, whenever things were going really well and God was moving, bringing opportunities, and advancing Sons of Thunder, there was always something to discourage or distract us from whatever He wanted us to focus on next.

One day, I heard a car pull up in the gravel drive in front of the main house. I had just gotten up to go see who it was when Sal rushed past me, nearly knocking me down on his way to the foyer.

"Lock the door behind me." The serious tone of his voice got my heart racing.

After doing as he'd asked, I went to the window, where I watched my husband stride toward a familiar-looking car. My breath caught. That car belonged to none other than the old missionary.

For the past eight years, all the drama surrounding this man had more or less died down. We hadn't spoken and only saw him and his wife on rare occasions while shopping in town.

I strained to listen, grateful that the hot afternoon had necessitated the opening of all the windows. The man got out of his vehicle and stomped toward Sal. By the fire in his eyes and the redness in his cheeks, I knew this was no friendly social call.

"I'm still a director." He waved his arms in a way that made me question if this might come to blows. "I demand to see the books."

*The books?* What the heck?

He told Sal he was still on the company records in Lusaka and still had rights.

As Sal tried to reason with him, I noticed that several of our staff members were doing exactly what I was doing—leaning out a window or peering around the corner of a building in an attempt to hear the dispute. Alexander was the only one who ran to the scene. He inserted himself between the two men and persuaded the old missionary to leave.

That drama started a series of legal actions that lasted the next three years and ended in 2017 with a judgment from the Supreme Court of Zambia to protect Sons of Thunder and all its inhabitants.

God fights the battle and vindicates.

## Chapter 34

IT WAS OFFICIAL. SONS OF THUNDER MEN WERE "DIFFERENT," AND it became noticeable to the outside communities.

Back in December, an older man from a neighboring village came to the SOT men's interdenominational meeting and gave his heart to the Lord. In March, the same man showed up at the clinic, feeling poorly. A group of SOT men gathered and formed a circle of prayer around him.

A few days later, word came that he had died during the night and was being buried the next day in the village. The men from SOT all felt the need to go, so they hurriedly assembled food—mealie meal, cabbages, cooking oil—and tools to help dig a grave in the stony ground. Then about twenty of them set out to attend the funeral. There were also a few women who went to lend support and comfort to the wives and family.

The man had two wives and nineteen children (no, I am not kidding). When our guys reached the man's home, they found out there was no food to feed the mourners. The family was surprised and very happy that, thanks to our men, they now had something to serve.

There had been a mix-up with the delivery of the coffin, so the SOT men stepped up to help, using their phones and talk time to fix the issue. While waiting for the coffin to arrive, our men went to dig the grave. It was a demonstration of the love of Jesus. "Love in action," as Alexander would come to call it.

About a week later, I was visited by the headman of the same neighboring village. He told me about the gift of food and demonstration of love and kindness from the SOT men.

"Things would not have been the same without them. They provided all the food for the funeral. We have never seen such a thing before."

Seeming to get a little choked up, he continued. "Even the senior headman was amazed and said we needed to come and say thank you. Since I can't manage to go to each man's door, I thought of coming to you and Alexander as the leaders. I know now that when I die, I will be buried nicely."

This might appear to be a small thing, but in rural Zambia, where everyone takes care of *himself*, this was a very big selfless demonstration of love. And by a group of interdenominational men, to boot!

The next Sunday, Alexander preached the sermon about *love*—specifically, *love in action*. He used a few key Scriptures, but the one I recall was 1 John 3:18: "Dear children, let us not love with words or speech but with actions and in truth."

It was an awesome message, with encouragement to the body of believers.

Not only were our men different, but Sons of Thunder was becoming well known to all the outside communities as a "different" kind of place. People at SOT cared. They were always there to answer a need. The clinic was open around the clock, and maternity calls were always answered with transport provided. Sons of Thunder became the place where everyone wanted to have their baby.

Our one-room, two-bed labor-and-delivery area in the clinic could not handle the onslaught of babies. Sometimes we had mattresses on the floors in all the rooms at the clinic to accommodate our laboring mothers. And whenever a woman had her baby, she had to wrap a chitenge around herself and walk through the waiting room of patients to go to the bathroom. It was less than ideal, by our standards.

Having heard God say *Raise the standard* long ago as part of our preparation, we knew this was one area that had to be addressed. But without money or any provision, we were not moving fast enough. So God "pushed" the plan to build a new maternity center, making us take the first step in faith. The maternity center was birthed in faith.

We decided to dig the footer, since that was something we could do without money. We would show God our faith, taking the first step with what we had. And of course, God was faithful in return. What He starts, He brings to completion.

The initial money came from friends who knew our situation and decided to stand with us in faith. For that seed, we were eternally grateful.

But there were other God stories that started happening. One was with Hope Church in Dayton, Ohio.

Hope Church was looking for an international/global cause for their "Christmas with a Cause." They were centering their theme around Mary and the delivery of the baby Jesus in a stable—because there was no clean, good place to be found (not unlike many of the deliveries here in the villages). Even the music that had been selected was around Mary and the birth, such as "Mary, Did You Know?"

Their committee met, and a woman who had been here before and knew about the need for the maternity center from my blog suggested with excitement the Sons of Thunder Maternity Center. The group agreed and took it to the pastor, who supported the cause wholeheartedly. The magnitude of their financial contribution cannot be understated.

The second story centered on a young wife and mother by the name of Jessica.

Jessica, longtime family friend of Pastor Jerry, lost her fight with pancreatic cancer at the end of 2013, leaving behind a devoted husband and four small children. By my estimation, the oldest a girl was about ten, and the three younger boys were approximately eight, seven, and five.

Over the course of her illness, she and her husband, J. D., had been visited by Pastor Jerry, and he would tell them what was happening at Sons of Thunder in Zambia. They would talk of how she would go with him once she was well. She was very much stirred with the maternity center and wanted to be a part of it. After her death, in her honor, her husband fulfilled her desire to see the maternity center completed by giving us a significant donation.

It was decided to name it Jessica's Hope Maternity Center.

The Zambians also wanted to recognize God's goodness. After all, it would be the surrounding communities that would benefit from this facility.

The Sons of Thunder Zambians planned a grand-opening event for the center. They hand delivered invitations to Chief Mukuni, the leader of

the Toka Leya tribe, located in the Southern Province of Zambia, requesting him to be the guest of honor. They also delivered invitations to the
mayor of Livingstone, the area councillor, the Ministry of Health, and
the senior headman, as well as twenty-six headmen from the surrounding
areas and their respective community members.

They invited two local television stations and the Mosi-O-Tunya radio
station to cover the event and provide tech support and a sound system.
They got the seventh graders from SOT Primary School to sing the national
anthem and hired a videographer to make complimentary DVDs.

They went to the army to rent tents and prepared to feed over a
thousand people. We bought a cow, a hundred chickens, and twenty bags
of the better mealie meal to make nshima, and the farmers all provided
vegetables. They set up two cooking areas: one for dignitaries and one for
the common folk.

On June 24, 2015, the representatives from Hope Church and Jessica's
family, kids included, came to Zambia to attend the grand opening and
dedicate the finished building.

It was a wonderful day filled with speeches, formalities, laughter, and
good food. We had a proper ribbon cutting and the presentation of a sign
for the outside of the building. J. D. and the four children were able to see
Jessica's desire fulfilled and knew that her name would be forever remembered in this concrete building of hope and new life.

Every time the members of Hope Church hear "Mary, Did You
Know?" or remember "Christmas with a Cause," they can be encouraged
that God called and they listened. They made a difference in Zambia.

The only disappointment that day was that Pastor Jerry and his wife,
Cheryl, were not able to attend the dedication. Pastor Jerry had to undergo
triple bypass surgery the week before he was scheduled to travel here.
Thankfully, he recovered nicely from the surgery, but he was sorely missed.

All of us at Sons of Thunder are very thankful for God's Providence
and gave all glory to Him! This story warmed my heart and let me know
that sometimes being obedient to what we hear from God means taking a
small step of faith, even when we don't see the solution or have the finances
and when others laugh or scoff.

In our case, that small step of faith—doing only what we could do with what we already had—was the very step that showed God our willingness to be obedient to what He was calling us to do. He took that mustard-seed faith and moved the mountain!

I guess 2016 must have been a pivotal year without us realizing it. Looking back, it was during this year that God sent many messages, all with the theme *Stay the course, and don't quit.*

As we prepared to go on furlough, I had been asking Sal if we could go somewhere for a little rest before heading home to the bustle of visiting with family and friends, going to doctor appointments, and supporting churches.

We received a card from one of our volunteers with a beautiful mountain picture on the front. When Sal saw the picture, he pointed to it and said, "I'd go *there*."

Looking at the postcard, I discovered that it was Glacier National Park in Montana. Before he could change his mind, I booked our flights home for furlough with a trip to Montana first. Neither of us had ever been there before, and it sounded like an adventure.

We found ourselves there at the end of May. The whole park wasn't open for the season because the snow and ice had not yet melted completely.

After some needed rest, we asked the concierge at the hotel what he recommended we see.

"Avalanche Lake." Spreading out a brochure, he pointed to a map. "Go to the end of Going-to-the-Sun Road, park your vehicle, cross over a little bridge on foot, and you're right there."

That sounded easy enough. Coming from Zambia, we were not equipped to hike. I had only flip-flops, and we didn't think to take water bottles, because it seemed so near according to his directions.

It turned out to be a five-mile hike! We would never have attempted it if we had known that in advance.

Sal had been fighting a cold since we'd arrived in Montana, and the journey to Avalanche Lake was a hike up the mountain. On the way up, Sal was coughing and had trouble breathing, and his hip hurt.

At one point, I asked him if he wanted to quit.

"No." He firmed his shoulders. "I want to see what God has for me. He called me here for a reason, and I don't want to miss it."

We both knew if we gave up, we would not try again. So we continued. Slow and steady with encouragement along the way, beautiful colored rocks, small waterfalls, and an occasional view of a mountaintop through the trees.

Each time we saw someone coming from the opposite direction, we'd ask them how much farther. Three times at three different places, we were told, "Thirty more minutes!"

It felt discouraging, but we trudged on.

Finally, we rounded a bend and stopped in our tracks. We had reached the goal, and it was more than worth it. It was breathtaking!

Avalanche Lake was beyond beautiful. The massive mountains to the left were covered in green trees and brown rock, the mountains to the right were snow-covered, and the mountains directly ahead had a small waterfall in the middle.

As we slowly walked toward the lake, we were speechless, taking it all in. We sat on a rock and felt so small in comparison to our surroundings. All we could think of was the majesty of God. It brought to mind the song "I Can Only Imagine," by MercyMe.

After resting *literally* in His presence and taking photos to capture the magnificence, we started back down the mountain. Sal was no longer coughing, but the way down was difficult for me. My legs and feet hurt because of my shoes.

As I struggled, God started to speak. I remembered some things from John Bevere's book *Relentless*, which I had felt led by God to read: The only failure is a quitter. To be relentless means to be unyielding, unstoppable, uncompromising, determined to complete the task at hand. A relentless believer continues despite the obstacles. He who finishes gets the reward.

If you quit before the finish, you miss out on all God has for you. If we had stopped anywhere along the journey upward, we would have missed the beauty and majesty God had for us.

Even after we arrived at home, God continued to talk about the mountain. We went to North Carolina to see friends and stayed a few days in their mountain home. While there, I read this from my daily devotional book:

> Together we will forge a pathway up the high mountain. The journey is arduous at times and you are weak. Someday you will dance light-footed on the high peaks; but for now, your walk is often plodding and heavy.
>
> All I require of you is to take the next step, clinging to My hand for strength and direction. Though the path is difficult and the scenery dull at the moment, there are sparkling surprises just around the bend. Stay on the path I have chosen for you. It is truly the *path of life*.[2]

# Chapter 35

THE RAINY SEASON ALWAYS BRINGS CHALLENGES.

One day, Sal delivered five babies in a twenty-four-hour period, three of whom came in the middle of the night. On the way to his third maternity call of the night, it was pouring rain, along with thunder and lightning. He did not have his rain jacket and hat because he had basically been out all day going from one call to the next.

He went to Makalanguzu, a rural village near Livingstone, and picked up his laboring maternity patient and her neighbor. On his way back on one of the village bush roads, the back tires of the vehicle slid in the mud, and they ended up in a maize field. He tried to get out but had no luck. If he'd continued, he would have sunk deeper into the mud.

Not able to reach anyone else, he called me at three thirty in the morning.

"I'm stuck in the mud!" He had to shout for me to hear him over the downpour. "Worse yet, I'm not sure any of our vehicles would be able to reach us." He explained that he had the patient and would probably end up delivering the baby in the back of the vehicle.

"Don't worry." I tried to sound reassuring, although I knew the situation was less than ideal. "I'll work on a solution." But when I got off the phone, I had no idea what to do!

I prayed. Then I made a few calls, but people still had their cell phones turned off for the night. I managed to reach Abson on his wife's phone (smart woman!), and he told me the only answer was the tractor. I sent the watchman to Padmore's house to get him to come and rescue Sal and the mom.

Abson, Japhet, and Padmore were the rescue team. When they reached Sal, they found him soaking wet without his raincoat, standing in in his bare feet in water up to the running board of the vehicle. Turned out he was in the valley of the area where all the rain water gathered!

They told him to get in the vehicle with the patient, and they began getting it unstuck.

Once it was out of the mud, Abson drove, with the neighbor in the front seat and Sal in the back with the patient. As they traveled over the many bumps on the back road, Sal delivered the baby in the back seat. He handed the baby to the neighbor and returned to working with the new mom—all while Abson continued driving.

This might sound like a catastrophe, but really . . . it's just life in Africa!

Life in Africa has been an adventure, to say the least. But as the saying goes, "You come to change Africa, and Africa changes you!"

Sometimes I can't believe how much Africa has changed me. Anyone who knew "pre-Africa" Renee would not even think that I could do some of the things I've done.

Imagine going into the bathroom, lifting the toilet seat, and discovering a frog looking up at you from the water. This became a regular occurrence because we had a frog living in the septic tank (gross, right?), and he would randomly pop up in one of two toilets that shared the same septic system.

I did not want to tell our visiting volunteers about our little frog friend, since they had already freaked over a spider on one of the banana bunches. However, one morning, my little friend once again greeted me from the bowl of the toilet. Every other time, he had been as frightened as I was and immediately headed down the drain and into oblivion. But that day was different.

That time, he didn't seem startled, and he didn't swim away. So I lifted both the lid and the seat and crept out of the room.

I closed the door and waited a bit. When I opened it again, I found him seated on the toilet tank. He let me close the lid and the seat, so there was no escape back to the prison of the septic system.

I then nudged him into a basket and carried him like royalty outside, where I set him free. A captive released! What a great way to start the day.

Between August 2016 and October 2017, we had twenty-four SOT ladies give birth.

After a four-month maternity leave, I noticed all these mothers having difficulty returning to their jobs, which they needed to help support their households. Zambian women always keep their babies swaddled on their backs in a chitenge. They do everything with their baby attached—convenient for breastfeeding on demand.

Some of the jobs they held, however, were with food and in places babies did not belong, such as the clinic and conference center. The solution was to open a childcare room to provide free day care so the moms could work hands free.

We renovated a bottom room in the tobacco barn by plastering walls, putting in a ceiling, and adding a window and a light fixture to make it brighter. We painted the room and added a new door with new hardware to lock. Our resident artist, Munkombwe, painted pictures on the walls.

Then we asked around for the consensus of who would be good caregivers for the babies. It was unanimous that Jenala and Eucaria would be ideal, and the two ladies agreed to take the positions. Both ladies went shopping for the supplies they felt were needed. Eunice even made uniforms and aprons for the two caregivers.

All the ladies with babies, or who were pregnant at the time, were called to a meeting in order to announce the opening of the new childcare room. It would be for babies and toddlers four months to three years old, at which time the kids would start preschool. Everyone was happy with the new innovative idea in Zambia.

Back in January of 2017, I felt my heart breaking for three kids whose life stories had stolen the opportunity for them to go to school. They were all good kids. And good students.

First was Given. He completed grade nine in the village at Zimba but failed his ninth-grade qualifying exam. His father and mother divorced, and his father told him that because he was lazy and not serious, he would not pay for any more schooling.

After Given sat out a year and didn't do much of anything, his brother-in-law, Pastor Winfred, brought him to live with him at SOT.

Given worked until he saved enough money to start grade eight at Global Samaritan School. He worked on Saturdays and after school, doing piece-work in people's gardens. He put himself through grades eight and nine without any help and passed his grade-nine qualifying exam with very high marks, getting posted to a boarding school.

Tuition costs in grades ten through twelve were much higher, and the cost of boarding and transport were not within his reach. He looked for a day school in Livingstone, which would not involve boarding and transport costs. But still, tuition costs were high. He had proven his commitment to education, so I prayed he would receive help.

Next was Naomi. Her parents were Winifredah and Enoch, the couple who started the patient feeding program at the clinic, growing vegetables and cooking meals. Unfortunately, Enoch was an alcoholic, and after years of trying to hide the drinking and other marital problems, Enoch left the farm and his family to marry another woman. Winifredah subsequently got a certificate of divorce and had been raising her three children alone. She worked as the head cleaner at the clinic and then transferred to the conference center to be mentored for Linah's position. Additionally, she had her own hair salon at her house and was one of the suppliers at the tack shop.

Naomi, her oldest child, graduated grade seven and passed the qualifying exam. She had been accepted at Global Samaritan School for grades eight and nine. Again, the fees for the upper grades are higher and put Winifredah in a struggle. There was no help from the ex-husband, as he was in poor health due to the history of alcohol abuse. He couldn't work and was being taken care of by his brothers. Winifredah thought of sending Naomi to her brother, who lived in another district, so he could help send her to school. But frankly, often young girls are sexually abused as a result of being sent away. We strongly discouraged that avenue.

So I prayed for help for this single mom.

Third was Gift, who graduated at the top of his seventh-grade class and passed his qualifying exam with excellent marks. His father, Chrispine, had just taken a second wife and was dismissed from the farm.

Chrispine had dropped off his first wife (Gift's mom) and the kids in the village with her mother, far away from Global Samaritan, where Gift had been accepted into grades eight and nine. Chrispine then went to stay with his new second wife and her two children.

When this happened, Gift walked to the farm to see me, crying because he wasn't going to be able to go to school.

My heart broke for him. We talked with his mom and found a place for him to stay at SOT so he could go to school at Global Samaritan. He was extremely happy and moved in with Justin, who worked at the clinic.

Gift worked during the break and on Saturdays. This boy had great potential and loved school, but his mom, whose world had been turned upside down, didn't know how she would continue to pay for it. I prayed for help for him.

Not knowing what else to do, I felt led to write their stories on the Sons of Thunder, Zambia, Facebook page. I thought, *Maybe, God . . . if I just tell their stories . . .*

Within *one* hour after posting these three stories, the SOT office in the US called to tell me that all three students had been sponsored!

I was shocked. Then I started thinking. If people were willing to help these three, maybe there would be a willingness to sponsor others. Education is so important for the advancement of not only the individual student but also of Zambia as a nation.

The program had to be a balance, a joint effort between the student, the parent, and the sponsor. It could not be just a handout. Everyone would have to do their part. So when the Student Sponsorship Program was developed, the idea was to raise support from the sponsor for tuition, uniforms, books, and boarding fees if needed. The parents would be responsible for food, bedding, shoes, and transport costs. The students would handle toiletries and other small school supplies like pens, paper, and notebooks.

Since the students would need a way to make money on their own, a work-study program was developed called the Blessed Fund. This program would involve students in grades eight through twelve and would take place during school breaks. The students would work four hours a day, stop for lunch, then return for some kind of lesson in the afternoon. At the end of the break period, a back-to-school shopping day would be provided for the students to learn how to budget their money and help their parents buy school supplies.

The program was intended to promote a good work ethic and teach the children how it feels to earn your own money and purchase what you need. The Blessed Fund and the Student Sponsorship Program have both been very successful. The seventh-grade graduates can't wait to start working with the Blessed Fund! It has become a rite of passage, and the kids feel excited to be part of it.

## Chapter 36

ALL MEDICAL PROFESSIONALS IN ZAMBIA MUST BE PROVIDED housing.

In 2017, we were surprised when the district health office posted an RN and a lab technician to the Sons of Thunder Clinic. Audrey and Rodgers were our first government-posted workers, and we were thrilled to have two medical professionals who would be paid by the government.

We just needed to be able to accommodate them, which thankfully, we could. We put Audrey in an apartment in the tobacco barn and Rodgers in one of the old classrooms that we'd renovated into an efficiency apartment.

At that time, we were in the process of building the first medical staff house in anticipation of Collin graduating nursing school in December. He had worked as a clinical assistant for over six years while studying on his own and completing both his grade-nine and grade-twelve qualifying exams, while also financially helping his sisters through school. He had been sponsored to nursing school by an individual donor who had met him while they were on a short-term mission trip here.

Collin graduated in December 2017 from nursing school, moved into his new staff house, and started work as an RN in January 2018.

When the builders completed Collin's house, they began construction of the second medical staff house, which was slated for Audrey.

But then something unexpected happened.

Pastor Winfred was one of our headmen and worked at the clinic as a clinical assistant. He also pastored a church that Sons of Thunder had built in Kasiya.

For years, he worked Monday through Friday at the clinic and went to Kasiya for the weekends to hold church services.

Some time back, Pastor Winfred said he felt he was supposed to move his family to Kasiya, but people at SOT kept telling him, "No, stay here."

Sometime around March of 2018, his mud house collapsed for no apparent reason. There was a random whirlwind that damaged only his house and no others in the village. The mud wall fell, damaging furniture, but thankfully, all the family was unharmed.

Again, he thought to go to Kasiya, but supporters from the United States, hearing his plight, sent money for him to rebuild his house at SOT. While Sal and I were on furlough, he began working with Pathias, the head bricklayer, to build a brick house.

The amount of money he was given should have been enough to complete an entire house, but because of a mistake with measurements, it only finished the brickwork. Sal and I offered to pay Winfred back the amount of money he had spent so he could build a reasonable house for his family. We would take over the building and use it for a hostel for medical staff. It was agreed upon, but before another house could be started, Winfred confessed that he felt he was supposed to go to Kasiya to pastor the church there full time.

After talking to him and hearing the story of how he felt God was calling him but he wasn't listening, we encouraged him to pray. The best place is always where God wants us to be. Even if we have fear, God promises to never leave us. He is the provider.

A couple of days later, he and his wife, Harriet, came to let us know they had decided to go to Kasiya. We all agreed. We gave him the amount of money he had been given for the house so he could have a pastor's house built near his church.

Pastor Winfred used that money to build a beautiful brick house near the Kasiya church—right where God wanted him. He and his wife were very happy there and were making a difference in the area. They still continued to be part of the SOT family. His children were included with the SOT Student Sponsorship Program, and they worked on breaks with the Blessed Fund.

God's plan is always better than man's plan. If the house had not collapsed, Winfred would not have been given money from supporters. If the mistake in the measurements had not happened, he would have built his house in the wrong place. And if the "mistake house" had not had all the brickwork completed, SOT would not have even thought to build a hostel for medical workers, which we have put to good use.

God is at work even when we can't see it—even when we make mistakes along the way.

"And we know that God causes all things to work together for good to those who love God, to those who are called according to His purpose" (Romans 8:28 NASB).

In March 2018, we were once again surprised. The district health office posted two more nurses, Felistus and Rhoda. Thankfully, we had one more apartment in the tobacco barn that they agreed to share.

The second medical staff house was completed sometime during the year, and Audrey moved in. We began construction on medical staff house number three. The hostel had also been completed by the end of the year, and since we had more females, we decided it would be for single ladies. Felistus and Rhoda moved in.

Things had been pretty much the same for the past few years—people working and farming their gardens, kids going to school and working on breaks with the Blessed Fund, meetings and workshops being held at the conference center, patients being seen and babies delivered at the clinic, short-term mission teams staying at the main house, and the builders moving from one job to the next.

But then, in November 2018, things changed.

After listening to a sermon by Pastor Michael Todd from Transformation Church in Oklahoma called "Recalculating: The Pace Has Changed," I felt God was speaking directly to us at Sons of Thunder. I felt strongly He was telling us that He was changing the pace for Sons of Thunder. No longer were we going to just be maintaining day to day, but He was about to be the "all of a sudden" God.

I told Sal and Alexander to hold on to their hats because I felt God was going to be moving fast and big things were coming.

I remembered the message Sal and I had received on our trip to Montana in 2016: *Don't quit; stay the course . . . there are surprises just around the bend.*

In the beginning of 2019, two full-time clinical officers, Mirriam and Mathews, were added to the medical staff, hired by SOT. Medical professional staff now consisted of three clinical officers (including Sal), four nurses, and a lab technician.

With the increase in professional staff, the district health office, for the very first time, gave us a catchment area (a geographic area of responsibility for medical services and statistical purposes) and officially named Sons of Thunder as one of their rural health centers. Our numbers were just too great, and we had been noticed by the Provincial and National Ministries of Health.

When we were given a catchment area, three communities were added that were very far away: Maunga, Makumba, and Libala. In order to assist their patient population and looking at God's provision of more staff, Sal suggested we see them in their communities. Maunga outreach was once a month, on the first Saturday. Makumba and Libala were twice a month. Makumba was the second and third Saturday of the month and Libala the third and fourth Wednesday.

We continued outreaches to Siandazya, which was added when we stopped going to Kasiya. The government had finally staffed that building, and now they had their own official rural health center under Livingstone District. We had also been seeing patients in Makoli and Natebe. Makoli had been started years earlier as a twice-a-month outreach, but now they were asking us to come to their new building—which had been officially dedicated—and see patients three times a week.

Natebe was an elderly community that had asked us to come to them because of the age and condition of their community members. Siandazya outreach was the second Wednesday of the month, and Natebe was the fourth Saturday. Mobile ART was still on Fridays to Kabuyu, Katapazi, Sinde, and Siakasipa. It was decided to make the three days a week to Makoli the same days as the main SOT clinic: Monday, Tuesday and Thursday. Staff would have to be scheduled to cover two sites on the same days.

Besides being open twenty-four hours a day, seven days a week, Sons of Thunder Medical was going out to ten different outreach sites every month.

Word also got out to the different nursing schools in the area that Sons of Thunder was a safe place with good accommodations and varied clinical experience for their three-week rural health rotation. Other schools from Livingstone, Choma, and Monze started to come.

But medical was not the only area of change and increase.

During 2019, Alexander was blessed to have a brick house constructed for his family, right at the end of the driveway and convenient to the main house. While his house was being built, Sal and I went home on furlough.

After coming back to Zambia, I felt I was supposed to transfer my phone number to Alexander. It was time for people to start dealing with him as director, and since my number had been circulated as the contact for Sons of Thunder since 2005, it only made sense to give it to him.

Sitting in the foyer of the main house talking to him about this, I focused on one of the bedroom doors. I can't explain what happened except that I jumped up and said, "Alex. That is supposed to be your office!" I motioned for him to follow me.

Together, we walked through the bedroom to an already existing office that we used for computers and accounts. My focus landed on a sealed-up door, on the other side of which was what we called the "red shed," where we kept diesel containers. Since it had its own outside entrance, this inner door was never used.

I immediately saw an office complex. We could turn the red shed into a reception room and unseal the door between it and the existing office. The bedroom could be renovated into a director's office for Alex.

It needed to be done. I felt an urgency.

So that was what we did. We followed God's direction to create a beautiful reception area, a business office, and a director's office.

Things outside were changing as well.

Farming is not just maize fields or vegetable gardens or cows. It's also fish!

Years before, some people from America had suggested we turn the swimming pool on the farm into a tilapia pond, but I was having none of it. God had not told me about tilapia, and I wasn't even sure we had them in Zambia. I already had enough on my plate without having to take care of fish.

Alexander—whom we were calling Alex by this time—started talking about fish again, but I wasn't listening. Until the Zambia National Farmers Union randomly showed up at our door, talking about how they wanted to help farmers.

Alex immediately asked, "Do you have anyone who could help with fish?"

They said yes and subsequently introduced us to Jairus, a government worker in the Department of Fisheries. Jairus helped us with turning the swimming pool at the main house into two fish ponds. After some renovations, they were stocked with five thousand bream fingerlings.

The pool was our experimental learning area, but Alex pictured expanding with a larger fish pond out in the old maize field along the driveway. He asked Jairus to go look and see what he thought.

On his return, Jairus reported that two ponds, fifteen by twenty-five meters each, would fit nicely, and he "just so happened" to be on government leave until January. He would be able to stay at SOT during the preparation and installation process of bulldozing, preparing the bottom with black dirt, sourcing liners from Lusaka, sealing them together to make them big enough, installing inlet and outlet pipes with a gate valve, and finally, placing the liner.

One pond had to be constructed at a time because of extreme heat and power outages of up to sixteen hours due to the drought. Over time, we ended up with four fish ponds constructed along the main driveway.

Once they were filled with water, bream fingerlings were sourced.

Remember my hesitance to turn the pool into a pond for tilapia because God had not directed me to do so? I came to find out that bream and tilapia are very similar in taste and appearance.

God has a sense of humor, even when it comes to fish.

## Chapter 37

BEFORE PLANTING SEASON IN 2018, SAL HAD STARTED TALKING TO Alex about increasing the maize fields. He was adamant about it and brought it up multiple times. He and Alexander seemed to be in agreement. I just sat back and kept quiet because I know my husband. Normally, Sal is all about medical and has no interest in farming. If he kept talking about increasing fields, I knew it had to have come from God. Sal is never one to tack "God told me" onto any suggestions he makes.

So additional maize fields were planted, some under rain and some under irrigation. God gave SOT a harvest in May of 2019 when the entire Southern Province had none! We had a small harvest of fifty-six fifty-kilogram bags of maize, which we kept in storage with Passmore, who was now responsible for maize—overseeing it. Not knowing exactly what God had in mind for the maize, I merely wrote a post about it on our Facebook page along with pictures. Within days, we received a call from Pastor Jerry, who informed us that someone had given a donation for a maize mill! I hadn't asked for a maize mill on our media page!

Another God-directed opportunity. It was quite a process to source a maize mill. Not knowing where to start, Alexander and Able—our lorry driver, senior headman, and director—decided to ask around town and found Mr. Kenny, a small miller who was willing to give advice and let them see his equipment. He had purchased his maize mill from a supplier in South Africa, since milling equipment is not found in Zambia.

They left that day with the contact information for his supplier in South Africa.

One of the sermons I was listening to at the time was by Pastor Michael Todd at Transformation Church in Oklahoma. He preached, "If God shows you a problem, just know you are the answer. We don't like being the answer . . . but when we are presented with a problem, God uses it as an opportunity for promotion."

The problem we were facing was that the lack of maize harvest had caused Zambia to experience one of the worst droughts since the 1980s, resulting in a lot of hunger and starvation. Our dilemma was not knowing how to be the answer if we could not source the milling equipment in time. When we talked with Mr. Kenny about our desire to feed the hungry and told him our situation, he offered to mill our maize for us when it was ready, since he and his guys had nothing to do.

That was all I needed for confirmation that we were on the right track with the maize and the maize mill. The only thing left to do was getting the printing done on the mealie meal bags.

Alex and I went to a company in Lusaka and placed the minimum order of twenty-five hundred ten-kilogram mealie meal bags with the Sons of Thunder logo and contact information on them.

Once we received the bags, we took them, along with our fifty-six bags of maize, to Mr. Kenny, who turned our maize into mealie meal and put it into our SOT ten-kilogram bags. We ended up with 226 bags of mealie meal.

Next, Mr. Kenny agreed to go to South Africa with Alex to Maize Master, the milling supply company, to meet the owners, see the equipment, and place the order. Everything was set with production, delivery, and training, until the COVID-19 pandemic closed businesses and shut the borders of South Africa. Here was another obstacle, giving us the opportunity to once again trust God's timing.

Waiting for the borders to open once again for cargo gave us the time we needed to prepare a place for the new mill. The only place with a high enough roof was the building we always called the "dairy." I guess that name just wouldn't do anymore—we would have to start calling it the "mill."

In order to clear out the building supplies that were being stored in the main area of the dairy (now mill), we decided to erect a structure that would encompass both a storage space for supplies and a much-needed personnel office.

When it came time to add the roof, Pathias suggested we try a steel roof using the fabricator that had been doing our water tank stands for the irrigation projects and door and window frames for the mill project. We agreed that, with all the termite damage we'd seen with wood over the years, it would be a good idea.

When the storage building was complete, Alex, Able, Pathias, and I went out to look at the finished project. It was much larger than I'd anticipated.

When all of us were standing inside the newly finished storage unit, I said, "This is not for building supplies. This is our maize storage."

There would definitely not be any leaking roof during rainy season. It was more than adequate for capacity. There were no holes for rats or other pests. It was close to the mill. We all stood in agreement with the same revelation: this was our maize storage!

As for the building supplies, Pathias said he would be happy with the old storage container that we had been using for maize. It was settled.

Two days after making that decision, Joseph, a man who had been hired to deliver river sand and pit sand for our building projects, informed us that he was ready to sell the maize he had been buying and accumulating. He had a thousand fifty-kilogram bags ready to sell and asked us first if we wanted them. Looking at the timing of everything and knowing there are no coincidences with God, we bought them, put them in our new maize storage facility, and waited for God's next step.

The maize mill equipment was made and delivered by a transporting company. There was no one for installation or training, but at least it arrived safely. Once again, we were able to reach out to Mr. Kenny, who graciously showed up with some of his workers to help with the installation of the mill. It took a full day to set up the mill and make sure it was operational.

Harold, one of the men who works with Mr. Kenny, came out to train our SOT team on milling procedures. After deciding that one day was not enough, Harold came to stay at SOT for an entire week. We then ordered twenty-five hundred Sons of Thunder twenty-five-kilogram printed bags from the printing company in Lusaka.

And we started milling mealie meal.

It was during this time that we hired an accountant to help out in the business office. We thought a young person would be beneficial with all the technology and transitioning to online accounts and banking. Unfortunately, that man only lasted a couple months before he relocated, but while he was still here, we started talking in the office at the main house about selling mealie meal, fish, village chickens, eggs, and vegetables. I had a lot of logistical questions. Where would people pay? How would we handle things in accounts? We would need to have receipts and possibly quotations and invoices for more substantial sales.

The accountant pointed in the direction of the maize mill and said, "We need a sales office out there."

When I heard the words "sales office," a peace came over me. I turned to Alexander. "Alex, let's take a walk."

When we got to the mill, we studied the space. There was an open room where I could visualize people waiting to place or pick up orders. Inside this waiting area was another door to an office. So the open area I saw as a receiving area, and the other room could be the sales office.

The main area in the middle was already designated for the maize mill equipment and storage of mealie meal after it was milled and bagged. The room around back that already had electricity was a great storage place for freezers to house fish and village chicken, as well as stands for egg trays. I imagined people coming to the sales office to order and pay for food products, and a receiving area for them to wait in while their order was filled and brought to them from the stores department.

It became a whole business center.

Pathias had once again made a mistake with a building project. We had selected an area and asked him to build a place for the raising of village chickens. The so-called village chicken house had been left unfinished because it was much bigger than I had anticipated.

When I looked out at the building that had been constructed, it did not at all remind me of a chicken coop. It was brick all the way to the roof level, with multiple large window openings and one doorway. It was placed on the driveway in front of Alexander's new house and right next to the Sons of Thunder shop.

What a dumb place! There would be a bad smell with chicken manure there at the entrance to the driveway leading to the office and main house of Sons of Thunder. Workers gathered there every morning to pray before signing in and starting the day's duties. No, it had not been a good decision to put it there.

So the roof remained open and undone. When I could stand it no longer, I decided to go take a look at the structure. As Alister—one of the ladies in the office—and I walked down the driveway from the main house, I prayed, "God, show me what You want."

When I entered the building, I saw the many open windows and thought about the bad smell that would permeate the air all around the building. No, this was not for village chickens.

As I continued to contemplate the building, I noticed it was already divided inside with a small brick wall that had been used as a feeding trough long ago. The floor was partial cement from days past. The division was one-third toward the back and two-thirds toward the front. In the back portion, I could picture people cooking with big nshima pots.

Then it dawned on me—this was like an outside Zambian kitchen!

I turned to peruse the front section and envisioned room for eight picnic tables, four on each side.

"This is a nshima kitchen," I said aloud.

A nshima kitchen—like a soup kitchen back home. A place to feed people. And it just so happened that we'd had a drought the previous harvest, and we were starting to see hungry people come to the door asking for help.

All of a sudden, it was very clear: God wanted us to feed the hungry during this time of starvation from the drought. A nshima kitchen it would be!

Now that the nshima kitchen was decided upon and the roof was being installed, tables were being built, and supplies were being purchased, the decision had to be made about whether to charge for the meals. I felt sure we were supposed to feed the hungry free of charge, but Able, Alex, and Sal were torn between charging and giving meals away for free. They even thought about asking for a donation.

When I walked into the building and felt it was to be a nshima kitchen, I remembered soup kitchens in America serving free meals to the homeless and hungry. So I was sure we were to feed the hungry during this time free of charge.

The problem was that everyone around me had other opinions, so I started to doubt myself and question whether I had heard from God clearly. So I went back to my source and asked, "God, are we supposed to give meals free or charge? Please let me know clearly."

Immediately in my spirit, I heard, *First fruits are Mine!*

First fruits? What first fruits?

Then I remembered. We had 226 ten-kilogram bags of mealie meal that Mr. Kenny had just milled for us. Currently, there were four fields of maize planted for the next harvest in different stages of growth. Absolutely then those mealie meal bags would be the first fruits of our maize. We were supposed to give those to God and use them for the nshima kitchen, feeding the hungry free of charge.

When I pondered further, I remembered we had five thousand fish in the swimming pool that were almost full grown and ready to eat. At the time, we had other fish ponds along the driveway already stocked with fingerlings. That meant that the first fish pond (the pool) was the first fruits of our new fish endeavor.

It seemed clear to me. The first fruits of mealie meal and fish were to be served to the hungry. Then as confirmation, I remembered exactly what Jesus fed the hungry—bread and fish!

So we finished the roof with timbers and iron sheets and put a door on the entrance. Within two weeks, we were ready to start feeding people.

From February through April of 2020, over thirty-nine hundred meals were served to the hungry at Sons of Thunder in the nshima kitchen during the year of drought in Zambia. As Jesus instructed His apostles in Matthew 10:8, "Freely you have received; freely give."

We called a general meeting for all the residents on the farm and told the story of God's direction to feed the hungry. Everyone was encouraged to volunteer as they felt led in what we considered a ministry opportunity to show the love of Jesus and give people hope. Since the vision statement of SOT is "To feed Africa physically and spiritually through the enabling of the Holy Spirit," we felt this was definitely an opportunity God was providing.

Everyone on the farm volunteered at some time and in some capacity. Some collected firewood, some cooked, some cleaned up afterward, some shared the Word, some led a time of praise and worship, some prayed, some talked, some organized a schedule and administrated. All did it voluntarily and with a joyful heart. It felt good to see everyone giving of themselves and even better to see the smiles on people's faces and hear their testimonies. All in all, it was a time of spiritual growth for everyone.

Due to the COVID-19 pandemic, the government said we were to have no more meetings of large groups. At first, we tried feeding smaller groups of families and giving takeaways. Later, we decided to give the remaining ten-kilogram bags of meal along with a care package of different side foods. We had no idea the number of families we'd be providing for but told them one family member should come through the line to collect the meal and sides for the entire family.

After giving out the packages, we still had forty-two ten-kilogram bags left.

Alex took a few SOT guys to visit the village of Natebe, where he had previously done FGW training. Natebe has an elderly population that are often forgotten, and they absolutely love it when they are visited and remembered. Alex had been stirred to go see them and take the remaining ten-kilogram bags of meal to give away, so he notified the headman and set up the meeting.

The morning of the meeting, all the leftover meal was loaded in the truck, uncounted.

When he reached Natebe, quite a number of people had gathered and were waiting. Alex shared what was on his heart from the Word, then the others were given the opportunity to share, including two headmen.

After that, they prayed together, then went to pass out the meal. Alex told them first that he had not counted the meal, so if anyone was left out, he would write their names down and bring them a bag in a few days.

*But* . . . as our God is an awesome God and provider, the number of bags matched the exact number of people. God never ceases to astonish me.

The day after Mother's Day, Pastor Jerry called to tell us that SOT had just received a very large anonymous donation, the likes of which he had never received before. He was not even sure the check was real, and he needed to have it verified.

On May 28, 2020, Pastor Jerry called to tell us the check was real! God is amazing. First, He led me to Proverbs 3:9–10: "Honor the Lord with your wealth, with the firstfruits of all your crops; then your barns will be filled to overflowing, and your vats will brim over with new wine."

Next, I thought about how a breakthrough comes "suddenly" and how God is in the small details. Our breakthrough was coming in the year of 2020 . . . the year of "perfect vision."

The very day Pastor Jerry called to verify the check's authenticity was the beginning of the three-day feast of Shavuot, which is the Jewish Feast of First Fruits.

You could say all those were just coincidences, but I have been on this journey with God long enough to know, He cares about the little things that are all divinely crafted and woven into His master plan.

## Chapter 38

WITH THAT LARGE DONATION, MANY THINGS HAVE BEEN accomplished.

Sal is all about medical, so the first thing that he did was purchase three used Land Cruisers to make up the new medical fleet. Then he completed medical staff houses three and four and started staff house five. Construction was also started on a new twelve-bed inpatient facility.

During 2020, the government posted Prudence—a data entry clerk—to help with data collection and statistics. SOT hired Enest—a public health nurse—to handle school and community, especially with COVID, and Jessie, another clinical officer.

Audrey was transferred by the government in 2020 after working at SOT for three years. The government posted Trebby—an RN-midwife—in January of 2021, to take Audrey's place.

And finally, Christopher knocked on the door in August 2021. He had just graduated as a radiology/ultrasound tech and wanted a job while he waited for posting. Since we do ultrasounds on every antenatal, we decided maybe God was bringing us the next step, so we hired him.

Medical has grown beyond our wildest imaginations. Currently, the medical professional staff consists of four clinical officers (including Sal), two RN-midwives, two RNs, one public health nurse, one lab tech, one ultrasound tech, and one data entry clerk.

That's a big difference from where we started.

Alex is all about farming, so he used the breakthrough to start a large Sons of Thunder garden and expand the orchard and banana plantation. He had a combination of drip and sprinkler irrigation systems installed in all areas. Two new boreholes were drilled to accommodate different garden-field areas. He purchased a ripper, a planter, and a new tractor, as well as a sheller, used to take the kernels off the maize cobs.

Finally, we were able to build the much-needed coop for our village chickens.

Just as the last wire was being put in place, Professor came to the door to tell me that he had heard a radio ad about an organization called Backyard Village Chicken. The advertisement had stated that they did trainings and community workshops for raising village chickens.

As I listened to Professor, I marveled once again at God's timing and direction. I smiled and thought, *Okay, God . . . I guess this is our next step.*

After a couple of introductory phone calls, a three-day training was set up for the following week at Sons of Thunder. Three men came from Backyard Village Chicken in Lusaka to carry out the training, and ten men were selected to take the class for Sons of Thunder. Out of the group, Gift, who had been interested for a very long time in village chickens, was selected to head up the operation, and Patrick and Caleb were chosen as his assistants.

After preparations were complete with the purchase of supplies and chicken feed, Backyard Village Chicken came with three hundred broilers and one hundred layers to get us started. We have had ongoing chickens being raised, slaughtered, and sold. All the families on the farm received a chicken each for their Christmas meal.

All I can say is God is amazing!

The final thing Alex did in 2020 was clear land and plant a seventy-five-acre maize field on the southern corner of the farm. That field harvested almost twelve hundred fifty-kilogram bags of maize. The maize storage facility was full, packed with all the bags from harvest plus what we had purchased from Joseph. Besides the initial one thousand bags of maize, we had purchased an additional three thousand over time.

When thinking of more storage space, a silo came to mind. We called the fabricator to discuss it, and he made one for us to try. We stored some of our maize in it for 2021, and it worked perfectly.

And me—I wanted the nshima kitchen completed with cement floor and painting. When that was done, I had the kitchen remodeled in the main house. The termites had infested and eaten away at the wood cabinets. Literally, one countertop had crashed down into the cabinet. It was long overdue. New cabinets—not made of wood—with granite countertops. It looked like a different house.

New appliances, including washers and dryers, were purchased not only for the main house but also for the conference center and clinic. Three new computers were purchased for the business office.

We also hired Innocent, a young man raised at Sons of Thunder, who had gone to teachers college through distance learning while working as an assistant at the clinic. Completing his diploma in secondary education, he applied for posting, without success. He acquired his driver's license and took computer classes while he was waiting.

The directors all knew him to be an honest and responsible man and felt he would be a good addition to the business office at Sons of Thunder. The position was offered to him, and he wholeheartedly accepted.

Since he has been in the office, technology has flourished in Zambia. Innocent has been able to step in where needed. Satellite internet has been added to the farm, providing Wi-Fi capability to the main house, office, and clinic. A lot of government payments and paperwork are now handled online, and Innocent has been able to take over. He has learned website design and has taken over operation of our website. He also handles the Student Sponsorship Program and the Blessed Fund kids, including all tuition payments and transport needs.

After being forced to close in 2020 due to COVID restrictions, the nshima kitchen opened once again in February 2021 using all SOT residents and anyone willing to volunteer their time and service to feed the hungry. We hired a cook and a cleaner to work during the slow months. Everyone on the farm is welcome to volunteer their time. They are very needed right before harvest, when people are hungry and numbers increase.

Abson told us he was finished driving trucks across borders and wanted to be home with his family. He asked me to find him something to do. As I was still contemplating, he came to me, obviously prepared for a discussion.

"Renee," he said, "what are the plans for dam three?"

257

Dam three was the largest dam on SOT and had not been functional for the seventeen years I had been there. But a year or so before, Alex had told me that he could picture another village there with cows. At the time I just listened. Now here was Abson asking me.

I hesitated, then answered. "I don't know. Alex says he sees a village there with cows." And then I added, "Why?"

Abson said, "I think we should fix it."

Since Abson was the bulldozer operator and knew that our bulldozer was down, I asked him, "How? We don't have a bulldozer."

He shrugged. "The council has heavy-duty equipment. We can ask them to do it."

"Well, go find out the details, and let me know what they say."

Not expecting too much, I was surprised when he came back the next day with all the answers. They indeed had the equipment needed—an excavator and tipper truck—and they had just finished all their contracts, so they were available to start the next day. I knew I still had funds from a donation, waiting to see what God wanted us to do with it. It was just the right amount needed, and seeing this as another lighted stone, we decided to take the next step.

After the dam had been fixed and prepared for rainy season, I stood on top of the riverbed, looking at the enormity of the dam. I definitely felt the presence of the Lord and His majesty.

As for a village and cows . . . I am sure they will come in time.

Next, Abson came with another concern, this time, regarding our truck. He had reviewed the paperwork and told me it was time to sell it before it started breaking down, and we should get a new Hino. He took care of finding a buyer, who came a couple of days later and purchased the truck for cash. Paperwork and everything finished in a day. Abson went to Lusaka, found a new truck, and completed everything within the week.

Absolutely nothing happens that easily in Zambia. It had to be God's direction.

I was still praying about a job for Abson, something we needed that he would be good at. After the purchase of the truck was completed, an idea came to mind. We needed a businessman who could take the business center to the next level. Upon discussion, Abson was excited about the opportunity. He became head over the business center, in charge of operations, marketing, and sales.

God is the one who knows the plan and has the map to guide us to complete what He has called us to do. The only way we have been able to walk this journey with God is by staying in right relationship with Him and hearing His voice as He directs our steps and lights our path. Our part is to stand still and wait for Him to light the stones. Only then do we take the next step.

That's the way it has been throughout our entire time in Zambia. I don't mean to say it's been easy. On the contrary, there have been challenges, discouragement, and adversity, but God has used those difficult times to test and build our character.

Looking back, it's obvious that there has been a lot accomplished at the direction and through the provision and guidance of the Lord. He used us all: Sal and me, the people at Sons of Thunder, and everyone who has provided support through the years, on the ground, financially, and in prayer, to accomplish what we now know as Sons of Thunder, Zambia.

God answered the prayers of a suffering and dying nation—riddled with HIV/AIDS, TB, and malnutrition, and filled with an ever-increasing orphan population due to maternal deaths. The deteriorating physical health of the people contributed to continued economic decline and poverty conditions. God sent many workers and nations and nonprofit organizations to Zambia so He could heal and restore the people and, consequently, the nation, all while opening their minds and hearts to Jesus as their only source of hope.

Sal and I were only one cog in the wheel.

It is easy to get caught up in how far we have to go instead of celebrating how far we have come. Whatever has been accomplished at Sons of Thunder, Zambia, is definitely the handiwork of our amazing God. All glory, honor, and praise belong to Him and Him alone!

Somewhere along my journey, I studied the tabernacle as God's model for entering into His presence and was so captivated that I always included it whenever I was asked to teach about worship. So when teaching the Tabernacle I always started with Psalm 100:4: *"Enter His gates with thanksgiving* and his courts with praise; give thanks to him and praise his name"* (emphasis added). I remember repeating over and over, "You don't even get through the gate without thanksgiving!"

Everywhere you go, there is always an entry, an entrance. Whether you're going through customs at the airport into a new country or entering someone's house or a public building or office, there is always an entrance.

Whenever you walk through an entrance for the first time, it is a bit uncomfortable, and you are treated as a stranger or a visitor. Over time, you become familiar and recognized. It becomes easier, and you are treated more like family.

In the beginning, when Sal and I would land at Livingstone Airport, we had to pass a certain way and stand in the line for Immigration to allow us into Zambia. When it was our turn, we answered questions while having our passports and employment permits checked. It brought anxiety and trepidation each and every time.

But after ten years of coming and going, we became permanent residents of Zambia with official documentation. Now, whenever we enter Zambia, immigration officers look at our passports and residence permits and say, "Welcome back!" They allow us to come through the short line of returning residents and greet us with a smile . . . because we are known. We have been this way before. In the beginning, we stood in the long line with all the other tourists and visitors, but now we are expressed through the returning resident side—we are like family.

Getting in to see God also has an entrance. Very clearly in Psalm 100:4, we are told that the key to open the door is thanksgiving.

During my time of preparation to come to Zambia, Pastor Jerry taught a year's worth of sermons on being thankful, and those were probably the messages that stuck with me the most. Just being thankful, however, is not enough. It's the beginning and prepares your heart. It says in the Word that out of the heart the mouth speaks, so we must verbally "give thanks" to God. Thanksgiving means "giving thanks."

The second half of the Scripture makes it clear: "Give thanks to him and praise his name." It is not thanks*giving* unless it is given. It reminds me of sitting around the Thanksgiving dinner table taking turns telling what we are thankful for.

At each step in our journey, we took time to thank God for what He was doing, each blessing that had been given, each challenge that had been overcome, every obstacle that had been hurdled, and most importantly, that He was *there* through it all. Having a grateful heart helped us see the progress made, protected us from discouragement and thoughts of giving up, and enabled us to see His love and faithfulness, freely given in abundance over not only us but all of Sons of Thunder.

We were also reminded to remain submissive. Submission requires not taking credit for what God has accomplished and not taking ownership of what is His. I know God uses people to carry out His plans, but it is our job to point everyone back to God and what He has done—what He has accomplished! God is always the originator of the plan. He is the one who provides and equips and directs the way. He is the author and finisher! When people come to Sons of Thunder and see what has been done or hear the stories or read the book, we want them to see our amazing God and what He can do with submitted hearts.

Joyce Meyer wrote in her book *The Power of Being Thankful*:

> We hear a lot of teaching about forgetting the past, and although there are times to do that, we should also be taught to remember with gratitude all the good things God has done in the past, passing the gratitude on to future generations. A thankful heart is a heart that remembers God's love and marvelous deeds and shares them with the world.[3]

That's exactly what we want to do—pass it on!

"Many, Lord my God, are the wonders you have done, the things you planned for us. None can compare to you; were I to speak and tell of your deeds, they would be too many to declare" (Psalm 40:5).

*Chapter 39*

AS I LOOK BACK OVER THE YEARS, ASKING MYSELF IF WE HAVE impacted others on this journey, I raise my head as if to scan both sides of the ocean.

The paramedic education company back in America that God directed us to start is now in its twenty-fourth year. It provided for our support for seven years during our time of preparation, then the entire time we have been in Zambia, which is almost seventeen years now. Not only did God use it to provide for us, but it was also the career path of our oldest son, Shaun, who has been director and administrator for seventeen years and is in his fourth year as owner.

It has also provided for our youngest son, Mark, first as an instructor and technical adviser, then marketing, and most recently, as the innovator and director of an adjunct ambulance company in its fourth year called AEC Emergency Transport and Rapid Response. AEC started in a converted bedroom and is now housed in a two-story, freestanding building with capacity in its parking area for multiple ambulances and chase cars.

When I ponder what God has done, I think of all the students who have passed through the training courses since 1998 and are now EMTs and paramedics, employed and providing emergency response and rescue to people in need. I think of the instructors and office personnel who have been employed either full or part time over the years, supporting their families or supplementing their incomes.

I think of the medical and nursing personnel who've been able to maintain their continuing education certifications through the training courses offered at their locations by AEC. I think about the EMTs and paramedics hired to staff the twenty-four-seven ambulance service, providing help to thousands of patients, not to mention organizations such as hospitals, nursing homes, and other private entities.

I also think of how hard it was for us to step out in faith at the beginning of this journey when we felt God's direction to start a company. Now I can't imagine not having done it.

Remembering our original call to Zambia: *Start a clinic on the farm.*

That medical clinic started back in 2005 in one small room and is now a licensed six-bed rural health center with a freestanding lab and a six-bed maternity center under the Kazungula District Ministry of Health in the Southern Province of Zambia. A twelve-bed inpatient facility is under construction.

The medical complex also includes three apartments, five individual staff houses, and a group hostel for some of the female employees.

Besides Sal and me, there are three clinical officers, seven registered nurses, one lab technician, an ultrasound technician, a data entry clerk, and twelve clinical assistants. There are also two drivers, six cleaning staff, one laundry worker, two cooks, one gardener, two yard workers, and a chaplain.

One of the nurses was sponsored to nursing school by Sons of Thunder donors, and five previously hired clinical assistants are currently in school for either nursing or medicine. The clinic has been used over the years for a clinical rotation site for different nursing schools, clinical officers, and now midwives.

Over eighteen hundred outpatients are seen every month at the main clinic and the ten outreach sites to surrounding communities. Family planning, Under-Five immunizations, antenatal care, cervical cancer screenings, and even male circumcisions are programs conducted at the clinic and outreach sites.

Sons of Thunder is an official antiretroviral treatment center with over eleven hundred HIV-positive clients currently being managed either at the center or one of the monthly Mobile ART sites. Anywhere from thirty to fifty babies are delivered at the maternity center every month, with transport provided when a woman goes into labor, then back home upon discharge following delivery.

HIV-positive moms are medically managed prior to conception and during antenatal care and have delivered healthy, HIV-negative babies that are even negative after eighteen months of breastfeeding.

The goal of the clinic and maternity center at SOT was to provide good antenatal care, including needed HIV prevention and or management as well as safe, supervised deliveries, thus greatly reducing and almost completely eliminating maternal deaths. The result: no more orphans!

But God didn't just stop at medical.

He also told us to *Raise the standard*.

At first, we thought God meant the standard of health care, but He meant so much more. We watched ourselves be used as teachers and trainers in all different areas.

The first people we trained were the assistants in the clinic, giving them practical knowledge to function as medical assistants taking vital signs, registering patients, drawing blood, giving injections, doing dressings, and eventually assisting with deliveries.

However, our roles as teachers and mentors extended beyond medical. We taught a variety of things, such as cleaning procedures, cooking in a modern kitchen, shopping and handling money and receipts, proper use of electricity and electrical appliances, hospitality, accounting, computers, office procedures, organizational skills, chain of command, and leadership.

We took people into the bank and other government offices for the first time, teaching them how to make deposits and withdrawals, submit paperwork, and pay annual licenses.

Many people were taught how to drive, and some were taken to trade schools for bricklaying, electrical, plumbing, and mechanics. A couple of guys continued on their own to upgrade their licenses to drive big trucks and operate heavy equipment.

On-the-job training continues as each one teaches the one behind him or her.

Teaching and training over the years also included Sunday-school lessons, Bible studies, and what we called marriage classes offered to the entire farm. Three men completed Bible college and are now pastoring churches. There are now both a Zambian-led SOT men's ministry and

SOT women's ministry that continue monthly meetings on the farm, as well as outreach to the surrounding communities.

Bible studies and cell groups can also be found in the SOT villages. Teaching about and demonstrating acts of giving has resulted in the unprecedented assistance being offered during funerals at different villages; individuals offering themselves and their finances for worthy causes; the building of houses in the surrounding communities for the elderly; and most recently, volunteering to feed the hungry at the nshima kitchen. We've also seen the adoption of an elderly man who needs a visit for prayer, food, hygiene, and housecleaning every couple of weeks.

In the way of formal education, there is now a childcare room for ages four months to three years, two preschools for children three to six years, and a primary school for grades one through seven. The government-posted headmistress at our primary community school is a woman raised at SOT.

Anna was the first clinical assistant hired at the clinic before she decided to go to college to be a primary teacher. She spent a year teaching here after graduation, until she was posted by the government to a school in Livingstone. After working there a few years, she was posted back at SOT as headmistress, where she has been for the past five years.

There is also a work-study program during school breaks called the Blessed Fund for kids in grades eight through twelve, as well as a Student Sponsorship Program, involving donations from the US, helping kids complete grade twelve. Some kids have even been sponsored for further education in college or trade schools.

In every area, leaders have been raised up to oversee and run their areas. They are busy training the one to follow them.

As for Alexander, my "Zambian son," I believe with all my heart that he was chosen by God and raised up for such a time as this. I have been mentoring him all these years to lead the entire SOT family.

Alex was born in the Kabuyu area of the Southern Province of Zambia. At the age of four, his parents divorced. He and two brothers went with their dad, while the youngest brother went with their mom. Their dad was a strict Catholic who would often get drunk and beat his boys.

School was sporadic, but Alex managed to pass his grade-seven exam at eighteen. Unfortunately, that was where his education ended, due to a lack of finances.

In August 1996, Alex asked Jesus into his heart as his personal Savior and was baptized in the nearby area of Milangu. In February 1998, Alexander married a woman named Agatha, after God confirmed her as the right woman for him in a dream.

Still needing to pay his lobola (bride price) to his in-laws, Alexander had another dream, this time about working at Sons of Thunder. He told Agatha he was going to look for work and proceeded to walk the twenty-plus kilometers (over twelve miles) to Sons of Thunder. He met the old missionary and was immediately hired as a herder.

That night, he walked back home to get some supplies and returned the next day with swollen legs, ready for work. He worked enough to pay the in-laws the full amount of the lobola—two cows plus a balance of cash.

In Alexander's early days at Sons of Thunder, he would only see his wife and baby daughter on his days off. Not happy with that arrangement, Agatha packed up everything and joined him in December 1998. They have been here ever since.

Alexander held different jobs in the early days, like cattle herder, night watchman, and border patrol. He was told to stay in a faraway area of the farm, alone with his family, in a place where the squatters were living. He literally had to stay near the enemy's camp.

In September 2003, while he and Agatha were at work, their house caught fire, and they lost all their belongings. His two daughters were with their mother at the farm proper at the time, and thankfully, no one was harmed.

Alexander is a strong man and was determined not to leave or give up. He stood and faced adversity, and God raised him up. God had a plan and a purpose for him at Sons of Thunder and was preparing his heart for the journey ahead.

He is now the head—the in-charge—of Sons of Thunder in Zambia. He is one of the directors, oversees all operations, makes decisions, handles all the finances as well as logistics, settles disputes, counsels, disciplines, organizes, and encourages. He does it all.

In essence, he has been raised up to do exactly what I do. He is the one to follow me.

As I see it, Alex walked a similar path to mine. We were both saved in August 1996, called by God, had our hearts prepared during an eight-year span, and were presented God-given opportunities that had to be seen and seized. We both had to partner with the right people, seek God's guidance, pass the character tests, fight discouragement, resist revenge, and show kindness, all while worshipping well . . . in order to live a life of significance and pass it on, leaving a legacy for the generations to come.

Besides the two directives mentioned above, Sal and I were also told to *Feed a nation.*

We were a little confused with this one, since the mission statement of Sons of Thunder is "to feed *Africa* physically and spiritually through the enabling of the Holy Spirit." We just figured that during our time on this journey, we would get to see the feeding of Zambia. We assumed that meant this ministry, and God's vision would increase after us.

In order to feed a nation, you have to start by feeding yourself and your family. When we originally came here, people were very malnourished. Some of those were HIV/AIDS related with TB as the most prevalent opportunistic disease at the time, but some were as a result of either low or no income and poor nutrition. People on the farm were not working, except trying to grow their own gardens. All the gardens were either dependent on rain or the Maramba River.

Once God put Sal and me in leadership after our first year here, he had Alexander pick seven areas for villages, and people were relocated into communities, each with a headman. New houses were constructed of mud instead of straw, with iron sheets for roofs, removing the risk of damage and possible injury or death by fire. All the men were given part-time jobs. Every family was given a garden plot to supplement their income. And that was how things began.

Now we have over eighty families on the farm in six villages, all with a headman. Everyone has at least a mud house, two have brick houses, and four more just completed building brick homes this year. Two of the villages have electricity to their homes, and soon we will be adding a third one. A lot of the ladies have refrigerators, and some have cook stoves. A few of the families even have vehicles.

Everyone has a job or the opportunity to do piecework. Not only husbands but also wives and even some of the grown and graduated kids are working.

Besides SOT residents, there are also people from the surrounding communities who have found assistance with employment opportunities. Almost every family has a garden and is using Farming God's Way instead of traditional practices. All gardens have direct access to water, whether irrigation from boreholes or the dam or the river. All produce is taken to markets in Livingstone every Monday and Friday.

There is even a very large official Sons of Thunder garden. The crops have expanded to include green beans; butternut; zucchini; Chinese cabbage; spinach; lettuce; red, green, and yellow peppers; cucumbers; carrots; okra; and *impwa*, as well as the original four (tomato, onion, cabbage, and rape). I think it was because of Sons of Thunder that you now see green beans everywhere. The Zambian ladies have found them easy to chop up small to make a nice relish to serve with nshima.

Besides vegetables, there is now a citrus orchard, a banana plantation, and over five thousand moringa trees. There are four operational fish ponds, as well as the stocking of a very large dam.

Village chickens are thriving. The new maize mill is operational, milling maize into mealie meal. There is now a complete business center with a sales office, maize mill, and stores department, as well as a spacious maize storage facility. Abson is over the business center, sourcing markets. Sons of Thunder mealie meal is being sold to all the surrounding communities. Seems to me we are on our way to feeding Zambia!

Part of the formation of this legacy happened as God easily brought it to pass, but some came with great price. There was definitely *persecution*, but surprisingly, it came from the family of believers, fellow Christians, and coworkers in the faith. I don't know why we didn't expect that, because when I look at the life of Jesus, that is exactly where His persecution also arose: Jewish leaders and Pharisees, the Sanhedrin and the high priest, and finally Judas.

There was *standing firm* in the face of opposition from all sorts of places wherever Satan thought he could stop God from moving. But the favor of the Lord was with us, and we soon discovered that no plan of God's can be thwarted.

There was an *oppression* felt over the entire farm in the beginning. It cropped up in different areas over the years, but God proved Himself as our deliverer through cleansing prayer, the Word, and praise and worship.

There was *heartbreak* as man fell into sin. Discipline had to be rendered, and hard decisions had to be made. Sometimes, we felt we advanced two steps forward then regressed three steps back.

There was *compassion* as forgiveness and restoration were given.

There was *prayer and practicing presence* as we sought God's direction and His heart.

There were *tears of discouragement* as we fought to never give up, but God provided "little kisses" just when we needed them from all sorts of places. He spoke to us from His Word at just the right time, giving encouragement and approval and sometimes even warning us about what was to come. He brought just the right people to the door at the very time we needed them to carry out the next step, even when we had yet to see the full picture. He equipped and provided always at the right time, never leaving our side. He walked with us through trials and storms, providing peace and taking away all fear.

There was a *determination* that rose up in each of us to run the race, finish the course, and above all, finish well as we wait to hear Him speak those words:

*Well done, good and faithful servants!*

# *Epilogue*

## Life Lessons

I WANT TO LEAVE YOU WITH A FEW LIFE LESSONS THAT I HAVE learned over the years. I hope you find them of value.

1.  Be a man or woman of your word. God says let your yes be yes and your no be no. If you say it, then make sure you do it. Many people disappoint because they do not fulfill what their mouth says. Do not make promises, because they can easily be broken. Speak truth always: "I will try," "I will see what I can do," "I will pray about it," and so on.

2.  Keep time. Real time. Hold people accountable to keeping time. Make sure you are on time for work, for meetings, and so forth. Keeping time helps people depend on you. They will come to know you as a man or woman of your word and a person they can count on.

3.  Whatever you do, do it as though working for God, and do it with joy. Every task you undertake, whether small or big, menial or important, do it with God in mind. How would He see you at the task?

4.  Always tell the truth, even if it hurts. If it was your fault, admit it. Take responsibility for your actions, and if needed, repent and ask for forgiveness. Don't try to cover up or lie about things. One lie leads to another, and we know who the "Father of Lies" is.

5.  You can't outgive God. Freely you have received; freely give. Your 10 percent tithe is just the beginning. The more you give, the more He gives back.

6.  When you think you hear God tell you something, take the first step. Just do what you can do. Remember the maternity center and how we took a step in faith to dig the foundation.

7.  Just do what He puts in front of you. Don't try to see around Him. Don't look at the big picture or the big need—just do what is in front of you, what He has allowed you to see. Imagine you are behind Him, holding on to His shirt. All you can see is what is between you and Him. You can't see what's up ahead.

8.  Don't take ownership. Remember, everything belongs to God. We are His servants. We are to be good stewards of what He has entrusted to us.

9.  Give all the credit and glory to God. Everything that occurs is because of His plan and His presence. We are just obedient servants. Thank Him for everything and give Him praise, honor, and glory. Let everyone know that it's because of God and what He's doing in your life.

10. Persevere and don't give up—don't quit! There will be obstacles; there will be persecution, but stand firm. Be strong and courageous and keep on. The only failure is a quitter. There is a quote from an unknown author that I like: "Remember that guy who gave up? Neither does anyone else."

Ten Lessons for a Life of Significance
Sermon Series by Pastor Dale O'Shields[4]

Lesson 1:     Be Prepared
Lesson 2:     See and Seize God-Given Opportunities
Lesson 3:     Partner with the Right People
Lesson 4:     Seek God's Guidance
Lesson 5:     Pass the Character Tests
Lesson 6:     Resist Revenge
Lesson 7:     Fight Discouragement
Lesson 8:     Show Kindness
Lesson 9:     Worship Well
Lesson 10:    Pass It On

# Follow Us

This book may have ended, but the story continues. You see, God is still moving forward at Sons of Thunder Zambia. For current updates with pictures, follow us on social media.

**On the web**
www.sotzambia.com

**On Facebook**
@sonsofthunderzambia
@SOTSponsoraStudent

# Endnotes

1.   Lindell Cooley, "It's Time," track 9 on *Open Up the Sky*, Integrity Music, 2001, compact disc.

2.   Sarah Young, *Jesus Calling* (Nelson), 205.

3.   Joyce Meyers, *The Power of Being Thankful* (FaithWords, 2014), 146.

4.   Pastor Dale O'Shields, sermon series, Church of Redeemer, Gaithersburg, Maryland, September 2019, https//church-redeemer.org/messages.

# ORDER INFORMATION

To order additional copies of this book, please visit
www.redemption-press.com.
Also available at Amazon, Christian bookstores,
and Barnes and Noble.

CPSIA information can be obtained
at www.ICGtesting.com
Printed in the USA
BVHW030815150223
658553BV00016B/128